The One Body of Christ in a Quantum Age

THE ONE BODY
OF CHRIST
IN A QUANTUM AGE

BERNARD TICKERHOOF, TOR

ORBIS BOOKS
Maryknoll, New York 10545

Founded in 1970, Orbis Books endeavors to publish works that enlighten the mind, nourish the spirit, and challenge the conscience. The publishing arm of the Maryknoll Fathers and Brothers, Orbis seeks to explore the global dimensions of the Christian faith and mission, to invite dialogue with diverse cultures and religious traditions, and to serve the cause of reconciliation and peace. The books published reflect the views of their authors and do not represent the official position of the Maryknoll Society. To learn more about Maryknoll and Orbis Books, please visit our website at www.orbisbooks.com.

Library of Congress Cataloging-in-Publication Data

Names: Tickerhoof, Bernard, author.
Title: The one body of Christ in a Quantum Age / Bernard Tickerhoof, TOR.
Description: Maryknoll, NY : Orbis Books, [2024] | Includes bibliographical
   references and index. | Summary: "Explores the intersections of
   Christian spirituality, quantum physics, and consciousness studies"—
   Provided by publisher.
Identifiers: LCCN 2023049410 (print) | LCCN 2023049411 (ebook) |
   ISBN 9781626985728 (trade paperback) | ISBN 9798888660287 (epub)
Subjects: LCSH: Christian life. | Quantum theory. | Consciousness. |
   Religion and science.
Classification: LCC BV4485 .T53 2024 (print) | LCC BV4485 (ebook) |
   DDC 248—dc23/eng/20240202
LC record available at https://lccn.loc.gov/2023049410
LC ebook record available at https://lccn.loc.gov/2023049411

In memory of my parents, David L. and Magdalen Tickerhoof

Contents

Part III: Spirituality and Consciousness

Acknowledgments

In a world where it is understood that all things are relational and connected, which is how I believe this world to be, addressing who has aided me in giving form to this book seems like a hopeless task. It has been an enriching process of weaving together a vast amount of collectible experiences and impressions I have picked up all along the length of my journey. The book builds on my previous writings and studies, but it more so draws from the experiences provided to me by each retreatant and directee with whom I have interacted over years of formative work and spiritual companionship. The first thing I want to do, therefore, is to thank all of them for their contribution, whether they were consciously aware of their contributive role or not. We learn from everything that comes our way.

In the actual writing of the book, of course, I was provided with several individuals who contributed in some specific ways that significantly affected its final form. I first mention Dr. Bonnie Thurston, who was willing to shepherd me through this process along its publication route. While I have learned much from Bonnie scripturally and theologically over many years, in this recent immersion into the world of publication probably the greatest teaching she has offered me is the importance of patience. I am also thankful to Dr. R. Dean Astumian, professor of physics and astronomy at the University of Maine, and a Secular Franciscan, who reviewed my physics and offered some important additions to this present work and some valuable suggestions for my future exploration. Another Secular Franciscan, Susan Burke, has been a faithful and sometimes demanding editorial presence through all of my published writings, this one being no exception. Others have read and commented on the entire manuscript through the course of its journey. With gratitude I mention Fr. Michael Higgins, TOR, from my own religious community, Dr. David

Kappel, and my sister, Ruthayn Tickerhoof, all of whom offered helpful comments and insights.

And finally, I thank Orbis Books for allowing me to share with them my manuscript, and especially Fr. Tom Hermans-Webster, who has worked with me through these months to bring that manuscript into the form that you now have before you. He has been supportive and encouraging throughout the entire process.

My thanks to all of you.

Introduction

Who are you? When I told some people I was writing a book about contemporary physics and spirituality, that was the first thing they asked me. Who are you?

To be clear, they were not asking about me. They already know who I am, for better or worse. They were asking about you. "Who do you think will read this book?" That was pretty direct. Or they might frame it in a softer way. "Who is your intended audience?"

Of course, I didn't know who you were. I still don't. I could only tell them who I imagined you might be. I felt that most of you would be what has long been termed "religious" people, and which now frequently is understood to be separated from others called "spiritual" people. If they are imagined to be two different groups, I presumed they would both be interested. But that is a very large group, and it has many subdivisions—people who still go to church, people who used to go but now don't, people who still go but are floundering, people who found other denominations, or started them, people who never went to any church but always felt some kind of pull in that direction. All such people might be interested in a book exploring the common ground between science and spirituality.

I imagine that the people in those groups have a range of feelings about my topic. Some are probably skeptical about my treating two such diverse topics as if they went together. Others might feel the opposite, wondering why anyone would think they wouldn't go together. I imagine that a large number of people in these groups would like to know more about one or the other, spirituality or science. They may have read books or articles that have sought to connect the two, but the connection was too complicated, too simplistic, or too obscure to be helpful. At times, I think I was in at least one of those groups, which probably include people like me, who have begun their own search for the connection and are looking for more information.

You may not, however, belong to any of the above groups. I imagined that some people would read this book believing there is no place in science for religion or spirituality at all. They may want to read the book to affirm their convictions or to give spirituality one last chance, even though they seriously doubt that it will be worth their time. In contrast, there may be people who would read this book hoping that I would once and for all cut religion's ties with a kind of science that could not possibly be in keeping with God's will. My guess is that this latter group will be deeply disappointed.

Finally, I imagine that some who read this book will be seekers, a group for whom I have great affection. They are people who have left open the box that asks for definition. They are believers, but maybe for too much. They are skeptics, but not able to really let anything go completely. They are people who don't color within the lines or maybe don't see the lines to begin with. For them, quantum theory may be a vast wonderland of possibilities, feeding on theories spawned from science fiction, where all things are possible. And there may be some who want to know what exactly is possible. Where is reality truly delineated?

So, who are you? I think you could be anybody, and you could have any number of reasons to believe that this might be a book that will prove important. I know writing it has been very important to me.

You may want to know who I am and why I wanted to write this book. Let me say, first of all, I am not a scientist, nor do I have any degree in quantum physics. But I do have some experience with spirituality and the spiritual journey that I believe we are all on. I am an ordained Franciscan friar who has spent several decades doing what I love to do, offering retreats and workshops of all sorts to gatherings and groups, as well as walking with many individuals on their spiritual path in the companionship called spiritual direction. It has all been a great gift that I have cherished very much.

In the process of acquiring the spiritual and theological education and formation to enable me to follow this path, a guiding belief of mine has been that theology, religion, and spirituality should harmonize with psychology and the human sciences. The studies I pursued, therefore, sought not so much to find a place in the academic world, but rather to make myself available for more direct work with groups and individuals who were walking along the spiritual path. In the course of these years, I have come to see that my guiding belief was still too narrow. For our world to be complete, spirituality and psychology also need to harmonize with the physical sciences. It was a simple realization: if spirituality and psychology could not fit into our understanding of physical reality as a whole, what was the point?

I, therefore, set out some years ago to understand quantum theory, which seemed to me to be more spiritual (read: indefinite) than the physical science that so baffled me in high school. As anyone who has studied quantum theory knows, it has remained rather indefinite, but, for me, it has also proved to be both enlightening and enriching. Therefore, it seems that making both quantum theory and holistic spirituality more accessible to all the groups I mentioned above, and doing it in such a way that the two disciplines could converse positively or at least frankly with each other, is a valuable effort to make.

We truly live in a global village. We hear this very often, and it is affirmed for us every day in a number of ways. People of different ethnic groups, each with their own cultures, living in other countries (or our own), and possessing different beliefs and values, are interacting with us all the time, if not physically, then through electronic communications of all sorts. We can be anywhere in the world in a matter of seconds in a number of ways. Some of the older folks among us have not yet fully allowed this reality to seep into their awareness. Some of the younger folks may not see why anyone would be surprised by that; it is all they have ever known. Whether anyone intends it or not, this contrast in itself has created a world of generational and experiential gaps. Both science and religion have been affected by it in different ways.

Needing to communicate with each other in this global village, we are challenged by both culture and language. As significant as the generation gap may be, our various cultural gaps have far greater impact. Culture lies beneath education and rationality. It is in our bodies, in our emotions, wedded to our lived experiences. Rational thinking cannot fully grasp it. Culture is conveyed through language, verbal and nonverbal. The culture of science and the culture of religion are only two of the many cultures that surround us, but they are important to our lives and our world. This book cannot fully bridge the gaps that exist between them, but my hope is that this conversation between science and religion may be helpful to further understand the ways in which we are currently dividing our world and our communities of faith.

This book is not an apologetic, a term that only theological types would probably recognize. It is not seeking to defend religion. It is not an attempt to critique science from a broadly Christian or a specifically Catholic doctrinal point of view. It is not attempting to prove or disprove either religious faith or physical theory. I envision it as more of a dialogue, or a conversation, allowing both science and spirituality to speak. Therefore, you may find yourself agreeing with some things presented or disagreeing with them. At least, be aware of where you are. I will not always be neutral myself, but I think you will know when I have questions about certain positions.

In our global village, we are immersed in an interfaith age. We are continuously being confronted with, and learning more about, the full spectrum of spiritual and religious beliefs and traditions, which is both challenging and necessary. Although I can attempt to present a variety of scientific positions on certain aspects of quantum theory (doing, I am sure, an inadequate job on all positions), I have no intention of adequately representing an overwhelming accumulation of religious beliefs. Instead, I can only speak for myself and for what I have experienced.

I am the product of a Christian—Roman Catholic and Franciscan—formation and background. As a young adult, I made a commitment to enter a male Franciscan religious community, and that decision has greatly influenced my spiritual journey as it has progressed forward to the present. Although I hope to remain open and accepting of all positions, I speak with this language and come from this worldview.

This book is divided into three parts. The first part is meant to set our historical context and identify some general themes and concepts of science and religion. The second part explores the development of quantum theory, beginning primarily with its historical roots and turning to a thematic background. You might be substantially unfamiliar with quantum theory. You might even feel a sense of anxiety or fear of the sciences in general and expect to feel stupid. I urge you to resist that feeling as unnecessary. I don't presume previous knowledge of either science or religion in the journey ahead, and I try to anticipate apprehensions. The third part of the book approaches quantum theory from the point of view of the human perceiver, you and me. It addresses mystery, neuroscience, and the development of consciousness. It concludes with some reflections on the individual spiritual journey, along with some comments concerning quantum theory and the communities of faith.

As for spirituality, it is addressed on the first page of the first chapter, and I think I touch on it on just about every page after that.

PART I

SCIENCE AND SPIRITUALITY IN DIALOGUE

1

Science and Spirituality

A Tale of Two Communities

Ours is a tale of separation, suspicion, and, then, of hope for restoration and a promise of renewed relationship and common benefit.

Two questioning communities have long lived side by side in Western civilizations: science and spirituality (religion). Living together has been mutually beneficial for a number of reasons, and these communities have maintained this long history of cooperation through Jewish, Islamic, and Christian traditions. In recent centuries, however, tension emerged between the two, fueled by new discoveries in science and pushback from traditional religious perspectives.

Why, some religious and spiritually minded people might ask, should we care what science holds to? Some adherents to religious beliefs would say that science and intellectual pursuits in general are hopelessly atheistic, antagonistic to spirituality, and should just be ignored, especially since it doesn't appear that we can eradicate them. Some in the scientific community may, likewise, want to write religion off as irrelevant to our contemporary world.

In the last century, this animosity in several ways has begun to change, given impetus by science and a variety of discoveries in physics, as well as an awakening of openness in many areas of religion. Neither of these hostile positions squares with the longer traditions of Western science or spirituality. Quite the contrary, as can be observed. No authentic religious faith expression seeks to hold false beliefs, and science, if it is authentic to itself, would not want to cut itself off from exploring the unknown. What we have come to recognize and ponder—if not fully understand—of the world we live in, as seen through the lens of quantum physics and other current theories, seems to defy much of what we call our daily lived experience. Yet for all our questions and puzzlements, this quantum world also, surprisingly, seems to resonate with what people of faith have long understood as spiritual experience and contemplative awareness.

This book attends the tale of these two communities and presumes a correlation between science (physical reality) and spirituality from a holistic perspective. Beginning from a Thomistic assertion that grace builds on (or perfects) nature, we seek to understand our natural world as the foundation upon which we build a sense of intelligibility and meaning in our human quest for wisdom. John Polkinghorne, quantum physicist and Anglican theologian (d. 2021), spoke in terms of physics and metaphysics. "Physics," he said, "does not determine metaphysics (the wider world view), but it certainly constrains it, rather as the foundations of a house constrain, but do not determine completely, the edifice that will be built upon them."[1] One can, we might say, build any structure imaginable, but it must rest firmly upon the foundation provided. Otherwise, it will eventually topple.

Mind the Gap

In searching through the physical world for what most people might refer to as "God and the things of God," we are necessarily brought to choosing one of three options. We can conclude that God and the world are the same thing, that God and the world are totally different and unconnected (and one or the other may be irrelevant), or we can land somewhere in between. In that third option, where most people are, we must recognize our dependence on *metaphors*.

Metaphors allow us to speak in approximations through a variety of analogies. This is like that, but it is *not* that—only to a degree. We may look to the physical world to understand the things of God, but they can never quite *be* God. In a retreat I once attended, the Indian Jesuit and spiritual writer of the 1980s Anthony de Mello used the Eastern image of the finger pointing at the moon. My finger points, and I say, "Look, the moon." But if I come to realize that I am actually staring at my finger and calling it the moon, I have fallen short. There may be features of quantum fields, dark energy, or quantum entanglement that possess aspects of what we believe about God, but that does not mean that these physical realities

---

[1] John Polkinghorne, *Quantum Theory: A Very Short Introduction* (Oxford: Oxford University Press, 2002), 90.

totally encompass how God works. They may, however, bring us closer to understanding how God works than a metaphor of a god who is always on my side, leading me into battle against my enemies.

Let us, then, think metaphorically for a moment. The First Letter of John says emphatically, "God is love, and those who abide in love abide in God, and God abides in them" (1 John 4:16). Is God love? I have heard many people affirm this to be true. And it *is* true, but not exactly true, or not true enough. We can all admit, from our own experiences, that love is a very complicated thing. We could even say that love is a mysterious thing or possibly many mysterious things rolled up in one. But love is not as mysterious as God, and love cannot encompass God, even if we could make a good case that it may come as close as we might hope to get.

Science is also metaphoric, using the limitations of language to articulate aspects of realities whose fine-tuning cannot be fully contained in their expression. Look no further than the basic conundrum of quantum physics, the relationship between a *wave* and a *particle* (please keep breathing; we will address the details later). How does physics speak of two discrete entities that are understood to be different in one sense and yet the same in another? Neither of the two expressions most frequently used, *wave function* and *superposition*, distinctly manifest what this entity is. They are just the best descriptions we can find. They are, if you will, metaphors.

Made in the Image and Likeness

While science may employ metaphors to express complicated or even paradoxical concepts, it is always intent on arriving at ever greater precision. In spirituality, in contrast, many metaphoric expressions are more easily tolerated because spirituality understands that the subject matter already lies beyond language's ability to fully comprehend and express.

Do we filter what we can know and articulate of God through metaphors, in part, because we ourselves are metaphoric, ourselves being images of *God's* reality in some way? The sacred writers of the Book of Genesis seemed to think so (Gen 1:26–27). The book's first story of creation explains that we have been made in God's image and after God's likeness, providing the scriptural basis for the gift of stewardship over the rest of creation to humanity.

That gift was a weighty responsibility. In Genesis, humans seemed to fail miserably at the task, and it would appear that, as we look around the world we currently inhabit, our contemporary generations are not doing much better. Humans seem to have a tendency to be self-serving, short-sighted, and highly consumptive. Yet we also understand that our higher aspirations and our belief in our own greater capacities yet untapped keep calling us to make greater efforts to fulfill the work we believe we have been commissioned to do.

This higher capacity, accompanied by our persistent frailty, puts an enduring enigma before us: How can we honestly strive toward human advancement—personally, socially, spiritually, and globally? The medieval response, during Europe's so-called Dark Ages, was often, "There is little hope; humans are stubbornly perverse." This approach presumed that most people would be lost unless they "left the world." Later, during the Reformation, this response was somewhat expanded to "Humans *are* perverse, but their faith in God can save them from destruction." The Enlightenment sought a radical correction: "Human reason itself can enable us to make ultimate progress toward our highest ideals." As many have recognized in our own postmodern times, this is a promise that remains unfulfilled.

The Latin root of the English word *science* is *scientia*, the noun that means "knowledge," related to *scire*, the verb that means "to know." Science is our human response to our curiosity about what we don't yet understand or of which we have insufficient comprehension, including ourselves. This response to our curiosities has been under way from the first appearance of humans, running through all of our imperfectly fashioned, tentative solutions. It is stoked in the embers of our own individual longings as well. All of us began our lives in utter ignorance, knowing practically nothing of ourselves or the world that surrounds us. For most, it is an intense and exciting journey of experience and learning, and it has taught us a great deal about the processes we use in our human investigations.

So, are we made in the image of God? Yes, but we are more image-tending-toward-likeness—a metaphor. We are living metaphors who seek to plumb the depths of self-knowledge and divine inspiration.

Knowledge and Faith

When we first seek knowledge, our search soon comes up against the realization that there is a lot we don't know. We start to chip away at the unknown, usually successful in some initial attempts. When we add to what we know, we begin to realize that what we don't know doesn't seem to diminish much, if at all. And as we keep going and for as long as we keep going, we soon come to admit that our uncertainty and ignorance always remain.

Adjusting to uncertainty is a huge challenge for both science and religion. Science honors certainty as *truth*, looking for a total understanding of the truth of physical reality. That the certitude of truth does not easily come into focus actually fires up science's desire for more. It stimulates further investigation, and it fuels scientific hunger. The challenge is accepted with relish.

Spirituality/religion seeks truth as well, but it perceives truth as something human investigation in itself cannot fully comprehend. Spirituality sees the gap between what we know and what we don't know and concludes that the questions cannot be totally answered by anything short of some kind of foundational *belief.* "Truth," then, for both spirituality and religion, taken as a whole, is an outcome of inspiration and discovery (including revelation) alongside human knowledge and investigation.

The roles of questioning in science and spirituality, therefore, are similar but distinct. Both are ongoing processes, but science specifically seeks (and possibly expects) an answer, no matter how incomplete. In spirituality and religious faith, questions are almost always understood to be open-ended. Questions are, we might say, more important than answers.

From spirituality's point of view, answers stop processes and are usually found wanting; questions open up further exploration. In a roundabout process, therefore, science and spirituality come to a common perspective. Ultimately, both keep the search alive. Although the quests of science and spirituality are not opposite (which is why they worked together for so long, hand in hand), at various times, they can appear opposite or contradictory. They have different foundational premises, and both can become very defensive when their respective foundations seem threatened.

And both science and spirituality, sooner or later, will hit a wall. I call it a wall of faith although some initially may want to resist that designation. The wall of faith is that place where the next step we take moves us into total darkness. Where do we go then? Everyone hits this wall, believers and unbelievers, clergy, seekers, and scientists alike. The wall is there, and it is "acknowledged" by all, even those who reluctantly come to admit it.

What, then, will the next step look like? There are three options:

- Recoil: "We can't go there. It's just magical thinking," or "It would be a betrayal of what we believe and hold to."
- Leap to the pre-given: "These are the tenets at which we will necessarily have to arrive." Many are here tempted to leapfrog to attractive "conclusions."
- Courageously continue forward with a discerning heart.

I will discuss how science's wall of faith appears to me later, so we can briefly consider spirituality here. Spirituality and religion always encompass faith at its most profound level. In fact, that is my working definition of spirituality—*my life lived in faith*. This is a holistic definition that implies that every aspect of life is spiritual because every aspect of life can lead me to a profound awareness that I stand at the door of Mystery. Approaching spirituality as the accumulation, or the sum, of my experiences encourages me to take the third option above, to continue onward into life's next moments with a discerning heart even when I do not know the way.

Religion and Spirituality, Religion or Spirituality?

To conclude this chapter, I return us to a question from the Introduction. Is there a difference between religion and spirituality? Many today see spirituality and religion as distinct. Some would say *religion* has to do with organizational structure, dogma, constraint, and repression, whereas *spirituality* is about freedom, wonder, inspiration, and community. This formulation only provides us with a simplistic dualism, however. Understandably, this dualism is often upheld by people who have encountered difficulties or frustrations in structural religions. There are many such difficulties, and many encounters have had tragic outcomes. Yet a deeper reality pulses underneath the tensions that exist between these two concepts—religion and spirituality. Both represent two points of location along a single line of historical process. Based on my lived experience of Roman Catholic religious life (technically, *consecrated life*) in the last decades of the twentieth century, and tied to my historical understanding of the evolution of the Franciscan charism, this has been called the process of *charism and institution*.

To briefly trace this line, think of an original spiritual movement that happens within either a person or a group. When at any time such a movement occurs, it is initially experienced as something called *charism* (grace, gift, inspiration). It is alive, free, and nurturing, and those who experience it, individually or corporately, surely want to keep it so. To do this for any length of time, however, presents its adherents with challenges. Many outside pressures (from family, society, Church, etc.) that already existed are perceived as threatening to its survival. In a short time, adherents recognize that this charism will require some sort of structure that can protect it from corruption or abuse. In corporate or communal circumstances, these could include certain "identity badges" or "bumper stickers," so we know who belongs and who doesn't. These could even be certain statements of essential principles and beliefs.

Initially, these structures appear simple and do not seem to be particularly worrisome. These structures, and especially those rules and safeguards that are permanently *instituted*, never automatically decrease. More protection always seems warranted. They work, but at a price. Such structures, which do not possess the same flexibility or vitality as the original core experience, become hardened and solidified over time, a process referred to as *institutionalization*. When a spiritual movement undergoes this kind of inevitable rigidity, it loses its life and vibrancy. Several outcomes are possible: the movement will disintegrate and disappear; it may also continue in a quasi-moribund form; or it must find a way to be rejuvenated, or *refounded*, and given new life and spirit, although usually not purely in its original form. The twentieth century, as a whole, was a time when religion and society, including the community of the physical sciences taken together, had to face these kinds of dilemmas. Today, we are still dealing with their conclusion, if in fact they are concluding.

Many people today claim to be spiritual but not religious. Few, I think, would claim the opposite, religious but not spiritual. The distinction drawn between the two, then, carries a kind of "us and them" dualistic ring. How can we speak of spirituality and religion today without conferring judgment on others who may perceive themselves as being at different locations within this singular historical process?

Let me at least offer this formulation: *religion*, from my perspective, is *the articulation of shared spiritual experience*. When you and I, even if it is only you and I (although it seldom is), share a common spiritual perspective, a kernel of religion is formed. Our shared experience can be enough to pray, to worship, to minister by offering service beyond ourselves, and to celebrate together. What we do with it from there will either deepen and strengthen it or cause it to deteriorate and putrefy. The "natural" development of any such religious and spiritual phenomena, when left to evolve through automatic communal processes, will only go in one direction, toward continuing institutionalization. It will require frequent, conscious vigilance to maintain the spiritual freshness that most adherents truly desire.

2

The Process of Investigation

Scientific Investigation

Scientific investigation is concerned with how we come to know. It does *not* so much focus on what we may *speculate* or *presume*. There are plenty of opinions around—we might say plenty of "science fictions"—but science has always highly prized certitude and verification, at least as an end result. Still, it does recognize that knowledge has its own processes. Many theories need time for germination, and many are incomplete. Some will be incomplete for a long time.

There is, therefore, a need to pursue truth and knowledge in a consistent and systematic fashion. The scientific method that emerged during the Enlightenment period, particularly as it relates to physics, has three basic pillars.

- Reflection and creative thinking (theoretical science), based on what is known or believed to be plausible.
- Mathematical formulation (equations).
- Experimentation and observation (measurement and verification).

The scientific process can actually begin at any one of these points. They do not need to be sequential. They do not even need to be proximate in time. The process remains incomplete, however, as long as any of those criteria are absent.

Although these pillars speak for themselves in many ways, another component of inquiry emerged during the Enlightenment and was felt to be a necessary component of scientific method—really an underlying companion that had accompanied science during the Age of Reason: *objectivity*. Science came to believe itself to be the cool and objective arbiter of truth (physical truth, for sure, but, over time, physical truth more and more tended to take center stage). As it has turned out, insistence on objectivity has become the part of the scientific framework that quantum theory would challenge and shake to its foundations.

The history of philosophy and the theological questions that spring from it are quite different from those of science. Spirituality, which arises within philosophical and theological disciplines, seeks truth through a distinct framework. Spirituality's investigation does not maintain the cool and detached approach demanded by science. The "pillars" of spirituality, for our purposes, include:

- The interaction between experience and inspiration (revelation). In spirituality, experience will always be central, for that is how Mystery is encountered. It could be common experience, but subjective experience is not dismissed out of hand.
- Reflective imagination, which stands alongside science's creative thinking.
- Conscious integration, understood as an ongoing life process.

In comparing these two very different lists, it should be quite clear that exploring something like quantum physics through these two disciplines requires a fresh spirit of open dialogue. This is not a bad thing, for it can enhance the shared process of creative thinking and reflective imagination. We can begin by asking deeper questions about knowledge.

A Rational World?

Knowledge. Certitude. Verification. Objectivity. These qualities make up a heavy agenda. So we might say that science sets a high bar in getting to the truth of the matter, getting to what is *real*. But that raises a number of different questions. What is real? Is it the same as what is true? Is there truth that is not verifiable? How important is objectivity? There are certainly spiritual traditions that believe the world around us is not real, that it is actually illusion. These are generally not part of the Western spiritual traditions, however. And there have long been philosophical schools that questioned realism.

Over 2,300 years ago, Plato and Aristotle respectively taught two very different views of the world around us:

- *Idealism*, championed by Plato, in effect held that what we see around us is not complete. There is much more to reality than what we experience in daily life.

- *Realism*, embraced by his student Aristotle, in turn emphasized that what is real is here before us, but we need to understand it completely.

In one sense, we could say that Plato and Aristotle never left us. Their differing views have substantially influenced Western philosophical thought down to our own time. In the late Roman period and forward, Neoplatonism influenced such Christian thinkers as Augustine, Pseudo-Dionysius, and Bonaventure. Aristotelian Realism, passed on through Islamic scholars such as Ibn Rushd (Averroës), led the way to the Scholasticism of Thomas Aquinas and others. These philosophical schools were shaped and reshaped through the Renaissance period, opening the philosophical door to the Age of Reason.

Although both positions had their proponents in the ancient world and through the Middle Ages, the position of idealism was more and more abandoned by the emerging fields of the physical and natural sciences during the Renaissance and the Enlightenment, which increasingly turned to realism and empirical verification. The impact of the Enlightenment (late seventeenth through the nineteenth century) touched practically every feature of Western society and culture. It spawned philosophical and political movements that continue to have an impact on our world today.

During the Age of Reason, the idea of God, invisible and intangible, was not out-and-out rejected, but God, we might say, had to settle for functioning in purely rational ways. Sir Isaac Newton (1642–1727), perhaps the most prominent scientific mind during the Enlightenment, held deistic religious views. The world was a large, highly functional machine that operated efficiently by reasonable laws that God had previously established. These laws provided for no substantial intrusion, even by God, who, in effect, was assigned only a maintenance role.

Predictability

As seen through the eyes of the Enlightenment, the physical world was governed by reason and was generally seen as an orderly place. Things that are in order, it was thought, happen as a matter of course and are, therefore, predictable. Things that are predictable have the advantage of providing us with firm, concrete answers to the questions we might seek. We may not know all the answers yet, but it was presumed that, in time, we would. Reason, brought to bear on human progress, would continue to open the doors to the unknown.

From the Enlightenment's point of view, the world was predictable because it was *deterministic*. Science was like a road map, or GPS, that would always lead us to the right address. The very reason we would want to do experimentation was that our experiments could be replicated, and, through their replication, confirmed. Equations, if they were true, would always produce the same results and would arrive at the same answers. Answers that are complex are good as long as they continue to be confirmed, and answers that are simpler are better and generally considered to be more trustworthy. And, if such answers provide solutions to *many* questions, then science describes such an answer as *beautiful* or *elegant*.

A deterministic world could, of course, look forward to what was coming, but it should also be able to look backward to what had come before. As much as determinism could predict what lies ahead, it was thought that it should also be able to identify what brought our present reality into being—in other words, the causes of things that now exist. From a deterministic vantage point, this causality would be as much rooted in physical phenomena as the present and future state of things. Such a scientific determinism left no room for non-physical, or *metaphysical* causation.[1] All causes would necessarily be physical.

As the world of science became more aware of subatomic entities (which we will soon discuss), this deterministic approach was carried even further toward what is called *reductionism*. Reductionism is a "bottom up" approach to determinism. The reductionist maintains that, as we eventually become increasingly familiar with the smallest pieces of physical reality, those "things" of which all of physical reality is composed, science will ultimately be provided with all the necessary information that we need to know everything. For instance, in what would be reductionism's supreme triumph, if we understood all the minute elements that go into the physical makeup of the human person, including complete data on neurological activity, we would be able to accurately predict the next thing that the person would say, do, or think.

---

[1] There are many definitions of metaphysics. Here some simple ones will do. The Oxford Dictionaries understand it as a branch of philosophy that treats the first principles of things, such as being, substance, cause, etc. Merriam-Webster sees it as being concerned with the fundamental nature of reality, including ontology, cosmology, and epistemology, among others. In general, it could be said that meta-physics deals more with abstract ideas and possibilities and not the concrete things of the physical sciences. For this reason, many materialistic approaches to physical reality would dismiss it.

Determined or Free?

The physics developed by and in keeping with Sir Isaac Newton, often referred to today as *Newtonian* or *classical* physics, is highly invested in determinism. As described above, predictability is the primary "advantage" of determinism. Historically, physical science has placed a high investment in reality's capacity to provide consistent answers. For a physical formulation *not* to provide such consistency would call into question the accuracy of the equations and the data. Even in the age of quantum uncertainties, determinism is still a preferred stance.

Determinism and materialistic reductionism, however, also raise some troubling questions. What, for instance, does a rationalistic determinism say about personal *value*? Values are those things humans hold as important and are measured on a sliding scale. Responsibility, sacrifice, service, integrity—such things are not ascertained by accuracy or predictability but by evaluation and proportionality. Determinism in and of itself cannot answer a simple question such as "Do I hold mercy as more important than justice, and if so, to what degree?" How does a reductionist view of the world create appropriate ethical standards?

Another area for questioning might regard the unexpected, that which is not predictable. How does determinism respond to the events that surprise us—serendipity, marvel, wonderment, or tragedy, collapse, disruption—or processes that are chaotic or random?

Freedom, presumed to be determinism's polar counterpart, lies at the center of this line of thought. Are we actually free? Or is freedom simply a social construct that is totally explainable through neurological investigation? Did I *choose* to do the action I just performed or say the thing I just said, or was I simply responding to a conditioned trigger lodged deep in some unrecognized area of my brain? Do we make choices or only appear to? Such questions lie at the heart of our spiritual reflections in the chapters ahead.

When we get to that part of our journey together, we will have to recognize that "freedom" comes wrapped up in a variety of packages, and we will spend little time on some of these packages. In the United States, for instance, we say that we live in "the land of the free and the home of the brave." We will not be pursuing issues of freedom in the sense of being at liberty, unhindered, independent, or possessing or lacking certain rights or permissions, privileges, or exemptions. These are juridical issues that seek to establish value questions for the common good.

Nor will we explore gratuity—no payment required. However, this is a little different, because this understanding can have spiritual meaning. Isaiah calls out God's invitation: "Ho, everyone who thirsts come to the water.... Come ... without money, and without price" (Is 55:1). God's love, we believe, is indeed free. It cannot be purchased or earned. It is a gift lavished upon both the righteous and the unrighteous (Mt 6:45). Our response to this offer of love, however, is a *choice* we either make or we don't. Our reflections focus here, on the kind of response we make and the process it requires.

Our point of reference, then, is the freedom of choice. Jewish, Christian, and Islamic traditions begin with the premise that God is free, free to create, free to enter into relationship, free to love. But how free is creation? How free are humans? If classical physics was moving ever closer to saying such freedom was just an illusion, the discovery of quantum mechanics has thrown the door wide open for a second look.

Reflections on Prayer: An Introduction

In each of the next four chapters, I present some aspects of prayer that correlate metaphorically with the chapter subjects. I say *metaphorically* because, while some do in fact have pertinence to the scientific area I am presenting, others may simply have similar processes that can help us, to some degree, better understand or appreciate the dynamics of prayer. Though I am not one of them, there are those who may feel that the spiritual agenda itself is simply about learning how to pray. They may *equate* prayer with spirituality. To me, this does both prayer and spirituality a disservice. It asks prayer to carry too much weight, and it too narrowly understands what spirituality is to be. Prayer is an essential part, but only a part, of the spiritual journey. *Spirituality* is a holistic enterprise, touching every aspect of our lives. *Prayer* also involves a response to the fullness of our lives, as the Lord's Prayer suggests (cf. Mt 6:9–15). They work together to weave the fabric of our relationship with Mystery.

In my life and (by way of definition) throughout this book, prayer is an attempt, with some degree of consciousness (at least in desire and intention), to encounter God in mutual presence and invited union.

Consciousness, as we shall see, means different things to different people. How am I intending it here? Let us, for now, call it an awareness of what is happening at this present moment. In this moment, no prayer is totally *conscious*—I, the pray-er, don't fully comprehend what is taking place—nor totally *unconscious*, which is true even in wordless prayer or mindfulness. I am conscious, at least of *desire* (longing to encounter God) and *intention* (the motivation of the moment).

Furthermore, prayer is a *relational* reality. Mutual presence, subject existing to subject, is at the heart of prayer. It is an encounter between two subjects, the Mystery of God and myself. It is a conscious attempt to share in a presence, an indwelling.

Prayer as such has a different focus from the kind of meditative practices that are intended to bring practitioners in touch with their truest being or to enhance relaxation. I, the pray-er, am not primarily intending to be the focus of my own prayer. Many, if not all, of the meditative techniques are commonly shared with prayer, however. This is particularly true of techniques that involve breathing, imagination, and various forms of centering. Using these kinds of meditation practices, which were developed over many centuries within the various spiritual disciplines, will facilitate our prayer as they also enhance our openness to the encounter with Mystery. This allows us, I might add, the opportunity to experience all the other benefits of meditation as well. We do learn to relax and to become more centered; we do come in touch with deeper and deeper levels of our own being.

But to this, prayer as such adds the dimension of faith. It places me, we might say, on a foundation of meaning and purpose. It is not essentially a matter of thinking theological thoughts or having emotional impressions concerning theological concepts. Prayer is holistically expressing with my life a point of view that seeks to affirm the fundamental goodness of my life and of all life, looking to something profound beyond me and to which all of life points.

PART II

THE QUANTUM WORLD

3

The Quantum Landscape

The World We Perceive

A note to the reader: The following three chapters should not be considered a complete introduction to quantum physics. That would take a much more thorough presentation than I intend or even feel qualified to give. They represent more of a bird's-eye view of the landscape, surfacing basic information and introducing concepts that will be helpful for understanding where we are heading in this work. I recommend, however, that you read a thorough introduction to quantum theory after this book. I suggest this as a good spiritual practice, which may seem strange at this moment, but I hope my intentions will become clear as we proceed.[1]

Instead of looking out at the physical world, let us begin by considering how it is we perceive in the first place. If science means *coming to know*, what can we know and where are the limits of that knowledge? Everything we know about the physical world, we know indirectly. We have no "firsthand information." Everything we have experienced has arrived at our brains through neurological transmission. I have never directly seen anything, or heard anything, or touched anything. I (whoever that is) have only received electrical impulses that my brain has processed and, in effect, has said, "I am seeing a river; I am hearing distant thunder; I am feeling pressure on the surface of my skin that I interpret to be a breeze."

This indicates a basic neurological fact that we seldom consider and presents us with a question: Are there things, perhaps many things, out there that our brains have never processed, and do not know how to do

---

[1] I found *Quantum Physics* from the Idiot's Guide series to be quite helpful with basic concept and terminology. Mark Humphrey, Paul V. Pancella, and Nora Berrah, eds., *Quantum Physics*, Idiot's Guide series (New York: Penguin Random House, 2015).

so? Are there things, even very close to us, for which our senses fail to provide neurological impressions that our brains would not be able to process anyway? We will return to these questions.

A basic evolutionary consideration about our perceptions is related to this line of thought. Physically, as a species, we have only perceived the information we have needed to know. Furthermore, we only perceive this information to the extent that we have needed to know it. We do not have the vision of an eagle, nor do we have a dog's capacity to smell. For one thing, we haven't needed them for survival or advancement. With a little help from corrective lenses, I, and many of us, do just fine sensing the world. Humanity has managed to survive and thrive.

Still, we also have a vast number of capacities that other creatures do not have or apparently need (or know exist), capacities that arise from our highly developed brains. We have, for instance, an insatiable curiosity that seeks to know what we do not yet know or understand. It drives us to learn more, and it is always smacking up against the current limits of our knowledge.

So, when you or I look around this world we inhabit, are there things surrounding us that we don't naturally feel or recognize? Are there things that our curiosity would want to know, but, using our natural abilities, we cannot get to? Undoubtedly there are, and our technologies and learning have enabled us to uncover and discover much of it. This curiosity and desire have led us to the vast knowledge of the arts and sciences that attests to human intellectual prowess. This has also, however, called into question the true nature of many things of which we previously felt convinced but have since proved to be untrue.

Ancient humans once thought of the world quite differently from how many of us think about it today. The book of Genesis, in addition to non-scriptural accounts, depicts a general understanding of the world as a flat but rugged plain, surrounded by water on every side, and, more or less, remaining in place. The land and sky, it was believed, were covered by a large dome, with more water above it. The sun, moon, stars, and other heavenly bodies were set in place below the dome and traveled in paths that were mysterious but somewhat predictable. As our processes and technologies of investigation have extended our perceptive powers, we know that this is not how the world—the universe, actually—really is. I hope I am not the first to tell you this.

As we study the world that we see around us today, we have available the perceptions gathered from our various senses. We have our "common sense," based on our own experiences and those that generations from the past have handed on to us. We make decisions, including crucial ones, on assumptions that we believe to be grounded in fact. But are they? Is what we experience around us the way things actually are?

Let us look at the dimensions we experience every day. Through much of human history, we understood there to be three spatial dimensions. Since the times of Pythagoras and Euclid, we have known the mathematics of geometry, which has shown us how to understand these dimensions, work with them, and utilize our findings for all sorts of good outcomes. We used these skills for a long time, but we never stopped to consider this "long time" as a fourth dimension. Isaac Newton believed time was something that flowed outside of the physical world, something that transcended nature. Then, in the last century, Albert Einstein, in his breakthrough work on relativity theory, demonstrated that time was not outside our physical world but was in fact a *fourth* dimension of it. In doing so, he completely redefined our world.

Is that it? Does that complete the picture, or are there more dimensions somewhere? If there are (and many think so), we have not yet *perceived* them as such. This lack of perception could be understood in several ways. Perhaps they are there but we have not yet recognized them. This, after all, is what happened with time. Perhaps they are lying at the edge of our perception—as some might consider, for example, telepathy or near-death experiences. Perhaps they are just not available to us now, or for a long time to come, or forever. There are, however, current theories of quantum physics, such as string theory, that rely on many more dimensions than four.[2]

How Does Reality Function?

Is what we experience around us, in however many dimensions there may end up being, the way things actually are? Well, yes, and no.

---

[2] As we will see, whether we accept ideas that would point to dimensions beyond the four we can perceive or not, there is good reason to acknowledge that some unknown features of reality must even now be given credence. They are not explainable by the dimensions of time and space that we have available to us. Such aspects of reality usually are referred to by the term *nonlocality*, the four dimensions we perceive providing us with all the coordinates we would need to *locate* ourselves in physical reality. There will be much to say about this in the chapters to come.

In physics, the view of the reality we perceive around us and function in every day is called the *macrocosm*, the *big* world. This familiar world lies between two other worlds, the *microcosm*—the very tiny world viewed through more and more powerful microscopes and other devices—and the *cosmic* world—best observed through telescopes. Such technological aids as these devices were first introduced in relatively recent centuries and have enhanced our ability to know beyond the edges of our natural capacity. Throughout the twentieth century, however, a problem emerged: the *microcosm* and the cosmic world, taken together, have revealed themselves to be describing a reality largely unlike anything we experience in daily life. Could that be correct? Are our common minds deceiving us?

Through the advances of physics in the past century, and especially through two very different areas of investigation in general relativity and quantum mechanics, it turns out that our perception of this everyday macro-world ends up seeming quite different from what we have come to know through our available senses of how reality is actually structured. Things sometimes are not as they appear. When we look at the world that we experience day in and day out, our perceptions fool us in some very real ways. Do the laws of physics reveal themselves one way in very small things, change in our everyday medium-sized life, and then emerge once again on a far more vast scale? Not exactly.

The laws of quantum physics seem to be consistent throughout. They are observable in the microcosmic and the cosmic but not directly observable in the macrocosmic, for the most part, because of a matter of scale. That is, we can observe very, very, very small vibrations in the microcosmic, for instance, and the vast extensions of light years at the cosmic level because they are so small or so great. We have, however, evolved to see our macroscopic "middle earth" as the way things are. Everywhere and all the time, there are factors existing around us that we cannot directly observe, much less measure, and yet still affect reality enough to change our lives.

In our macrocosmic world, we clearly see the evidence of two physical forces—gravity and electromagnetism—and both of these forces reveal to us the importance of *fields*. In general, a field is a region of influence that stores potential energy. When certain entities within those regions interact, their stored energy is put into motion. Your prized vase, accidentally brushed from its shelf, falls to the ground and shatters. The incoming low-pressure weather system interacts with a warmer, high-pressure system, and a thunder storm erupts.

Isaac Newton studied gravitational fields and came to some important conclusions for classical physics. Gravity, he concluded, was a matter of attraction between objects that possessed certain quantities of mass (weight). Their attraction was a straight force, like between your vase and Earth. He then continued to establish mathematical theories that seemed to answer every question about the force of gravity—end of discussion. Only, as we shall see, it wasn't exactly the end of the discussion.

Not knowing at the time that electrical and magnetic fields were two variations of the same force, both having to do with light, Newton also postulated that light was made up of small particles he called corpuscles. They traveled in straight-lined rays. While we don't usually think of *light* as a particle, we understand the general idea of what particles are—small pieces of certain substances that can be divided again and again into smaller and smaller quantities, which ultimately can be counted (if we are able to do so). We do not often think of light that way, but Newton had his reasons for doing so. This, however, was not as universally accepted as his theories on gravity. Christiaan Huygens, for instance, was a fellow physicist who disagreed with Newton. He felt that light was transmitted as *waves*.

Almost two centuries later, James Clerk Maxwell (1831–1879) provided mathematical equations that proved electricity and magnetism were two aspects of the same physical force, electromagnetism. This force was related directly to light, and Maxwell agreed that light traveled through space, not as a particle-like entity but as a wave. Maxwell's equations successfully provided solutions to all the relevant questions of his day. His understanding of the functioning of the electromagnetic field became accepted by physicists in the late nineteenth century.

We know waves from, among other things, standing on a shoreline, watching the water continuously approach the land. We see the waves moving particles of sand and, we understand, hydrogen and oxygen (molecules of water) as well. But we have the "common sense" to recognize that the wave itself does not consist of the various particles it seems to move. With a little more knowledge of physics, we know that every wave possesses two characteristics, frequency and amplitude, oscillating (moving back and forth) at a certain speed (velocity) as it passes through some medium. A wave doesn't seem very much like a particle at all. Who was right, Newton or Maxwell? In the nineteenth century, it seemed like Maxwell's understanding of the wave-like nature of electromagnetic fields had won the day.

The Quantum Perspective

As the decades proceeded, however, and as physics moved closer and closer to the microcosmic level, this apparent contradiction of the nature of light became increasingly significant. In 1900, a German physicist named Max Planck postulated a mathematical formula demonstrating that light intensified in discrete (singular) and even (evenly spaced) energy levels, packets of light he called *quanta*. Building on this, a few years later Albert Einstein published his theory of the *photoelectric effect*, for which he won his Nobel Prize in physics. Einstein designated a single quantum of light a *photon*. Einstein's theory brought together the discoveries of Planck and others and, in the process, showed that light demonstrated properties of *both* waves and particles.

As the knowledge of physical science moved forward in the twentieth century, therefore, light was understood to be somehow an incompatible amalgam of two very different types of physical reality. But how could this be? How could the quality of granularity we associate with particles coexist with the seemingly immaterial undulating motion of a wave? As the scientific community turned slightly toward another physical problem, however, the world was about to get even stranger.

Light doesn't weigh anything. Quanta of light have no mass. It was understandably difficult, therefore, to equate a certain quantity of light packets, for instance, with a kilogram of sodium or a liter of water. Physical elements possessing mass, however, had been known and somewhat studied for a long time. The ancient Greeks had wondered what would happen if you took a certain substance and started to divide it again and again into smaller pieces. What would it be like to get to the smallest piece possible of that substance? They did not have the means to do such a thing, but they imagined what it would be. They called it an *atomos* (something that could not be divided). The atomic quest—the desire to arrive at something basic and indivisible—began in antiquity.

Through many centuries, there was little more the scientific community could do than speculate. How small was an atom? How many kinds of atoms (elements) were there? It was not until the late nineteenth century that mathematics and technology advanced sufficiently to arrive at some sound information about an atom's nature. From that vantage point, however, it was quickly recognized that these little things were actually misnamed. The atom was not indivisible after all. Atoms had parts—but not that many—and they were the same parts as all other kinds of atoms, just in different proportions. Furthermore, by nature, these parts carried electromagnetic (positive and negative) charges. Science had entered the *subatomic* realm.

In the first decades of the twentieth century, knowledge of the atomic structure continued to grow. It was soon discovered that atoms had a nucleus where its positive charge resided. Negatively charged electrons carried on sustained movement around it. Still, understanding how these atoms worked remained elusive. Then, in 1913, a Norwegian physicist named Niels Bohr, working in England at the time and drawing on the findings of Planck and Einstein on quantization, presented a new model of atomic structure. After developing his quantum theory in the following years, he arrived at an explanation of the atom's structure and energy, theorizing physical matter as having both particle and wave characteristics. It was the original *quantum leap*.

What Is the Structure of Physical Reality?

This new quantum theory seemed to be practically impossible to explain —it was some sort of paradoxical reality. Attempts to establish definitive information about a particular entity through experimentations (usually referred to as *measurements*) were continuously stymied by an inability to arrive at a complete answer. Seeking information, for instance, on an electron's exact location removed any information one could gather on its momentum, and vice versa. Bohr proposed a principle of *complementarity.* Subatomic particles possessed features of both waves and particles simultaneously, but these aspects were not in conflict. Instead, they complemented each other in different ways. Physical science never asked a particle to do something that required it to be both a wave and a particle at the same time. Both features were present in one physical entity at the same moment, and both had to be taken equally into account.

By the early 1920s, Bohr had moved the center of his work to his native country and established himself in Copenhagen. There, he was joined by a young German physicist, Werner Heisenberg, who was attracted by the older scientist's innovative ideas. Heisenberg continued to work closely with Bohr and, in 1927, published an important addition to the quantum model, the *Uncertainty Principle*—which maintained that precise measurements of the complete particle could never be definitively established. This was not because of an error but was a result of all physical reality consisting in conjugate pairs, momentum and location being just one of those pairs. This theory held that many aspects in physical reality seemed to have a kind of dualism (or dipolarity) that might seem contradictory but, in fact, was complementary. No matter what measurement one would attempt, the outcome would always remain somewhat unclear.

Such uncertain outcomes created a major difficulty for the classical physics presumed since the work of Newton. *Uncertainty* was not how science was supposed to work. This new theory postulated an uncomfortable position that challenged one of the foundational assumptions of scientific method at that time—its determinism. You will recall from the last chapter that determinism and predictability were central to the Enlightenment understanding of reality. In the eyes of many in the scientific community, there must be something wrong, or at least incomplete, in this new quantum understanding.

The Dilemmas Underlying Quantum Theory

Along with its indeterministic features, another problem with quantum theory soon made its presence felt—the *measurement problem*. The measurement problem involved the experiments that were set up to work with the theory. These experiments, set up to ascertain aspects of subatomic particles such as velocity or location, produced amazingly accurate results, yet they seemed to *always* produce the outcome they were intended to observe. If the experiment looked for a wave, that was what it found. If it measured for a particle, it always encountered a particle. It began to seem that the entity was following the will of the observer who had constructed the experiment. Not only was that rather startling, it also challenged the long-established scientific belief that science was *objective*. It now seemed like the scientist was unduly inserting herself or himself into the experiment.

All of this was leading to an uncomfortable situation. Quantum theory worked; in fact, it worked consistently and produced measurement outcomes that were extremely reliable. Yet its indeterministic nature and this untenable threat of subjectivity in the process led many scientists to believe there must be something missing. This could not be a complete theory. Bohr and Heisenberg, however, stood their ground. They were also joined by a number of other physicists working independently in different parts of the world who were arriving at results that reinforced the general theories of quantum mechanics.

One such contributor was Erwin Schrödinger, who developed a complete formalism (mathematical equations) that described how the same wave packet (or *wave function*) behaved as both a particle and a wave at different times. Schrödinger had hoped to demonstrate how this new theory could be explained through classical physics. Instead, his equations became the basic mathematical formalism still used in support of quantum mechanics.

German physicist Max Born was another important contributor to what came to be known as the Copenhagen Interpretation of quantum theory, providing a lasting homage to the Bohr-Heisenberg contributions. Born developed the formalism of quantum *probability*. Born said, in effect, that one cannot fully identify where an electron actually is, but only where it probably is, and the degree of probability will be spread out over many possible locations. This, however, seemed to add to the growing uneasiness of some in the scientific community. Now, not only were things undetermined and possibly subjective; they were also being defined as *necessarily* probable.

Taken together as it developed through the 1920s, quantum mechanics, with its paradoxes, uncertainties, and probabilistic tendencies, called into question the predominant scientific view of how reality itself was constructed. The physical world had turned upside down, and this new world was working quite well. Not all climbed onboard the quantum train, however. Schrödinger, who had created the quantum equations that demonstrated its functioning, felt unsatisfied when he realized that they had not safely returned quantum theory to the classical world. Einstein, whose photoelectric effect had paved the way for the theory, was incensed by the very idea of probability. For several years thereafter, he carried on a series of debates with both Bohr and Born but was not able to disprove the general theory.[3]

Quantum Theory on the Defensive

In the decades that followed, while the Copenhagen Interpretation has continued to be used, however tenuously, to advance the scientific understanding of quantum theory and remains a relevant view today, several important challenges have been presented that seek to reestablish a deterministic view of reality. Some of these depart significantly from

---

[3] Central to Einstein's focus of debate was what became known as the Einstein-Podolsky-Rosen (EPR) thought experiment. This will be dealt with in greater detail in the chapters ahead.

the classical world of Newton. In general, these seem to fall into two very different approaches: theories around *hidden variables*, and those generally referred to as *many worlds* (or the multiverse).

Both of these interpretations set out to offer alternative understandings of quantum theory's measurement problem, understandings that do not assign a deciding role to the observer. Both presume that what the observer measures is correct but explain the observation in different ways. In the *hidden variable* interpretations, it is posited that what the observer discovers had already been established in the instant before anyone looked. This outcome would be accomplished by the presence of something undetectable that accompanied an electron, for instance, and ultimately determines the result of the measurement. In the most viable form of this interpretation, formulated by David Bohm in the 1950s, the particle and the wave are separate (inadmissible in the Copenhagen Interpretation) but travel together, the wave providing necessary information but remaining undetected. While the theory satisfies Schrödinger's equations, most physicists, it would seem, have judged Bohm's process contrived, and the theory's influence on contemporary quantum physics has been relegated to the sidelines.[4]

While the *hidden variables* approach attempts to redefine the entity being measured, the *many worlds* interpretations more or less seek to redefine reality itself. The observer does not determine the outcome of the measurement because both possible outcomes actually happen; they happen, however, in different universes. The measurement in effect splits reality into two different worlds, both identical but for the measurement's two distinct outcomes. Life then continues in totally separate realities, even to the point of a complete unawareness of what just took place. Such an identical split occurs with each subsequent experiment, resulting in an infinite number of deterministic parallel universes. A variation of this approach, called the *many minds* interpretation, is understood to happen internally at the level of the observer.

The introduction of the *many worlds* model was first proposed around the same time that Bohm was developing his theories. Hugh Everett, a young graduate student from Princeton University, made the proposal in a draft of his doctoral dissertation, but his theories remained undeveloped until the following decades. While the sheer scope of possibility that so

---

[4] David Bohm reappears in our discussions, however, in connection with holography and the implicate order in Chapter 6.

many parallel worlds would come into existence naturally, as well as during innumerable scientific experiments, seems truly overpowering, forms of this interpretation have many proponents in the scientific community. This could be due in part to the fact that the Bohr-Heisenberg model itself seems something of a fantastic stretch. Still, it does cause a scientific layperson like me to wonder what benefit such an extravagant model of spontaneously generated universes would offer.

Some current readers with a philosophical bent may recall the axiom of Occam's razor (attributed to William of Ockham, a fourteenth-century Franciscan friar), which states that "entities are not to be multiplied without necessity." It is a guiding principle rather than a strict rule of logic, but it does seem relevant. Why would we want to multiply universes? Of course, one obvious answer is that it inserts determinism back into the quantum theory. It speaks, I suppose, to the strong investment contemporary science has made in determinism.

Something else to consider, however, is that it eliminates the need for a conscious observer to play a role in the process, thus also bringing objectivity back into the mix. The loss, however (since most important decisions have gains and losses), is verification. Since the split in universes goes unnoticed, we will just never know if it is true.

Determinism and objectivity, threatened to some degree by the Copenhagen Interpretation, have an honored place in classical scientific method, as we have seen. To restore them would be a high value in such a method as *many worlds*, but is it worth the threat of the permanent loss of verifiability? In a similar way, in regard to the theories of *hidden variables*, what is introduced when we advance a theory whose premise presumes an entity that remains imperceptible? And if we say it is worth it, then where else are we willing to set aside perception? In Chapter 1, I spoke of hitting the wall of faith, beyond which lies the gaping abyss of mystery. I said that both spirituality and science will hit that wall sooner or later. Is this such an example from science? The answer to lost verification is "Well, we just don't know." We need to remember this, because along our journey ahead, we will come to this point rather frequently.

The Role of Faith in Perceived Reality

Faith is, of course, a word that seems to throw us directly into the realm of religion and spirituality, but that is *not exactly* what I mean when I use it here. Let us call it an indirect entry. I said above that faith implied that every aspect of life is capable of leading me to a profound awareness that I stand at the door of Mystery. This is not the kind of faith that equates with dogma or conceptual belief; it is the faith born of our human experiences.

In the early 1980s, James Fowler wrote a book titled *Stages of Faith*. It looked at faith from a human-development viewpoint, describing it as something that grew and unfolded over the course of our lives. This is how he speaks of faith:

> Faith is not always religious in its content or context. To ask these questions seriously of oneself or others does not necessarily mean to elicit answers about religious commitment or belief. Faith is a person's or group's way of moving into the force field of life. It is our way of finding coherence in and giving meaning to the multiple forces and relations that make up our lives. Faith is a person's way of seeing him- or herself in relation to others against the background of shared meaning and purpose.[5]

Searching questions that open human knowledge to the investigation of life's meaning and purpose cannot be seen as lying apart from scientific investigation. If all we wanted from science were "just the facts," to make our lives a little more efficient and a lot more complicated, of what useful purpose would its time and energy ultimately be to anyone?

Continuing Our Quantum Investigations

While the controversies around indeterminism and probability continued, the essential discoveries of the subatomic world brought about by quantum theory increasingly led to a deeper and richer understanding of the essential structures of reality. The elementary parts of the atom came to be seen as more and more complex. Protons and neutrons, for instance, were themselves determined to consist of even smaller particles, given the name of *quarks*, held tightly together in a variety of different combinations. With the construction of large atom smashers, more and more varieties of subatomic particles were consistently being discovered and studied.

The sum result of all this theoretical and experimental work in the latter decades of the twentieth century was the formulation of what is referred to as the Standard Model of particle physics. While deemed incomplete, it is currently held in common by all varieties of quantum

---

[5] James W. Fowler, *Stages of Faith: The Psychology of Human Development and the Quest for Meaning* (San Francisco: Harper Collins, 1981), 4.

theory. It attempts to explain mathematically all the interactions and exchanges of the various kinds of subatomic particles and to present them in a symmetrical format that would appeal to that sense of beauty and elegance that science honors and trusts. Beyond that, the Standard Model proposes theoretically to bring together three of the four fundamental forces at work in all of nature. To understand what is termed the Grand Unified Theory (GUT), however, we must better understand the *forces* of nature. We will investigate these in future chapters.

At the conclusion of this brief and tightly condensed historical overview of the early development of quantum theory, we should take a step back to regain perspective, assess where we are, and determine where we need to go from here. In the early decades of the twentieth century, the neat and certain view of reality provided by classical Enlightenment physics was shaken in two ways: first, by the publication of Einstein's theories of special and general relativity, which completely redefined Newton's theories of gravity and our understanding of space and time; and second, by the startling development of quantum theory, which first challenged and then refashioned our understanding of the structures of physical reality.

It is significant to note that quantum theory was not the result of some maverick or sensational ideas that someone or even many individuals concocted. It came about by piecing together new solutions to fill the gap of emerging cracks in the theories of the day. It was built on the standard methodology of science—theoretical reflection, mathematical formulation, and experimentation and observation. The fact that it brought surprising features of uncertainty, probability, and dipolarity as it developed was not in anyone's plan. It presented a theoretical logic that was not consigned to *either/or* but embraced *both/and*. The wave function (the entity to be observed or measured) cannot be considered either a wave or a particle until the measurement is completed. Until that time, it remains somehow both, existing in what is called a *superposition*. This line of thought provided a springboard for even more creative experiments and surprising conclusions.

So far, we have explored the structures and functioning of quantum theory. Before we move on to an exploration of how the theory developed in the concluding decades of the last century and where it might be moving in the decades ahead, we will need to place quantum theory into a wider framework of our general understanding of physical science. We

will focus on two areas: how quantum theory fits into the evolving sense
of cosmology, particularly its place in a universal reality that is in constant
motion, and how we see the theory in regard to systemic wholeness. The
next two chapters will address these areas.

Reflections on Prayer #1: Prayer as Superposition

Recall my definition of prayer from the previous chapter. Prayer is *an
attempt, with some degree of consciousness (at least in desire and intention),
to encounter God in mutual presence and invited union.* We might then ask
the question, What does *an attempt* mean? And what is happening when
I, the pray-er, attempt it? We want to look briefly at prayer as a *thing*, but
what kind of thing is it?

Prayer could be viewed very simply as something I do—I set some
time aside and I pray. There are many ways I could do this. I could
reflect on scripture, say devotional prayers such as the rosary, or use a
technique such as centering prayer to quiet my mind and open myself to
the presence of God. The options, actually, are almost unlimited. These
could all be termed methods of prayer.

We can also speak of various forms of prayer. We can think of a
form of prayer we could call *praise*. It has certain features attached to it,
a particular way of using scripture, or certain kinds of verbal constructs,
or even certain gestures. We could also think of prayer as *supplication* or
petition, where I am mostly asking something of God. Or we may think of
a prayer of *thanksgiving*. The list goes on.

In all of these forms and methods of prayer, we could notice some
very general structures into which we place the form or method. These
structures have something to do with time and space. When do I pray and
where do I pray? These structures can be very formal and regular, but they
do not have to be. I can "generally" pray around this time of day (usually
one that works best for the rest of my daily schedule) or "frequently" in
this room, looking out this window, or in this chapel.

In all of these variations, I have been speaking of the *particulars* of
prayer. All prayer has a particular aspect to it. Even if I use a wordless
and imageless approach to prayer, what might be called *apophatic* prayer,
this is still the particular way I choose to enter into the experience. But,
in all of this, something emerges within us that might say, "But that is
not all my prayer is." We don't want to just "put in time" or cover all the
bases so we can say, "I prayed today." Prayer is, after, all, an attempt at

presence to and union with God. It exists as a relationship that we hope has breadth, depth, and duration. We could even go so far as to say that it *sort of* undulates. It is not always even and regular; it often intensifies, and then seems to diminish, and then once again is strengthened and confirmed ... for the moment.

Encouraged by this chapter's overview of quantum theory, we could understand that prayer often presents itself, metaphorically, like some kind of a wave function. When I stop to look at what is happening in my prayer, as I might do in spiritual direction, it always looks like *something*. While it may not at first be easy, in time, I can learn to articulate that. But that formulation can never contain the whole scope of my prayer. It continues to spread out and deepen in ways I cannot fully appreciate, locked, as we will see, in the mystery of relationship. Much as a wave function, prayer is not contained in the usual boundaries of our macrocosmic world.

Understanding prayer in this spread-out way means that I could experience prayer as overlaying my entire life, distinct from my life journey, my life lived in faith, yet intertwined with it. This understanding resonates with Paul's urge in First Thessalonians, "pray without ceasing" (1 Thes 5:17). This call to *pray always* does not mean to go around whispering devotional prayers. It means to have a growing and deepening attitude of openness and communication with God in all the circumstances of life, positive and negative. Our prayer reflects our life, and our life, in turn, reflects the movements of our prayer.

Our prayer, or the lack of it, will always be particularized. What I do in prayer, what I say in prayer, how I sit, how I kneel or stand, even what I think or the sense that I should do more of any or all of these—they are the objective elements that make up my form and method of prayer. They all have meaning, and I can bring a sense of discernment and evaluation to them. The rest of my prayer, however, is a much less certain mysterious journey. It has the flavor more of becoming than being. While I am active, I am also profoundly receptive. Prayer endures through space and time and gradually unfolds.

4

A Universe in Motion

Change and Motion

Change certainly does complicate our lives, for better or worse. Some of us may wish that were not the case and might say, "If things didn't change, my life would be much easier. I would feel more in control. I could learn tasks at my own pace." The older we get, the more complications life seems to bring about. If we can't go back to where we were, can't we at least stay where we are now? Others (generally younger people) might say, "No, I look forward to change. If things didn't change, life would be boring. I enjoy the challenge, the adventure." And, if I'm really young, change means having opportunities I don't presently have—driving a car, getting a job, starting a family. "I can't wait for things to change."

Whether we like it or not, change is here to stay. The world is always changing. Everything is changing, from the galaxies we observe in space to the subatomic particles that make up reality. In a relativistic sense, nothing remains the same for very long. Change is a product of *motion*, and everything is moving—continuously. There is no way we can ever totally stop the movement of life. The universe was set in motion by the original singularity, the Big Bang, and it has never stopped. It is in perpetual motion from "top to bottom," from the galaxies and stars all around us to the components of atoms. Motion affects every part of our lives, but beyond the sometimes chaotic and stressful activity around certain events that attract our attention, we actually perceive little of it.

From our "big" *macrocosmic world* perspective, many things might appear not to be moving, but that is only our perception. Consider many meditation practices that advocate silence and stillness. Even as we sit motionless, our hearts are beating, our lungs are in rhythmic movement, our circulatory, digestive, and neurological processes are continuing, and every atom in our bodies is undergoing constant activity. On the *subatomic* level, everything is constantly moving, vibrating, shifting, appearing, and disappearing.

On the *cosmic* level, everything is expanding and moving. Our galaxy, the Milky Way, is moving away from every other galaxy at a tremendous speed. Our star and every other star are expending energy and radiating. Our solar system is perpetually revolving, our planet is perpetually rotating, and so on. The tremendous concentration of mass that unleashed its energy at the Big Bang propelled everything outward in all directions. We will continue to move as we proceed into the future.

At the moment of the Big Bang, the universe began to expand, but the universe as we know it didn't just pop out. For one thing, it was too hot. It was at its hottest at the exact moment of the original singularity. The universe was so hot, in fact, that nothing could hold together—no elements, no molecules, no atoms, no protons, no electrons—an intense primordial soup. As it moved, it was also cooling, and, as it cooled, it started to change. It has never stopped.

This initial process of change is the first and essential demonstration of what is called the Second Law of Thermodynamics, the law of *entropy*. It states that the entropy of a closed system never decreases. Entropy essentially means disorder, but the law is stated in a kind of double negative, which may not help in understanding what this means. Let's restate it this way: *the disordering of a closed system (like the universe) always increases.* Remember, this is a law of thermodynamics, so we are talking about the loss of heat. The loss of heat causes a closed system to become more disordered, and it never goes back.

To explain this further, let us look at our sun. The universe had to go through a great deal of disordering for it to begin dispersing galaxies and stars. Our sun is not nearly as hot as the primordial soup, not by a long shot. It is a total mixture of hydrogen and helium, two of the most basic elements in existence, so it possesses low entropy, not much disorder. Yet the sun is continuing to lose its heat through the process of radiation, which extends outward in all directions. A small portion of that radiation comes our way. The Earth and everything else in our solar system depends almost entirely on this thermal energy. The Earth takes that radiated heat and breaks it down further. Some of that is "disordered" into, for instance, a tree. We are out on a cool summer evening having a cookout, and we need some heat. We take the energy stored in the tree and burn some of it, disordering it all the more. So it goes.

The universe will continue to cool off as the vast array of galaxies and stars expend their heat, in the process becoming more and more "disordered." This disorder, however, is often what we generally call evolution, progress, productivity, and specialization. It usually doesn't look so disordered to us. Our sun is about halfway through its fuel, having only about six billion years to go.

Interaction

Let us go back, however, to our primordial mix. As the temperature of the universe cooled and expanded, everything was in motion. Things move because, in some way or other, they are influenced by something else. This physical influence is what is called *interaction*. An older and more familiar name for this is *force*. Contemporary physics generally favors the new designation since it eliminates the sense that a bigger and heavier object is imposing itself on something smaller. Concepts like "bigger and heavier" really mean very little in a relativistic world. In reality, everything interacts with everything else.

At the earliest stages of the universe, the physical interactions (or forces) that we can identify today were probably undifferentiated, but, over time, as the cooling process continued, certain interactions began to separate. Today we recognize four fundamental interactions that power all we know of the *physical* world.[1] It seems these interactions emerged from one another sequentially as the early universe unfolded. The first to separate was *gravity*.

We will remember that Sir Isaac Newton was particularly interested in the force of gravity. He viewed it as an attraction between objects possessing certain amounts of mass. Their attraction was a straight force, but its strength decreased as the distance between the objects increased. In Newton's theories, space and time were absolutes. His gravitational theories could correctly calculate the paths and positions of all physical bodies. In fact, they still generally work very well in our macrocosmic world. The microcosmic world and the cosmic world, however, soon revealed the need for a more complex understanding of gravity with a different framework.

---

[1] Scientists are always open to the addition of new interactions, although so far none have been determined. New claims have recently been made, which we will mention later. Here we will only treat the physical forces that all acknowledge.

That framework was formulated by Albert Einstein in a little over a decade in the early years of the twentieth century. As just about everyone knows, it was called the Theory of Relativity. It is really two theories or perhaps two various applications of one overall theory. In 1905, the same year that Einstein had published his breakthrough work on the photoelectric effect, he also wrote a paper on what he called the Special Theory of Relativity. It was special in that it only addressed relativity in a certain circumstance, which was when two observations of light were made from two different frames of reference (such as, for instance, Earth and space) when both observers were traveling at constant (although not the same) velocities.

The Special Theory of Relativity maintained, contrary to the presumptions of Newton, that space and time were related and were not absolute after all. They only appeared to be absolute because we were all sharing a similar frame of reference on Earth. Space and time together made up a framework of four dimensions called *spacetime*. What *was* absolute was the speed of light, which remained the same for all frames of reference. The next time you are on the top of Mt. Everest, for instance, and I am safely here closer to sea level, your watch and mine will be keeping different times (and neither will be incorrect). But the speed of light will be the same for both.

While this was a major breakthrough (one does not frivolously contradict Isaac Newton), it was clearly incomplete. It only applied to observations with constant velocities (as, for instance, two cars traveling at constant but different speeds). It did not take acceleration (changes of speed or direction) into account.

Einstein's *General* Theory of Relativity, on the other hand, dealt with changes in acceleration, bringing about a completely new understanding of gravity. Dealing with changing velocities was vastly more complicated, and it took Einstein years to appropriately refine his theory, which he finally presented in 1915. It is based upon what he called the *principle of equivalence*, which states that the interaction that gravity produces upon an object (related directly to its mass) is equivalent to the effect of its acceleration. We can get a sense of this equivalence as passengers in a car when the driver suddenly takes off at a green light and we feel our backs being pressed to our seats.

Einstein realized that both mass and acceleration have a profound impact on the four-dimensional spacetime around them. A gravitational field is then created that *bends* or curves spacetime. The amount of matter–energy present and the speed and direction of its acceleration will determine the degree of curvature of the surrounding spacetime. Gravity, therefore, is completely explained geometrically through the distortion of spacetime by the presence of mass and energy in the universe. General relativity, therefore, does not exactly treat gravity as a force from "outside," because the particles of mass are simply following straight-line paths and are being bent relative to the curvature of spacetime itself. Its effect is simply a fact of nature. Wherever mass and energy are, gravity will be present.

Einstein's work on relativity relied completely on classical physics. It challenged and ultimately superseded Isaac Newton's theories, but it never departed from Newton's understanding of the principles of physical science. The gravitational force itself has little to do with quantum physics (at least so far), except to present it with a problem. It is better to say that relativity and quantum theory have been a problem for each other. For the moment, we can state the problem and promise to return to it in time.

Both relativity and quantum theory work amazingly well. For over a century, both theories have been demonstrated to be accurate and useful with high consistency. The problem is that they have never been able to work together. In fact, to attempt to do so has only led to meaningless results. Furthermore, we could say that decades of attempts to solve the problem of their incompatibility have made this elusive solution *the* goal of contemporary physical science, what physicists refer to as the search for the *Theory of Everything*.[2]

The emergence of the physical interactions in the aftermath of the Big Bang return us to our developing exploration of quantum theory. Following gravity, three other forces separated and emerged from the ever-cooling cosmic soup. Taken together, they were just the forces necessary to give some order and structure to the universe. The force that we have already addressed to some degree, the one most noticeable to us in our everyday macrocosmic life, is *electromagnetism*.

As we have seen, electromagnetism has to do with how light functions, but its usefulness does not stop there. Just think, for instance, of all

---

[2] As the Grand Unified Theory is often simply referred to as the GUT in scientific literature, the Theory of Everything is frequently abbreviated as ToE. Such abbreviations occur often enough that some lay readers, like myself, may find it helpful to make the mental effort to hold them in mind, as we do with a term like DNA, for instance.

the ways electricity touches our lives—electric appliances, televisions, computers, light bulbs, and so on. Electromagnetism, however, has far greater impact on us than its reflection in our electric bills. It also holds us in our chairs, resisting gravity's pull to the center of the Earth, just as it keeps the chair from falling through the floor. And at another level, it holds our DNA together, and it enables our cells to function, among countless other uses.

The remaining two interactions of nature are only encountered at the subatomic level, both being necessary for the structure and functioning of atoms. The *strong* nuclear force holds the nucleus of every atom together. By all expectations, electromagnetism should pull every atomic nucleus apart, but the power of the strong force overcomes the positively charged protons' desire to repel each other and keeps the protons and neutrons together. The *weak* nuclear force functions in the interactions of electrons and other related particles.

Since the emergence of quantum theory and the discovery of the strong and weak forces, science has reasonably asked the question of how all these interactions are related. Considering the three latter forces, excluding gravity, we may get a sense of some common features, as they all seem to involve some sort of dipolarity—positive and negative charges playing a relevant role in how they function. Quantum theory has, therefore, sought the theoretical framework that would explain how they fit together. The complete answer to this quest, referred to as the Grand Unified Theory (GUT), would be a quantum theory that unites the interactions of the electromagnetic, strong, and weak forces. The development of what is called the *Standard Model* has been an attempt to present such a theory, but it is still a theory in process.[3] The present stage of development of this structural model could be judged as *functionally* successful. It works in that its theoretical structure is in agreement with experimental data, but many physicists continue

---

[3] Going too deeply into the model's specific aspects is beyond the scope of this book. In the journey ahead, I will offer pertinent information to the particular discussion, and I commend comprehensive descriptions of quantum science's quest for the GUT to your reading. There are a number of books and online sites that could prove very helpful in providing good background. I have already suggested from among the many, the *Idiot's Guide* series: Mark Humphrey, Paul V. Pancella, and Nora Berrah, *Quantum Physics* (New York: Penguin Random House, 2015), chaps. 17 and 18 (in part), 231–52.

to feel that its complicated construction gives evidence of theoretical incompleteness.[4]

While a fully satisfying theory of the Grand Unified Theory still eludes science, the Theory of Everything (ToE) seems to remain significantly farther away. The Theory of Everything, as already mentioned, would unite the interactions of all four forces, including gravity. There is a natural desire in the scientific community to accomplish this. While the two most important achievements of twentieth-century physics remain fundamentally at odds with each other, a huge question mark hangs over the scientific community and not for lack of trying to bring them together. Albert Einstein spent the last decades of his life in what was ultimately an unsuccessful effort to accomplish the task. Several others have given much of their careers to the cause, and there have been some theoretical breakthroughs that offer a degree of hope for the future, as we shall see in chapters ahead.

What about the force of gravity makes it so difficult to fit it into the quantum framework? For one thing, the relative strengths of the four interactions are at great variance with each other. Relatively speaking, gravity has a very weak interaction. Consider that the power of the strong nuclear force holds every atomic nucleus together. Short of atomic fission, no power that we possess can overcome it. Yet I can walk into a room, pick up a book lying on the floor with one hand, turn around, and carry it out—no problem. Each of us overcomes the interaction of gravity countless times in a single day. There are striking differences in how relativity theory and quantum theory understands something as basic as light. In relativity theory, light has no mass, so it plays no role in gravitation. In quantum theory, every quantum of light (each photon) is accounted for. Other difficulties exist between the two theories in dealing with quantum uncertainties at a subatomic level.

Scientific investigation has not identified any other physical forces beyond the four we have briefly looked at. It would seem, at least for the moment, that fully understanding these four interactions would be the only necessity in order to explain the functioning of the universe we live in and experience around us. But could there be other forces at work in the

---

[4] For readers who may want to further explore the limitations of the Standard Model, I suggest Michio Kaku, *Hyperspace: A Scientific Odessey through Parallel Universes, Time Warps, and the 10th Dimension* (New York: Anchor Books, 1995), 126–31.

universe, or in our lives, that are not being recognized? If we were to ask such a question, perhaps our further investigation would have to be pursued in a different way from how science has proceeded up to now. From our current view, by way of the natural sciences, there are still many unknowns lying before us. What might yet lie beyond the edge of our perceptions?

Philosophy, theology, and spirituality can and have asked such questions frequently. Generally, this exploration has carried the conversation into the realm of metaphysics. As a rule, reductionists, materialists, and positivists sometimes like to go there because they feel such questions can then be treated (and dismissed) as fantasy. Metaphysics, however, is not nearly so easily set aside as they might hope.

I believe there is still some ground between physics and metaphysics that has not yet been sufficiently explored. I have already suggested that our present journey through this book will lead us to what I have termed many "walls of faith." I do not intend these walls to be understood as barriers separating the physical sciences from metaphysics, nor do I mean *faith* to be the same as doctrine or dogmatic formulation. Instead, in this context, faith is a trusting encounter with the imperceptible, with that which is beyond our usual perceptions but remains connected to and in some way is interacting with physical reality. From there, faith reaches into the realm of Mystery and suggests a profound conviction based on essential trust and wisdom. That is the Ground, it seems to me, from which metaphysical reflections can fruitfully proceed.

Quantum Field Theory

The development of the Standard Model introduces us to a new and important feature of quantum theory, that is, the *quantum field*. The model itself, in fact, has been constructed to provide for its inclusion. So what is a *quantum* field, and how does it differ from other kinds of energy fields with which we are already familiar, such as a gravitational or a magnetic field? In Chapter 3, I spoke of a field as a region of influence that stores potential energy of some kind. Certain interactions that occur within such regions put this stored energy into motion. Locations within a classical field are established in three dimensions. Mathematically, every point in space is, therefore, identified by three numbers. A quantum field, however, includes special relativity in the picture. It does not exist in space (three dimensions) but in spacetime. The overall effect of this is described succinctly by physicist Sean Carroll:

The basic idea of quantum field theory is simple: The world is made of fields, and when we observe the wave functions of those fields we see particles. Unlike a particle, which exists at some certain point, a field exists everywhere in space; the electric field, the magnetic field, and the gravitational field are all familiar examples. At every single point in space, every field that exists has some particular value (although that value might be zero). According to quantum field theory, *everything* is a field—there is an electron field, various kinds of quark fields, and so on. But when we look at a field, we see particles. When we look at the electric and magnetic fields, for example, we see photons, the particles of electromagnetism. A weakly vibrating electromagnetic field shows up as a small number of photons; a wildly vibrating magnetic field shows up as a large number of photons.[5]

In quantum field theory, reality essentially exists in wave function state. Everything is in superposition unless it has been measured or observed. Depending on how the observation takes place, the thing will collapse into either particle or wave form. Even then, its underlying nature, we might say, remains wave-like. As Carroll has suggested, the visibility of particles is to be understood as vibrations or agitations occurring in various quantum fields. Much of reality's movement, then, doesn't move very far, vibrating and oscillating at the subatomic level. There is a ubiquitous "shakiness" to the subatomic quantum world.

Another important feature of quantum field theory is its understanding of its components' interactions. If we look at an atom and its major parts—protons and neutrons, both of which the standard model understands as being composed of various combinations of smaller particles called *quarks* (the name was picked more or less out of the air, and carries no functional meaning), and electrons—we could ask how they function in relation to each other. The simple answer would be that they relate through the interactions of the three forces that we have detailed above—electromagnetism, the strong force, and the weak force. But how do these exchanges happen? In quantum field theory, they are accomplished by three even smaller particles, together known as *messenger particles*. These

---

[5] Sean Carroll, *From Eternity to Here: The Quest for the Ultimate Theory of Time* (New York: Plume, the Penguin Group, 2010), 269–70.

messenger particles, each having its own specific force charge, are passed between the larger particles during each subatomic interaction.

Taken together, quantum field theory describes a dynamic subatomic world, maintaining itself in endless movement that never shuts down. It is somewhat mind-boggling that you and I and everything else in this whole universe consists of frenzied relational interactions such as these. And that is one of the spiritual takeaways from our consideration of quantum field theory: From our understanding of the physics of wave functions, reality at its deepest level seems to be closer to vibration, movement, and energy exchange than to solid structure and location. This is quite different from what classical physics and our commonsense perception would have thought.

In addition to vibration and energy exchange, we have to remember that quantum uncertainty is always present. The blurriness associated with quantum wave functions cannot allow us to definitively identify location in spacetime. This is a feature of the Uncertainty Principle and is a related aspect of the strange phenomenon known as nonlocality, which will later be discussed in greater detail. The quantum fields occupying all positions in time and space are probabilistic. That is, I see myself here, and experience myself present in this room, reading this material, but that is never more certain than a very high probability.

Most, but not all, of the particles currently theorized as belonging to the atomic structure in the standard model have mass. Some, however, most notably the photon, are without mass. In the 1960s, physicists predicted the presence of another quantum field, later named after physicist Peter Higgs. The Higgs field would, in this theory, give mass to all the particles that pass through it. Without the Higgs field, reality would be imperceptible to you and me. The search for the Higgs particle, a quest of some fifty years, finally seems to have come to some level of fruition in 2012, when its presence was detected at the Large Hadron Collider in Geneva, Switzerland. It was expected that this would lead to the detection of numerous other as-yet-unknown particles. So far, this has not happened, much to the disappointment of many physicists.

This quick, superficial overview of quantum field theory, in some ways, resurfaces a question from the first chapter. "Are we made in the image of God?" Thinking with quantum field theory, now we may ask the further question, "What *is* our image of God?" Many different religions in the world would have vastly diverse responses to this question, including that we should not even *have* an image of God. In the vast extent of the Christian tradition, Christians have not generally held that position, especially because we believe that Christ himself is an incarnate image of God. God's images appear innumerable times in Christianity's long history, including in liturgy, art, architecture, prose, and poetry.

Though acknowledging the ineffability of God, Christians still picture God in many ways. By far, most of these depictions comfortably reside in that "solid structure and location" context of our commonsense perceptions. In Christian Trinitarian art and architecture, physical impressions of Jesus are ubiquitous, pictured in scriptural scenes, in imaginative contexts, in celestial glory, and so on. In a similar way, the image of the Father, who we understand to be pure spirit, still is manifested in works of art and architecture in long flowing robes, well placed in clouds or mist, or perhaps, even in a contemporary context, in male or female form. The Spirit is, of course, the least figured, but, even here, we make the attempt—as fire, dove, wind, or something even more creative if we can imagine it.

I am certainly not saying these attempts are wrong. They are even quite understandable and devotionally admirable. Our quantum context, however, prompts reflection on a different take on reality—on personal presence, and on what we understand God to be like. If we feel, as Genesis says, that we are made in the image and likeness of God, therefore in some way being like God, how do we comprehend the likeness that we and God can share? If you and I are wave-like, our physicality and locality oscillating and interacting within fields of energy, immersed in mass, and shot through with consciousness, what do we understand God to be? If the quantum fields in which we exist stretch across the universe, how does that affect our imagination and experience of God's presence?

Or let us question the opposite. How might our pervasive anthropomorphic imaging of God shape and, to some degree, limit what we allow or permit ourselves to apprehend about God? To what extent do I think of God as being like a human parent, and how might such an image be shaped by my own parental experience? Do I feel that God is always judging me, belittling me, or testing me? Do I try to placate God, or manipulate, or appease, or bargain with God? Do I attempt to rebel against God and liberate myself from the caricature of God I myself have created? How do we attempt to confine God within our own metaphors? If, at times, we would prefer that the things we do, the thoughts we think, the emotions we feel would be better off somehow hidden from God's vision, do we actually think there would be a realistic chance this could happen?

Engaging these questions should not revert us to some kind of faith in a deistic God who is cold, impersonal, and unconcerned about the well-being or the very existence of humans, or any other form of life, for that matter. Instead of denying God's intense involvement with and engagement in the world of our experiences, I am saying that we cannot allow ourselves to confine our understanding of God within the projections of our own flawed formative journeys. The insights of the sciences challenge us to expand our theological and spiritual imaginations.

Time, Change, and Directionality

In many vast and minuscule ways, we have been considering a universe completely in motion in this chapter. We must remember that this is not just a matter of moving through three-dimensional space. Reality itself is continuously in motion and changing, but we live in *spacetime*, so the movement of time cannot be left out of the picture. Even by our own macrocosmic world commonsense perception, it is very clear to us that moving through space and moving through time are vastly different experiences.

Time

Our earliest and most enduring realization about time: there is just no going back. Time, unlike space, seems to be one-directional. In three-dimensional space, I can move to the left or the right; I can go backward or forward; I can climb up or down. In time, it would seem, all I can do is keep going ahead. I can't walk backward in time to examine in greater detail the place I visited yesterday, nor can I fully relive what I did or said when I was there.

Humans, and to some extent some other living creatures, do have memory, but memory is totally a function of our brains, not an objective structure of reality, and it is very uneven. I have heard it said that a goldfish has a memory of one second. For the goldfish's sake, I hope this is not literally true, but having watched fish in an aquarium for even a very limited time, I have also thought that this could be a merciful blessing for the fish. For humans, though, the neurological process of our forming and retaining memories is quite complex, and, as time moves forward, our retention of memories will invariably be affected.

As best we can determine, therefore, time is one-directional. Could it ever be otherwise, and, if so, under what circumstances? Some contemporary writers have thoroughly explored such ideas.[6] It would seem that, if time were ever to be reversed, at least one major law of physics would need to be dealt with—the Second Law of Thermodynamics, our old friend entropy. Entropy (disorder), you will remember, is also one-directional, never decreasing in a closed system. Time and disorder seem to have a lot in common. Both the events of time and the process of disordering tend to accumulate. My desk, for instance, seems to bear witness to that.

If we look directly at entropy in relation to time, we cannot escape facing what many in the science community would see as the endgame for our universe. At the opposite end of the spacetime spectrum from the Big Bang (low entropy), we would come to the cool drift. As the energy of the stars burns out billions of years from now, each star going through a final flair and ending as drifting white dwarfs, the universe would be a cold and lifeless expanse. Is that it? Not with a bang but a whimper? Could the expanded universe, at some point, possibly reverse and go backward?

That would seem to go against the Second Law. Entropy would begin to decrease. If there were a way that it could, would time then go backwards, like a movie running in reverse? Could it continue forward but with a 180-degree turnabout, letting gravity slowly pull everything back together again? And what would all or any of this say about what theological studies call eschatology, the study of God, creation, and the end time?

Before we get too far in this line of speculation, let us ask an even more basic question. What is *time* in the first place? We have already heard that Isaac Newton thought time was an *absolute* in the universe, the attributes of which never changed. Then, in 1905, Einstein said it was not so, that it was a *dimension*, more like the three spatial dimensions. So, what is a dimension? While it seems that just about everyone in quantum science speaks of four-dimensional spacetime or the many dimensions of hyperspace, very few have simply stated what a dimension is. Etymologically, *dimension* comes from the Latin word for measurement. We could say that a dimension is a way to measure, perceive, or fathom the fundamental aspects of reality.

---

[6] See, for instance, Carroll, *From Eternity to Here*, and Carlo Rovelli, *The Order of Time* (New York: Riverhead Books, 2018).

Time is a dimension, but what do we really understand that to mean? If we can perceive four dimensions, does that mean that these are all that actually exist? Could there be more dimensions than these four? It may not surprise you that many physicists believe there are. In fact, there are a number of physicists who are, in effect, staking their careers on it being so. Such a view of reality is sometimes referred to as hyperspace. The search for additional dimensions will be an important question in some of the chapters ahead, but, for now, let's not drift too far from exploring one of them—time.

If we could somehow step out of our dimensional existence, however many of them there are, what would we experience? How does God, for instance, perceive and understand time? This is, of course, an impossible question, at least for us creaturely humans, but that has not kept philosophers, theologians, and even some physicists from asking the question. At stake here is how one would understand divine action in the present. If I, or you, or all of us prayed to God to allow something to happen, something that seemed to be impossible, and God did so, what exactly did God do? Did God change the future, reconfiguring all future events? Or did God already know the future, and it just *seemed* to us impossible, but God intended it that way all along. Are we then just scripted, living out a role already predetermined, believing we are free, but not really being so?

Part of the answer to these questions, if there is one, will depend on how we understand time. There seem to be two very different metaphysical views of time, the *block universe* and *flowing time*. In a block universe, with God being outside or above it, past, present, and future events are seen in their entirety. God knows how things came to be and, more importantly, knows how things will play out. When applied to science, this is something similar to basic determinism, although many reductionists would like to keep God out of that picture. In a block universe, God doesn't need to change anything, for it is all laid out "ahead of time." Whether that would leave any purpose in our attempts at prayer would need further explaining.

When we turn to consider the idea of flowing time, we find that God is seen as being more embedded in our human experience. God's role here, perhaps, has best been expressed by one of its major proponents, John Polkinghorne:

Modern science discerns a world that is dynamically open and evolving and not statically mechanical and deterministic. The theological counterpart to these ideas is the conception of cosmic history as an unfolding creative improvisation rather than the performance of a divinely pre-ordained score. The scientist-theologians believe that, as part of the divine kenosis involved in the act of bringing into being the created other, allowed to be itself and to make itself, God has freely embraced temporality in addition to divine eternity, even to the point that, in a creation that is a world of true becoming, God does not yet know the unformed future, simply because it is not yet there to be known.[7]

Both of these positions have had numerous proponents. The block universe would probably represent the views of classic Christian theology. Polkinghorne, elsewhere, mentioned Augustine and Boethius as influential in the idea's development.[8] The position of flowing time is more represented by contemporary process philosophers and theologians. The emphasis here is placed not so much on creation as being, but as *becoming*. From the point of view of quantum physics, with its uncertainties and probabilities, this latter view likely finds a better fit.

From my perspective, such discussions persuade me to believe that time as a dimension and dimensions in general, for that matter, are fragile things, much more porous than we would like to admit. Perhaps God is outside of time, looking in, and choosing to act when most suitable for reasons we may not know, or perhaps God is embedded in time, but not locked into it and not limited by it, moving freely between both. Or perhaps God does both, paradoxically, defying our beliefs that God can only act the way we would expect.

Change

Whatever time might look like in its entirety, one thing seems clear—it is moving, and its movement seems different from that of the spatial dimensions. Still, as the movements associated with all the dimensions, it results in *change*. In time, things are always changing, and, as Ecclesiastes

---

[7] John Polkinghorne, *Science and the Trinity: The Christian Encounter with Reality* (New Haven, CT: Yale University Press, 2004), 54.

[8] John Polkinghorne, *Faith, Science & Understanding* (New Haven, CT: Yale University Press, 2000), 136.

3:1–11 would suggest, there is a suitable time for everything, whether we want it or not. But what do we make of this *suitable* movement? Things are always changing, but is it change that is going somewhere, change with direction, or is it just change? Often, changes in our world appear as spontaneous and haphazard. A volcano erupts, the wind blows out our candles, a chicken crosses the street—does any of it have any meaning? Stepping back a bit, some aspects of spontaneous change seem to be directional. Unpredictably, they seem to have an impact; they matter. It is not simply a matter of changes being more complex. Were such changes *purposeful*?

Many in the scientific community would answer no. They would not say, however, that they are haphazard either. Many scientists see change as deterministic. This is particularly true of advocates of reductionism. In the reductionist understanding, change begins with, or is reduced to, physical or chemical interactions at the subatomic level, where what takes place is always in keeping with the structures of the atoms and molecules that are there. From there, changes continue in accord with the determined processes that these interactions produce. It is a purely bottom-up experience. In reductionism, there is nothing from above that is pulling forth a desired outcome out of nowhere. If a particular outcome is desired—by an experimenter, say—the necessary ingredients must be there initially or be added at the properly determined time. If there is no experimenter, changes simply follow their determined course in one-directional time.

There is a great deal of "physical logic" to this position, but does it then leave no room for purposeful action? Does the universe not possess directionality? When the initial singularity (the Big Bang) took place, the cosmic soup that emerged contained in potential all the physical material that is currently in the universe. For the reductionist, all we see around us is the deterministic outcome of the processes that were initiated at that moment. But, in contrast, could there be a purpose, an intention, a blueprint of sorts that has, however subtly, aligned itself with the current state of the universe we see around us? Could we say that, in some fashion, the very physical laws that seem so deterministic actually have an imperceptible bent within them that tends to pull the universe in time toward something not yet perceived?

Purposeful action that seems to move events somewhere toward desired outcomes, or at least intended results, strongly suggests a *faith question*. Does God, or something, know where all this is going? Is there an end, or are there several, toward which creation is moving? Are there desired eventualities to the changes that emerge from the movements of the universe? Reductionists would say that these are questions we cannot answer, so we need not or cannot ask them. From the other side of the faith question, we would say that these are questions we cannot answer, so we cannot afford to close the door on them. They must remain open-ended, and we must remain searching.

Time changes things, and, quite often, we humans have had some pretty intense feelings about that change throughout our journey as a species. Earlier periods of history did not always look at change as something to be welcomed. Change meant instability, uncertainty, scarcity, disruption ... the list could go on. Change introduced political upheaval, natural catastrophe, and social unrest. Admittedly, change was not always seen as bad, but, generally, it was met with an attitude of suspicion—the stranger in town, the foreigner, the heretic, the newfangled contraption.

Since the beginnings of the Enlightenment, however, and particularly since the industrial revolution, we have tended to view change with greater openness, even with eager anticipation. The modern era introduced an important change-related concept that has taken our world by storm, the wonders of *progress*. Progress presumes that change is not only acceptable, but desirable. In the modern worldview, progress signals that things are getting better, advancing, improving. This is often a very subjective estimation, and it has frequently been wedded to free enterprise, technological innovation, and capital profit. Still, most of us, at least in Western society, and often uncritically, look for and expect progress to be made in our institutions, our organizations, and our own personal life plans. In the United States, we uphold the right to the pursuit of happiness and look forward to experiencing the American Dream. In such a "First World" society, many have come to hold to the belief (unfounded, and actually dangerous) that progress and personal betterment should be considered something of a birthright, a destiny. We somehow feel we are entitled to personal and societal fulfillment, falling unwittingly into what I call an *addiction to positive outcomes*.

Progress is enticing, but its shiny wrapper does not always match the substance within. Admittedly, we have frequently tended to overrate the changes that happen around us, "in our times." We feel that we are at the doorstep to great advancement or that we live in a special time. This is much like what essayist and novelist Marilynne Robinson has referred to as the *threshold illusion*.

A model that shapes contemporary writing across any number of fields is the crossing of the threshold. It asserts that the world of thought, recently or in an identifiable moment in the near past, has undergone epochal change. Some realization has intervened in history with miraculous abruptness and efficacy, and everything is transformed. This is a pattern that recurs very widely in the contemporary world of ideas....

... In denominating any moment in history, whether real or imagined, as the threshold moment, a writer or a school is asserting a prerogative, the right to characterize the past and establish the terms in which discourse will be conducted from this point forward. Some transformative concept has obliged us to rethink the world in a new light, assuming pervasive error in previous thought or its survivals.... In culture as in nature there is no leaving the past behind, but to have done so, to have stepped over a threshold that separates old error from new insight, is the given from which these schools of thought proceed, as posture and as method.[9]

We can probably see where this way of thinking could be very alluring to science (although theology and spirituality are by no means immune to it). Science, after all, is explicitly interested in acquiring new information, divulging new discoveries, unveiling new principles. I do not mean to imply that science does this in a slipshod or careless fashion. That kind of science never gets past quality peer review. The scientific method is demanding from beginning to end, but there are still hoped-for outcomes, and reputation, recognition, and respect are at stake. Science and theology alike need to take these "revolutionary breakthroughs" with circumspection. Today's monumental discovery may be tomorrow's discarded theory, and spirituality attaching itself too closely to the newest scientific innovation could lead to disillusionment ahead.

Directionality

Is directional movement *evolutionary* movement? Is even raising the issue of evolution, an issue that in the past seems to have identified the critical battle lines between the communities of faith and science, a prudent thing

---

[9] Marilynne Robinson, *Absence of Mind: The Dispelling of Inwardness from the Modern Myth of the Self* (New Haven, CT: Yale University Press, 2010), 3, 20.

to do? It is an *obvious* thing to do. It is a necessary thing to do. And if evolution theory is a battleground, it is not mine, nor does it seem to be a place of battle for the vast majority of theologians or spiritual writers, nor for practically all scientists. For those willing to accept the physical and scientific evidence that is everywhere around us, evolution is hard to deny. It is not just a biological issue. We are evolving in all areas of life. We are evolving historically, sociologically, and, perhaps most importantly, consciously. The evolutionary process is part of the integral fabric of life.

The contemporary philosopher who brings this idea of "creative emergence" clearly to the forefront is Ken Wilber.

> The *continuous* process of self-transcendence produces *discontinuities*, leaps, creative jumps. So there are both discontinuities in evolution—mind cannot be reduced to life, and life cannot be reduced to matter; and there are continuities—the common patterns that evolution takes in all these domains. And in that sense, yes, the Kosmos hangs together, unified by a single process. It is a universe, one song. . . .
>
> . . . As we were saying, evolution is in part a self-transcending process—it always goes beyond what went before. And in that novelty, in that emergence, in that creativity, new entities come into being, new patterns unfold, new holons issue forth. This extraordinary process builds unions out of fragments and wholes out of heaps. The Kosmos, it seems, unfolds in quantum leaps of creative emergence.[10]

This kind of evolutionary concept is going far beyond a Darwinian sense of survival of the fittest, or the most adaptable, or even the most generative. It is not an idea of evolution that only looks back at chance occurrences found in where we have been. That, of course, plays a significant part, but this concept is more concerned with what is coming forth and focuses on the directional movement of where it may be taking us.

Perhaps past and future are all of one fabric. Perhaps the events that arise from the past and move toward an emerging future are part of a much broader design, or a holistic inclination. We have already looked at the physical interactions of nature present in our world. Humans,

---

[10] Ken Wilber, *A Brief History of Everything* (Boston: Shambhala, 2007), 34.

and to a degree some other animals, have learned to use some of these forces to shape and direct certain changes, inventing tools, mastering technological capabilities. Did animals "invent" this capacity through survivalistic trial and error over many eons, or has it always in some way been there, hidden deep within unseen structures of creation? Is there something within the heart of life's vital principle that leans us toward advancement?

Evolution seen from this vantage point presents us with two distinct takes. The first is what we could call cosmological or universal evolution. This is what we usually think of when the topic of evolution comes up, a movement of change across the board, the universe seen as unfolding through countless experiences and having an impact beyond individuality toward the greater whole. Language, for instance, does not just come to one individual (what would be the point of that?), but it becomes universal. All *Homo sapiens* come to stand and walk on two legs, freeing our arms and hands to master (manipulate) countless technical tasks. Changes move through individuals, possibly on many fronts at the same time, toward lasting imprint in a species, a genus, a phylum, etc. As has been stated, this is evolution that goes beyond the biological, embracing the very structures of the cosmos.

But there is a second take, and that lies within the life journey of each individual. It encompasses the recognition that not every personal experience is encoded into the entire species. The events of our lives and the impressions they make upon us, everything that goes into us and becomes part of our personal formation—all of this contributes to our personal evolutionary identity. Each of us has been learning in one fashion or another from our very beginnings, acquiring not just skills or knowledge, but also experience and wisdom. Each of us has evolved into the individuals we are presently and toward whom we shall yet become.

Our personal evolution, however, has not always been what we would consider desirable or positive. Sometimes, we have learned the wrong lessons from our experiences, or we drew the wrong conclusions. Sometimes, perhaps even with the best intentions of our early caregivers, our formative experiences were greatly flawed, and we ourselves were wounded. Perhaps we were able to overcome them and reinterpret them. Perhaps not. In the traditional language of spirituality, our process of going forward has borne the name *conversion* or *transformation* and points to a reality of constant experiential and evolutionary motion.

Both takes on evolution, the universal and the personal, bring us clearly into the realm of emerging consciousness. How is the journey you and I are now making—individually, together, and in conjunction with all of creation, including the decisions we make, the innovations we produce, and the beauty we create—allowing us to be continually changed by time and experience? What would it look like to embrace a new narrative for our lives, to move from the confines of seeking utilitarian progress and embrace a more *transformative evolution* that seeks to plumb the depths of the creative secret we all are carrying within us?

Before addressing these questions, we must first come to terms with the startling awareness that we are actually all in this together.

Reflections on Prayer #2: Movement in Prayer

For anyone who has been pursuing a spiritual path that includes a regimen of prayer or meditation, recognizing the presence of movement within his or her experiences would not be difficult. Making sense of what that movement means could be a much more complicated task. Images may come and go; distractions may do the same or sometimes seem to linger far beyond their welcome. Sometimes the journey looks clear and open, only to become obscure when we begin to walk it.

So many people today who take up a practice of prayer are looking for something. They are seeking God or something beyond themselves. Sometimes, they are dissatisfied with life or feel there must be more to life. Often, they are lacking substantial guidance. They have a spiritual hunger, and they want something that can take them farther, but the movements in prayer are confusing. They wonder if they are doing something wrong.

If my prayer consists exclusively or *almost* exclusively of devotional prayers or pre-established formulas, then the movements in prayer may not be easily noticed. Maintaining an objective, predetermined track may not be conducive to noticing subtle changes in my inner life. But for those whose prayer or meditative practices include varying degrees of self-observation and self-reflection, noticing the movements in prayer can seem quite obvious. The living process of prayer experiences is always changing, and if it isn't, the lack in itself may be significant.

Movement in prayer generally takes on two modes of being or levels of observation. At one level, movement is seen throughout life in the continuous flow of consciousness. In my prayer time or during my meditation practices, I, the journeyer, become aware of changes in attitude, in temperament, in emotion. Images or thoughts emerge, sometimes passing, sometimes lingering. Are they important—elements of life needing to be explored further? Are they distractions more to be eliminated? At some mental level in my prayer, it seems that I am being asked to choose. Is further exploration best, or should I just let them go?

The second mode or level of observation deals with chronology. Movements in our prayer or meditation can be perceived and noted over the course of our life journey. If we were to look back at what we would consider our earliest prayer, whether in childhood, adolescence, or young adulthood, we would clearly see that our experience and understanding of prayer has changed, and continues to do so. We could possibly plot out the "steps along the way." We may notice that these changes can sometimes be perceived as occurring cyclically. Our prayer journey periodically may seem to be going over the same ground during a longer period of time, sometimes years. This may be a sign to us of our spiritual deepening and enrichment, or we might feel that such repetition means we must be doing something wrong. How would we know which it is?

Attempting to address the question marks at the end of the two previous paragraphs is a matter of *discernment*, itself one of the most important aspects of the spiritual life. The difference between these two modes of experience, however, is more simply a matter of definition. I find that Ken Wilber offers a helpful distinction. Wilber distinguishes between states of consciousness and stages, or levels, of consciousness.[11]

The continuous flow of consciousness from one moment to the next, in or out of prayer, is a parade of conscious *states*. It is how the brain processes all the information with which it is continuously dealing. In times of meditation or prayer, these shifting states constitute the movement and process in our prayer experiences. They are not in themselves signaling anything permanent, although they can sometimes be dramatic experiences.

When we speak of *stages* of consciousness, we are recognizing the development of our prayer journey, its ongoing movement and procession. The stages of life and prayer through which we move chart the developing evolution of our consciousness, the enriching of our soul.

---

[11] Wilber's fuller basic distinction between the two concepts can be found in *Integral Spirituality* (Boston: Integral Books, 2007), 3–7, but these concepts are scattered throughout his writings, where, taken together, they are treated much more fully.

We would expect that these stages or levels would be relatively permanent but continuously deepening as we move through the life cycle, although trauma or some kind of personal disintegration can potentially throw us off course, or even into reverse.

These two modes of experience, the moment-by-moment flow of prayer experiences and the overall progression of our prayer journey, meet in the transitional moments of life. Life is full of *transitions*—some great, some small—and the transitions we encounter along the way can shake us up, disorient us, or even throw us into depression. Often, life transitions are perceived as crises, times of challenge and uncertainty. This is in part because we have convinced ourselves of our immunity to change. The word *crisis* comes from the Greek word for separation. It names an experience that separates us from past perceptions and life solutions that are no longer working. What we found comfort and meaning in is gone. But transitions are not just *from* something; they also lean *toward* something. What emerges from the transitions in our journeys are new possibilities, new occasions of growth and transformation.

Our life transitions, along with the movements of prayer that accompany them, are all perceived within the spacetime continuum that has been the general focus of this chapter. We come to recognize, however, that these experiences are discovered in a different range of awareness largely outside the four physical interactions (gravity, electromagnetism, etc.). In our prayers, our imaginations, and our investigations, the implications of these movements invite us to also consider our evolution of human consciousness woven into the wider cosmic background.

5

Wholeness and Relationship

Reality in a Holistic Framework

The story of the common journey of science and spirituality that we are telling could be viewed as a contemporary work of art in relief, with high-tech visual effects that change and shift, focusing now on one thing, now on another. The holistic nature of the universe has been in the background of our story from the very beginning. An essential component of the entire piece, it is now time to bring this into clarity. It is now time to recognize that everything is connected, that everything is a part of the one great whole, and that it all fits together.

In one way or another, this has been stated from the beginning. We have seen that the microcosm, the macrocosm, and the cosmological world we inhabit all function through the same quantum principles. We have also recognized that, in quantum theory, the quantum fields exist everywhere in spacetime. Likewise, everything is in motion, consisting of vibrating energy, powered by physical interactions that are universally at work. It is all interrelated. Everything is in a process of evolving and shifting forms of order. Nothing is purely in isolation from everything else. Though we do not fully understand nor can we adequately explain these relationships, it all belongs together, and you and I are integral parts of the whole.

Quantum physics recognizes that everything is in relationship with everything else, and this fact has universal implications. Interrelational reality was one of the startling conclusions that Bohr and Heisenberg recognized early on in formulating what came to be named the Copenhagen Interpretation. Science can no longer claim to be an objective observer, standing "here," apart from what is happening, and believing it has no part in what is taking place "there." Observation changes the nature of what is observed, pulling the observer into the mix.

A growing interest in the holistic nature of reality, however, has not been true only in the area of particle physics. The fundamental nature of wholeness and interrelational structure is being researched and embraced by practically every aspect of human investigation—cosmology, chemistry (along with medicine and holistic health), biology, anthropology, sociology, psychology, and theology, just to name the most obvious. We are recognizing that everything is capable of influencing everything else at many levels. The understanding of the initial development of our universe is a case in point. Physically, everything has a common origin, the primal singularity, the Big Bang. This becomes a symbol, a tangible metaphor for our common life and purpose; so, too, the common origins of all members of our species, verified by our DNA coding.

Science was not always totally on board with holism, however. The Enlightenment science of Newton and the scientists of his day was decidedly more mechanistic. Like any machine, the universe was envisioned as being put together with component parts, each having a role to perform so that the overall machinery would work properly. Each part fit together for the good of the final product, but the parts themselves were viewed separately, distinctly, and often interchangeably.

If we were to ask where in the development of the physical sciences the movement toward wholeness began to gain momentum, we could possibly look toward the gradual recognition of the nature and functioning of the physical interactions. James Clerk Maxwell's publication of equations demonstrating the unity of electricity and magnetism in the 1860s and 1870s, followed in the early twentieth century by Einstein's revolutionary work on general relativity and gravitational theory, allowed us to look at our everyday life in new ways. In succeeding years, the discovery of quantum physics and the strong and weak nuclear interactions has presented us with the basics of our holistic framework. While still not theoretically complete, our understanding of the physical forces indicates the commonality of how reality works.

While contemporary science for the most part embraces the discoveries that seem to lead us more and more toward a holistic view of reality, it is not always a perfect fit. Questions could arise as to how determinism, that benchmark of classical physics, fits with an overall holistic outlook. Some physicists, for instance, would see holism as being in opposition to reductionism.[1] Reductionism, a theoretical stance that presumes complete determinism, begins with the smallest subatomic entities and builds deterministically from the bottom up. All that exists is reduced to the physical and chemical interactions of the elemental bits and pieces of the physical world. The results of the world (universe) around us are strictly cumulative. Pure reductionism is critical of what it sees as holism's top-down approach, and, of course, the only plan at work is the plan of elemental reactions.

Yet the case could be made that holism doesn't really start from the top down. Instead, it seeks to encounter reality in its completeness. Any plans, directives, or incentives at work are working throughout the whole process. Holism does not view this process as the building of a great master plan from a precise blueprint, but as a flexible or fluent unfolding, with sensitivity to all the incremental changes along the way. From holism's point of view, we are interconnected top-down, bottom-up, and everywhere in between. This implies one central feature of holistic reality: the importance of *systems*. A holistic understanding of physics and spirituality alike is a *systemic* understanding.

Systemic Understanding

The very fact that holism affects such a wide variety of fields of human investigation makes it difficult to articulate *one* definition of a system that adequately satisfies all. Biological systems, organizational systems, family systems, cosmological systems, chemical systems, sociological systems, and so on—each of these brings its unique processes and elements into the mix. The kind of definition with which we are left may fit all, but it may also adequately fit none. A system is a single configuration of elements understood as a whole that consists of interconnected relationships existing over an indefinite time frame. If something exists in systemic relationship, the various "pieces" that make up the whole are all connected and must be viewed corporately to be fully understood and appreciated. This is true of subatomic particles, molecules, solar systems, galaxies, and everything in between. Wherever you have relationship (everywhere!), you have *systems*.

---

[1] For a more thorough treatment of the holism/reductionism debate, see Michio Kaku, *Hyperspace: A Scientific Odyssey through Parallel Universes, Time Warps, and the 10th Dimension* (New York: Anchor Books, 1995), 318–21.

Some authors, including Ken Wilber and Ilia Delio,[2] use the term *holon*, first coined by Arthur Koestler, to speak of something that is itself a system composed of interconnected elements and, at the same time, is an interacting part of a larger system. Viewed in this way, all of reality consists of holons.

Some systems may never change, as, for instance, all the subatomic parts of an oxygen molecule. If something in this system did change, it would no longer be an oxygen molecule and would not work the way such a molecule would be expected to function. However, many systems change frequently, such as a single family unit living at home, where family size and makeup change over time in indefinite ways as new members are born, leave home, or die. Elements within such systems are *mutually reciprocal*—a change in one element will automatically bring about compensatory relational changes in all the other elements. Whether systems change or don't change, as we have seen, they continue to move. Essential to reality's wave-like nature, all the interconnected parts of reality do not stay put.

Quantum field theory recognizes the entire universe as existing as one systemic whole. Sean Carroll describes:

> In quantum mechanics, no matter how many individual pieces make up the system you are thinking about, there is *only one wave function* [italics in original]. Even if we consider the entire universe and everything inside it, there is still only one wave function, sometimes redundantly known as the "wave function of the universe." People don't always like to talk that way, for fear of sounding excessively grandiose, but at bottom that's simply the way quantum mechanics works. (Other people enjoy the grandiosity for its own sake.)[3]

The systemic nature of reality has produced some surprising outcomes in quantum theory, none more significant than that of *entanglement*. Entanglement is a phenomenon that occurs only in quantum physics, having no place in the classical physics of Isaac Newton. In quantum

---

[2] See, for instance, Ken Wilber, *A Brief History of Everything* (Boston: Shambhala, 2007), 27; and Ilia Delio, *The Unbearable Wholeness of Being: God, Evolution, and the Power of Love* (Maryknoll, NY: Orbis Books, 2013), 34–35.

[3] Sean Carroll, *From Eternity to Here: The Quest for the Ultimate Theory of Time* (New York: Plume, 2010), 245.

theory, particles that closely interact can become systemically bonded. They form a single wave function, and they can no longer be viewed separately as long as they remain in this entangled state. Interestingly, this bonding remains intact despite changes in time or space between these components. Even over great distances, action taken upon one particle in such a system causes a spontaneous and instantaneous complementary action in other parts of the system, even if separated by vast spatial distances. In the process, the expected limitations of time and space are both overcome.

This idea of entanglement was famously disputed by Albert Einstein. To him, it demonstrated a fundamental flaw in quantum mechanics because it seemed to contradict his relativistic theories of spacetime, particularly in relation to the speed of light. In 1935, he and some collaborating physicists published a paper on what came to be known as the EPR Experiment.[4] It was formulated as a *thought* experiment, the necessary technology not yet in existence for an actual experiment. Quantum theory would require one entangled particle moving in the opposite direction of its counterpart to instantaneously adjust to changes made on the other. Given that nothing can travel faster than the speed of light, however, this instantaneous adjustment seemingly contradicts Einstein's special relativity. Any correspondence between two such entangled particles should require some minimum time for this information to reach one from the other. Einstein and his associates felt that this correspondence without a time difference was an impossibility and concluded that quantum physics was, therefore, incomplete.

The Copenhagen physicists were not moved, believing their research to be correct. This theoretical impasse (not so rare in scientific research) existed for several decades. At first, those who were uncomfortable with or opposed to quantum theory felt that some hidden variable must be present that could account for the apparent paradox. David Bohm and Louis de Broglie separately presented such a position. In the 1960s, physicist John Bell proposed a theoretical experiment (then still not practically feasible) that might bring closure to the issue. Bell's approach had an interesting twist to it. He created a formalism (mathematical equations again) that would *disprove* entanglement, therefore disproving the completeness of quantum mechanics. If the equations did not work, it would also *prove* quantum mechanics correct. His theory carries his name,

---

[4] Einstein, Boris Podolsky, and Nathan Rosen each contributed the first initial of their last names.

Bell's Inequalities. Over the subsequent decades, several experimental physicists, working separately, were able to construct actual experiments that confirmed that quantum theory's original understanding was, in fact, correct.[5] Hidden variables seemed to be ruled out. Confirming the theory of entanglement, however, does not *explain* the theory.

Einstein's theories of light as the ultimate speed of anything that can exist in spacetime have, in fact, also been confirmed through innumerable experiments. How can information pass between systemic components instantaneously, overcoming both space and time? How is such a thing possible?

This feature of an entangled system, now verified experimentally, is most frequently referred to as *nonlocality.* The word itself suggests something that is not subject to the expected norms of three-dimensional space, yet since we understand that our perceived reality exists within spacetime, we must remember that nonlocality is also *nontemporality.* The spontaneous correlation of two entangled particles over potentially vast distances in space defies the "classical" limitations of relativity. And, of course, it also defies our common macro-world perceptions.

With the verification of Bell's proposed experiment, the majority of the physics community moved away from the idea of hidden variables; most, but not all. David Bohm, who had earlier formulated the mathematical equations that could replicate, in a classical (non-quantum) framework, Heisenberg's quantum theories, continued to explore ways that might offer an alternative explanation. Seeking to move away from indeterminacy, he reasoned that there must be some "sub-quantum mechanical level" of experience that could account for the EPR paradox. He called such a level the "Implicate Order." Bohm's ideas presumed an arrangement of reality that was in continuous holistic movement, folded over into regions of space and time rather than presenting itself as a linear series of events. "Now the word 'implicit' is based on the verb to 'implicate.' This means to 'fold inward' (as multiplication means 'folding many times'). So," Bohm wrote, "we may be led to explore the notion that in some sense each region contains a total structure 'enfolded' within it."[6]

---

[5] Alain Aspect (USA), John F. Clauser (France), and Anton Zeilinger (Austria) received the 2022 Nobel Prize for Physics for their work in this area.

[6] David Bohm, *Wholeness and the Implicate Order* (New York: Routledge Classics, 2002), 188.

In Bohm's view, every aspect of reality has, at some level, all of reality enfolded within it. Each part, in some way, contains the whole, a major outcome of his theory of implicate order. In order to demonstrate the nature of implicate reality, Bohm focused on a photographic process known as a *hologram*, which uses a complex process of interference patterns to create an image that gives a three-dimensional effect. The hologram as a model (we could perhaps call it a *demonstrative* metaphor) intends to convey the idea of a reality that contains the whole in each of its parts. Each region of the image, taken separately, can reproduce an image of the whole.

Bohm's implicate order is, technically, not part of quantum theory since it relies totally on classical physics. It salvages determinacy from the threats of quantum uncertainty, but in the process it creates another insoluble dilemma for physics, once more driving us to the edge of our perception. How do we confirm the underlying premise of the implicate order? Applying it to the EPR paradox, could it account, in another way, in an unprovable way, for what quantum mechanics theorizes and experimentation confirms? The physics community as a whole has not embraced Bohm's ideas of the implicate order while crediting them with the legitimacy of theoretical accuracy.[7] The holographic model, however, will return to our story in the next chapter, as we explore some of the mysterious edges that allow us to look beyond what we cannot yet know.

Theoretical physics has certain preferences when it comes to hypothesizing about systems. There are certain kinds of shapes and structures that create a sense of rightness. In a previous chapter, I mentioned that such theories, providing simpler answers to physical problems, were preferred to more complex propositions. I referred to this kind of simplicity as possessing qualities of *beauty* or *elegance*. Expressions of such preferred formats are often sought through something called *symmetry*. Something is symmetrical when its form or arrangement is similar or identical on all sides of a shape. We might think of a circle or a square, both of which maintain their symmetry if rotated in either direction. When something is symmetrical, rotation does not change the overall picture.

---

[7] See, for instance, Robert Russell et al., eds., *Quantum Mechanics: Scientific Perspectives on Divine Action*, vol. 5 (Vatican City: Vatican Observatory Foundation, 2001), especially articles by James T. Cushing, "Determinism versus Indeterminism in Quantum Mechanics," 100–106, and Robert Russell, "Divine Action and Quantum Mechanics," 325–27.

Symmetry can exist even if two sides of something do not appear to look like each other. The basic symmetrical structure in mathematics is expressed in the *equation* (=). Every math problem seeks to establish a symmetry on either side of that symbol (1 + 1 = 2). Presumably, such symmetry establishes *fact* (taken for truth) in physics, as in mathematics. Schrödinger's equations for quantum theory, for example, were accepted as a verification of the theory *because they were equations.*

Some physicists hope to find that reality is all symmetrical. They hope to arrive at that elusive Theory of Everything, knowing and perhaps mastering the four physical interactions in the beauty and elegance of simplicity. That is the hope, but we are not yet there. Even the Grand Unified Theory (GUT), as it has developed over recent decades, holding together electromagnetic, strong, and weak interactions, is only piecemeal, awkward, and not what physics would call elegant in its symmetry. Symmetry, while perhaps desirable, is, fortunately, not a requirement. In science, awkward theories that still work allow the theoretical and experimental processes to continue, often with the expectation that "there is more to come."

Some theories, however, challenge the premise that simpler and symmetrical are necessarily better. You may remember the reflections, offered toward the end of Chapter 2, on determinism, reductionism, value, freedom, and verifiability, and focused on science's desire for *predictability.* For many in the scientific community, predictability is very highly valued. Many holistic systems are quite predictable, but some are not. Some are, by definition, *chaotic.* Chaotic systems have no predictable outcome for the next iteration. No possibility of prediction, no answers; no answers, no verification. Chaos theory explores some very fascinating developments in contemporary science that seem to suggest that, even in unpredictable, chaotic systems, there is a paradoxical indication of some kinds of order and meaningful structure.[8]

Holistic Reality and Relationship

If, as a child, you collected marbles and stored them in a large pouch, or you kept all your old baseball cards in a box, or all the dolls you might have played with are still kept in your attic, none of these would, in

---

[8] *Chaos theory*, which is separate from quantum mechanics, is an important subject in contemporary physics in its own right, and may have certain spiritual or metaphysical implications not unlike quantum theory. However, it will not be treated in these pages. The decision to do this is simply to keep our project manageable.

and of themselves, constitute a system. Instead, all of these are various collections. Collections may be connected and stored side by side in three-dimensional space. To someone, in this case presumably the various owners, the collections may have meaning or emotional attachment. They lack, however, a relational interaction. The interconnection existing within systems has to do with processes that relate and are related to all the elements that constitute the systemic structure, allowing the system to function. When it comes to systems, relationality is primary.

We have always known that relationships are important, even essential, for reality. When each of us came to recognize the first system we could clearly identify, our family, we each understood, at some inchoate level, that we needed these people to survive. Without them, we could not even exist. As each of us grew in wisdom and knowledge, we slowly came to see the importance of a variety of systems. We came to understand developing friendships, socialization, religious affiliation, educational institutions, and so on. But we often presumed that relationship was basically a "human thing," having to do with affection, nurturance, family affinity, and so on. Relationship provided emotional and cognitive opportunities. It also caused a fair amount of pain and difficulty. Such relational systems were the perpetrators of many of our successes and failures.

We recognized, of course, that there were other kinds of systems— solar systems, traffic systems, operational systems—but they were just names attached to certain groups or processes. They all seemed to stand more or less separate and unconnected from each other. Slowly, however, we are coming to understand that the *human* part of our perception of systems is just a small fraction of what systemic structure and process is all about. We can expand our appreciation of relationship to include animal life and all living things. But, clearly, relationship and interconnection go far beyond that. Quantum theory, for instance, makes clear that relationship and interconnection are systemically structured into everything. Even the very makeup of an atom has relational structures that cannot be eliminated or terminated.

The universe is relational through and through, from bottom to top, from back to front, and from side to side. It consists of an enormous number of systems, from galaxies and solar systems to microcosmic systems like the atom. We have never seen a large part of the universe, and we likely never will—galaxies moving so fast away from the movement of our own Milky Way that their light will never catch up with us. Still, we are systemically and relationally connected with the whole of the universe. Our earth, likewise, consists of an intricate web of ecosystems, all interdependent on the air that supports them, the earth's nutrients that sustain them, and each other upon which all living things feed. The biosphere (the sum of life on this planet) is a part of and interconnected with these ecosystems and with each other, as is our web of social systems in the human domain. As individuals, each of us is part of these systems. In turn, we consist of intricate interlaced chemical and biological systems, all controlled by a master system, the brain and its neurological components, which systemically manages everything we do. And it all comes down to the subatomic particles that form all we can scientifically perceive. Everything is in relationship and is interconnected with the various "pieces" of this vast network, which must function systemically. That is how this entire work of creation manifests itself.

The interconnection of everything was recognized in a startling way even in the theoretical and experimental beginnings of the field of quantum physics. At least in the Copenhagen Interpretation, this interconnection called into question the very presumption of objectivity in the observation process. The observer could not fully separate from the experiment. Observation itself seemed to determine, or at least influence, the nature of what was observed. As we have seen, this unleashed a tidal wave of questions, theories, and disputations that continue to this day. The Standard Model, as it unfolded over the decades, wedding itself to quantum field theory, has not solved the many questions of quantum theory. In many ways, it has created new questions and new theoretical horizons needing to be explored and integrated.

The scientific community will continue to pursue all this, as it should, but the community of spirituality/religion had already embraced a holistic understanding of the universe (creation) long ago. East and West have approached this differently, however, sometimes understanding God, the human person, and physical reality in significantly different ways. Eastern thought, in its various forms, has many articulate voices to express its understanding. Even though my thoughts in this work rely on aspects of the Western spiritual tradition from which I have come, Eastern and Western spirituality, often articulating spiritual understanding in quite dissimilar ways, are as dependent on interconnection as everything else. Approaching discussions about spirituality as a matter of "which side is right" completely misses the nature of nondualistic thinking. Having a thorough and respectful depth of knowledge of both is the only way to move forward in our global communities of faith.

The apostle Paul was clear in witnessing to the Christian community in Rome that we humans cannot fully comprehend the inner workings of God. "How unsearchable are his judgments and how inscrutable his ways. For who has known the mind of the Lord? Or who has been his counselor?" (Rom 11:33–34). Yet we Christians have come to a firm belief in some aspects of God. For instance, we believe that *God is a loving and merciful God who wants to be in relationship with us.* Hopefully, we have come to this belief out of our experiences. Even if we have not experienced this yet, we still believe it because it is the *essential revelation of Jesus.* For the Christian, it is the one statement that Jesus taught us without even uttering a word. It is the basic manifesto of *Incarnation.* As the Gospel of John famously proclaims, "God so loved the world that he gave his only Son, that whoever believes in him may not perish but may have eternal life" (John 3:16). The Word became flesh. God's irrevocable commitment to the cosmic process is the revelation that anchors our faith.

Furthermore, that God is loving, compassionate, and *intensely* desirous of relationship leads us to recognize a few more things:

1. *God, in the inscrutable communal mystery of Trinity, is shown by extension as being in relationship, not just with humans, but with all creation.*

We humans are creatures of the land, water, Earth, stars, and galaxies. All the physical material that constitutes each of us was present in some form at the Original Singularity. God chooses to interrelate through this very "stuff" of the cosmos. This most profound process is how God has manifested relationship in Jesus—*Incarnation*—and how God is in relationship with humankind.

2. *God's desire for relationship with creation is what holds all things together. This relationship implies systemic Unity.*

If God and creation are intricately and intimately connected, what does that say about my connection with all the others, personal and otherwise, that lie beyond my perceived personal boundaries? Our understanding of this unifying process envisions God as *freely* entering into relationship with each of us—actually, with everything. God is, therefore, connected to us in some profound systemic way. We, in turn, are also connected to each other and everything else. The Franciscan tradition has honored this understanding most symbolically and poetically in the Canticle of Creatures, composed by Francis of Assisi in 1225.

This line of thinking could further ask us to consider some of the implications of quantum field theory that we have been exploring and our comprehension of reality from its vantage point. As we develop an appreciation of the vast network of relationships that totally surround us through the course of our lives, we recognize that we share the common benefits, responsibilities, and limitations of the rest of created reality.

3. *God's desire for relationship witnesses to an understanding that this systemic relationship is, ultimately, about love.*

Everything is interconnected, and everything is in a process of shifting forms of order and complexity. The sustaining of my life through this moment is a wondrous sign of the sustenance of all life, of all existence, of all energy, in all its forms.

Recognizing the sustaining phenomenon of interconnectedness witnesses to the belief that reality is all a *gift of love freely given*, and that I am, amazingly, free to respond. I may feel totally inadequate to make a response, but that hardly matters because life's sustenance will continue whatever my response is. The opportunity is always there and is never withdrawn. It is based on the free love of the Giver, and my attempts at a free response, no matter how seemingly insignificant, allow me the opportunity to enter into a cooperative relationship with this movement of energy around me. My cooperative response makes me a participant in this great Work that I can hardly even comprehend. It is my part to do, if I so choose.

The spiritual life is, therefore, one of *co-operation*—cooperation with God, with physical and spiritual nature, with one another, and in an intra-connectedness within myself. This is true at the most elemental levels of creation; it is also true at the most profound levels.

What does God's invitation ask of us? Simply, that we respond in this present moment.

> A scribe asked Jesus, "Which commandment is the first of all?" Jesus answered, "The first is, 'Hear, O Israel: the Lord our God, the Lord is one; you shall love the Lord your God with all your heart, and with all your soul, and with all your mind, and with all your strength.' The second is this, 'You shall love your neighbor as yourself.' There is no other commandment greater than these." (Mk 12:28–31)

The two great commandments—loving God, creation, others, and self—the Spirit is bringing together all things. Relationship is a spiritual imperative.

Reflections on Prayer #3: Solitude and Solidarity

Is it possible that prayer is systemic, interactive, and relational? It is, of course, a relationship with God, but is it systemic in a wider sense? Does it connect me directly with others? We may never have thought so. Prayer is seemingly something I do in my *alone* time. It is solitary, isn't it? Jesus says that we should go to our room, shut the door, and pray in secret (Mt 6:5). We take a great deal of time and effort in prayer trying to clear space, keep focused, tune out the world around us. Furthermore, we might reflect, are there not solitaries, hermits, and recluses who, presumably, set themselves apart from the cares and concerns of the world as contemplatives and monastics who leave everything to live a life of prayer? Is prayer not intended primarily to allow each of us to be alone with God, if only in the in-between minutes that our schedules provide?

Yet there is, of course, *communal* prayer. There are times when we pray together. We gather for liturgical services; we celebrate communion; we go to prayer meetings and revivals; we have healing services. But are not these times purposely set apart in separate formats, with rituals and common prayer forms? Still, we do make supplication (petition) for the needs of others, and we ask others to do so for us and our loved ones. That is a lot of indirect connection, but is any of this prayer systemic in the sense we have proposed above?

You will remember our definition of prayer. Prayer is a *relational* reality, which seeks abiding presence, *an attempt with some degree of consciousness—at least in desire and intention—to encounter God in mutual presence and invited union.* I have suggested above that the spiritual moment (the moment you and I are presently living in, and certainly the moments we create for prayer) offers us an opportunity to participate cooperatively in the manifestation of the two great commandments, loving God holistically (with all your heart, your soul, your mind. and your strength) and loving others as we love ourselves. The spiritual moment is an active moment of living out the interchange of love. So prayer is a relational reality, a desire for some form of mutual presence, including but beyond the confinement of one-on-one time only with God. Prayer is indeed systemic.

It is true, however, that we do not usually perceive through our sensory impressions or the accumulation of cause-and-effect data that we are interrelated with one another by prayer. By now, however, our survey of quantum physics should suggest that encountering the sensory limitations of reality might warn us not to discount what lies beyond our four-dimensional perception. Nor is our interconnection through prayer a new or unusual concept, as can be witnessed to by the assertion of the Church's belief in the Communion of Saints in the ancient confessional statement, the Apostles' Creed. Christians have, from the beginning, felt the presence of the bonds of faith in their prayer for one another.

Still, this does present us with something of a paradox. In one sense, we think of prayer as the domain of solitude, what I do when I am alone. Of course, we can now understand that pure solitude is relative. In our reflections on God, we come to see that we can never be purely solitary, as in, "I am now fully on my own." In the Mystery that is God, I can never be cut off, I am never on my own. But what about *them*, all those others—people, events, processes, created things, ethical works of justice, peace, and truth—all the things I care about and hold important? Is my prayer also interacting with them?

As with any true *paradox* (keep in mind, *not* a contradiction), both "sides" are true: in my prayer I am alone, solitary, and at the same time in solidarity with all things. But how is such a thing possible—for prayer, or for anything? How can I be both singular and interacting in solidarity with everything at one and the same time? We might try turning to quantum theory and reflecting that it is possible for a wave function in quantum field theory in four-dimensional space to have the potential of singularity (particularity) and yet be extended out across spacetime as a wave. A wave function in superposition has value everywhere across a field stretching through the universe. Beyond time and space, as we have seen, such a wave function also has capabilities of systemic entanglement and nonlocality. Am I suggesting that there could be a wave function for prayer, that a "prayer field" could exist? The *least* I am suggesting is that quantum field theory provides a rich and exciting metaphor for what we believe about prayer.

Could we go further? Could we maintain that such a prayer field is more than metaphoric? Under what preconditions would this be possible? It would clearly ask us to move beyond our spacetime continuum, our four-dimensional perception, while, of course, remaining rooted in it.

It would require our movement into what is often called hyperspace, a reality of some higher (or deeper) dimensions, a discussion we have not yet had, but one that lies ahead in our next chapter. Hyperspace is one of several items that remain untreated and that carry our journey to what we might call our quantum frontier.

6

The "Invisible" World

The Edges of Perception

I should first acknowledge that the title of this chapter, "The 'Invisible' World," is purposely misleading. The issue at hand is not our inability to experience or detect an invisible world. There is a great deal of the world/ universe around us that cannot be experienced through our visual sense, and our inability to see it has not kept us from learning about it. The sense of the chapter title arises from the metaphoric use of *vision*, or in this case its lack, indicating something that is undetectable and, therefore, unknown. Invisibility is only one of several perceptual difficulties we will need to face going forward. All of our senses, separately and taken together, have their perceptual limits. In time, some specific areas of limitation may, and likely will, be overcome. Others will not.

Limitation is a fact of our human existence. We all know we are limited. At some point in life we may have felt that we had no limits. Most of us got over that delusion quickly, and some a bit later. If we didn't, we are probably, to some degree, pathological. Looking realistically at ourselves in relation to our world, it should be fairly obvious to us where our limitations are. We are limited by space and time, by our talents and abilities, by the opportunities life has afforded us, and a host of other things. Still, paradoxically, none of us knows exactly where our limits actually are, and few of us have ever reached our limits. Reaching our full potential is an area of great interest to both science and spirituality.

Limitation is part of the human experience, but what happens when we get to our limits? What happens when we get to a place in a certain area of investigation where we just do not know what comes next? I mentioned in the first chapter that, short of unexpected tragedy, we all hit a wall sooner or later. I called it a wall of faith. The limitations we encounter, our unanswered questions, our educational deserts, individually and communally, ask everyone at some point to take positions of faith, if for nothing else than facing our mortality. Again, I am not speaking only of dogmatic faith; I am speaking more of an *ontological* faith, the faith that life will make sense and can provide us with meaning for living. This kind of faith always has its implications in terms of the choices and decisions we make throughout the life journey.

Faced with such limits, scientific and spiritual communities (as well as others—philosophy, psychology, etc.) have a common solution: *theorize*. These communities say to themselves, in effect, "Don't just stand there; think of possibilities." Spirituality and religion, following initial philosophical lines, move into areas of metaphysics and theological investigation. Some of this theoretical reflection situates itself in religious doctrine along particular lines of denominational belief, but a great deal of theological and spiritual investigation, particularly in areas of spiritual experience, is shared commonly across religious lines.

The physical sciences, of course, would generally like to believe that their theoretical pursuits steer clear of such "magical, mystical" thinking. They would want to remain in the real world, looking at things as they "actually are." Yet we have seen that this is easier said than done. There are hidden variables, parallel and multiple universes, enfolded holistic realities, and some other phenomena we have not yet encountered—maybe ... possibly ... still theoretical and undetectable. Such theories, along with imagination and technological know-how, have expanded our understanding of our physical world immeasurably. Yet the limitations remain.

One of our primary limitations is imposed upon us by our senses. We discover that we must live with the incompleteness of our perceptions and the knowledge that can flow from them. Taken together, they ask of us some important questions regarding the physical and cognitive limitations that situate us in our world. How, for instance, are we intellectually bound by our four-dimensional perceptions? What are the parameters of what we can know? To what extent can our theoretical investigations provide us with further insight? And then what?

Certainly, the advances in our knowledge through the field of neuroscience, particularly in the short decades of the twenty-first century, have revolutionized our understanding of what we can know and how we know it. The ability to see the brain at work through technologies such as magnetic resonance imaging (MRI) and positron emission tomography (PET) has taken us to levels of information and knowledge that have completely transformed our self-understanding. But still, our brain functions in order to deal with the realities we have evolved to experience. Can we suppose that what we experience is all that is "out there"? For me and many scientists, if they choose to admit it, this is an active question.

Before considering possibilities beyond our experience, let us take stock of the extent of our perception. Just what can we or do we experience through our senses? Daniel J. Siegel, MD, clinical professor of psychiatry, identifies seven senses at our disposal. There are, of course, the five senses through which we experience and engage physical reality. Siegel also identifies a sixth sense, which he calls *interoception*, through which we are able to perceive our internal bodily states.

> This sixth sense would include balance and proprioception—knowing your position in space—as well as the sense of hunger and thirst and internal signals from muscles, teeth, and pain sensors in the skin. Even sensual touch is a part of this interior data. Having a visceral sense—the feelings of your viscera, such as the heart, lungs, and intestines—would also be included here and has been called "enteroception." Taken together, knowing the internal world can be called "interoception." The spinal cord layer called lamina 1 carries this internal data upward to the various parts of the brain in the skull.[1]

Siegel calls his proposed seventh sense *mindsight*. "What mindsight does is enable us to sense and shape energy and information flow. That's the basic definition, the deeper truth, the fuller picture." Here, Siegel parts company with a number of physicists who see the brain and the mind as indistinguishable. "With mindsight," he writes, "we gain perception and knowledge of the regulation (mind), sharing (relationships), and mediating neural mechanisms (brain) at the heart of our lives."[2]

We will return to Siegel's understanding of mindsight in Part III of the book. My purpose in introducing it here is simply to demonstrate the extensive nature of sensory perception. The scope of our senses is broad and rich, yet still it is limited. For instance, where does nonlocality fall? We

[1] Daniel J. Siegel, *Mindsight: The New Science of Personal Transformation* (New York: Bantam Books, 2011), 272–73.

[2] Siegel, *Mindsight*, 57–58.

know it is there. We see its effects, but we really have no explanation for how this comes about, or even what wonders it would open up for us if we knew. Will we ever know? What are the spiritual implications of not knowing or of coming-to-know? These questions continue to lie open before us.

Let us metaphorically assume that we are standing at a *point* of limitation where we say to ourselves or others, "I don't know what comes next." It actually is not a point but a *line*, and I will call this line an *edge*. Let us imagine that this edge forms a boundary of perceptual possibility—something like a road map that we open and stretch out. Instead of a two-dimensional representation our map is the four-dimensional universe that we can experience through our senses. We could further imagine that this "map," like the old charts drawn by early cartographers, goes only as far as the "known world." You may have seen the early maps of Eurasia and Africa with such a designation. They end at the edge of the page, some of them having the figures of strange beasts and words akin to, "Beyond this, there are dragons." These early cartographers probably didn't really think there were dragons "out there." It was just a way of saying, "If you know what's good for you, you won't venture beyond this point."

But, of course, no one paid attention to these warnings. Explorers ventured forth in ever-increasing numbers, and they found wonderful things awaiting them there. And they found that eventually it led them back to themselves, but now in a new place, with the promise of richer and fuller lives. Humans had the curiosity to take the risks. Many, not all, were successful, but all of their descendants were enriched by their journeys.

How might we be invited to see beyond the edges of our spacetime continuum? When we come to this place I am calling *the edge*, three life stances are placed before us. Each of us can in some way do one of the following:

- I can stop and say in one way or another, "This is all there is. We just can't go farther."
- I can stop and say, "It looks dark out there, but I *know* what happens next. I know this because something or someone else has told me . . ., and I know this is what will happen, so we needn't bother."
- I can stop and say, "It looks dark, but I will keep searching and moving toward the darkness. I will wait upon the darkness to show me, step by step, where to move next."

All three choices involve some stance toward trust. The choice we make of how we interpret our limitations will be highly influenced by our "faith" system. What are we willing to believe about reality and about our lives? Limitation asks of everyone at some point to engage a position of faith. For now, we could say that this faith is where we stand in relation to our perceptual limitations. Faith always has direct implications for our lives. At such a place (and time), there are no faithless people. I can say, "I just don't know," and that might be sufficient for this moment, but, in the very next moment, my actions will matter. Not to decide is to decide. Everyone must make some kind of faith decision. The question is whether the decision I make is *strong* enough to support my life going forward.

Walking Along the Edge

Although I am only now introducing this metaphor, it would be important to recognize that we have been walking along this Edge for most of our journey up to now. Certainly, for many in our world today, spirituality is itself an edge of which they are wary. Some people have been hurt by religion or religious people. Others have found spiritual practices to be feeble or judgmental by nature. Some are recovering from cults and tend to view all religion as cultish. Others have rejected the religions of their families or the beliefs that their families superficially avowed but never practiced. In a similar way, many religious people find secular science to be unethical, impersonal, and pompous. Those on both sides of this aisle have felt judged and categorized by the other. Sometimes, taking a step toward dialogue could seem like some sort of betrayal or infidelity.

There is, of course, also plenty of disagreement to be found among proponents *within* either side. Quantum theory itself, for a long time, was something of an edge experience within the community of science. That is certainly how established physics understood it, as we have seen from the response it received from people such as Albert Einstein and many others. At some point in almost every theory of quantum mechanics, reality as we would understand and perceive it from our common perspective moves to the unknown, the imperceptible, even the unimaginable. And so there has often been pushback from the more traditional scientific community.

We could look, for instance, at the criticism initially charged against the Copenhagen Interpretation, which was holding fast to the Uncertainty Principle and threatening the demise of determinism. Further, quantum theory led to the acceptance of nonlocality and entanglement. Again, we could think of resistance to the position held by proponents of quantum field theory in regard to the wave function and superposition as being the basic structure of reality. How could reality be two things at one time, not only occasionally but as its universal feature, a complexity of potentiality and actuality rolled into one?

For many scientists who otherwise embrace quantum theory, the Many Worlds Interpretations seem to be overreach. Is this how far scientific investigation would have to go in order to salvage determinism and reductionism from uncertainty? Acceptance of the multiverse theories in some way leads to an infinite number of unknowable and imperceptible universes, and the unknowability of these interpretations will not be solvable by scientific advancement—just as theories of holography and the implicate order lead to undetectable wholeness, a movement that pure reductionists would sometimes hold suspect. Whether in religion or science, anytime we get too close to the edge of our "known world" beliefs, resistance tends to mount around us.

Looking Over the Edge

We have been walking tenuously along the edge of our known world, keeping an eye open for dragon-like apparitions, but now it is time to courageously stop, kneel down, and peer over the edge—just to see what might be there. There are still some significant theories in contemporary quantum physics that I have not yet addressed.

Science and theology differ a bit in how they approach experimentation "at the edges." Scientific agendas regarding human limitations continuously seek to expand our knowledge, pushing the envelope, sometimes unwisely, beyond the edge of social accommodation. Theology, in contrast, usually "honors tradition" inasmuch as it wishes to test the firmness of the edges it seeks to investigate with doctrinal belief in hand. Investigating in this way seems to avoid the slippery slope. With this nuance in mind, it is still true that both science and spirituality have the capacity to be either dogmatic or brash.

So if we are voyagers at the shoreline of perception, carrying both our microscope and our catechism in hand, what is at stake? The following topics represent some areas of physical science that encourage us to look over the edge, in some way or other, beyond the limits of what is presently known. Standing at the edge of what we know, acknowledging what we don't, what do our minds and our faith invite us to consider?

Nonlocality

To some degree, we already addressed nonlocality in regard to entanglement, and I have referred to it often in other places. Entanglement—predicted by quantum mechanics, vehemently disputed by Einstein, and eventually verified by experimentation—describes the systemic binding between subatomic particles that defies and overcomes our four-dimensional perspective of reality. Although entanglement seems to be well established experimentally, that does not mean that it is well understood. This "spooky action at a distance," as Einstein termed it, still is unexplainable. It carries us out of familiar spacetime, into something else that remains beyond our present reach. With that in mind, it leads us into many other questions that are, as yet, unexplainable.

Recall that nonlocal entanglement is when two entities bind within a system in such a way that they remain bound even though sensory experiential observation would suggest they should not be. This idea raises some interesting considerations. Can entire systems be entangled? Is the entire universe self-entangled? Is that what it means to say that everything is connected? Is that what Sean Carroll meant when he spoke of one wave function for the entire universe? Or is the universe inextricably entangled with God, and God with us?

There is another consideration, however, still to come, and that has to do with hyperspace and the presence of multiple dimensions in reality. Nonlocal activity, action at a distance, if you will, could be a *doorway* to unperceived dimensions. Could entanglement, therefore, also point to engagement between entities in ways that lie beyond spacetime, beyond our sensory perception, and beyond the physical body's ability to neurologically track such interactions? If we do not know how two electrons halfway across the universe can instantaneously affect one another, how do we know what is possibly occurring between two people, or five people, or a hundred people who are bound together in entanglements we might call love and commitment?

Out There/In Here in the Darkness

One would think that, after more than a century of studying cosmic reality from subatomic particles to clusters of galaxies, science would have a pretty good idea of how much reality is out there in the universe. While science, at least, has its calculated guess, it can't seem to find it, and doesn't know where to look for it. Estimations vary in small degrees, but, if we took all the "ordinary" matter we can distinguish—stars, planets, space rocks, gases, etc.—and put it all together, we could account for about 4 percent of our gravitational calculations. Where is the remaining 96 percent? Scientists believe it is divided between two "substances," *dark matter* and *dark energy*.

Dark matter essentially gets its name because it doesn't respond to electromagnetism, which means it neither emits nor absorbs light. Because of this, it is hard to find. It does seem to respond to gravity and is much heavier than our ordinary matter, so it figures into calculations of the general amount of matter, making up an estimated 26 percent of reality's substance. Other than educated guesses, there is no real sense of what dark matter is for or even where it is.

While dark matter is defined by its gravitational force, *dark energy* repels gravity. It is the energy inherently present in "empty space" and, therefore, is often spoken of as vacuum energy. Dark energy makes up about 70 percent of the matter/energy in the universe. If dark matter is something out there somewhere, dark energy is uniformly present throughout spacetime. It maintains a constant density throughout the universe, including the space around which you now sit. It cannot be seen or experienced, and (you may have guessed it) we don't know why it is there (here). We do know, however, the effect it is having on the universe as a whole. It makes the universe expand, and the universe is continuing to expand. In fact, the universe is accelerating and likely will continue to do so for billions of years, until all the energy of the stars will be exhausted and physical reality will be led to a final entropy that will bring everything to its rest, its equilibrium. And this is where reality will continue to be . . . adrift forever.

A minority of cosmologists hold to another scenario. In the struggle between gravity and dark energy, gravity will ultimately win out, and the cosmos, eventually, billions of years in the future, will begin to come together again. This outcome, however, does not necessarily lead to a happier ending, since the universe would eventually collapse into its pre–Big Bang state. Science seems to offer no Goldilocks solution, where everything ends up being "just right."

This does raise some interesting theological questions in regard to what is called eschatology, the end time. Scripture, particularly the New Testament, provides a considerable amount of reflection on the End, and it situates it in unspecified but still rather familiar circumstances. The world as we now experience it will still be functioning in some fashion, and it then will begin to rather abruptly conclude, sometimes in a series of cataclysmic events. What follows would be what the Book of Revelation calls "a new heaven and a new earth" (21:1). Current scientific theory doesn't seem to offer much hope for a literal interpretation of that picture. Certainly, our planet, Earth, could replicate something destructive very similar to Revelation's picture, either from outside itself or from within. Such events are happening to individual stars and planets throughout the universe all the time. But if such a thing happened to the Earth, the rest of the universe would go on, including any as yet undiscovered life forms that might exist in the potentially millions of earthlike planets that likely populate the galaxies.

Resolving such ultimate questions is not where time and space permit me to go in this book. Any number of theologians have entered into this forum, and their works would be worth reading. Writing in the 1940s and '50s, Pierre Teilhard de Chardin, a Jesuit priest and paleontologist, looked for an Omega Point, a place and time when all would be drawn back into complete oneness.[3] This line of reflection is what many today would refer to as the emergence of the Cosmic Christ, a title that draws mixed theological reviews. Yet when Teilhard reflected on the end time, he basically was reflecting on the "end of the world." The vastness of the universe as we know it today still lay ahead to be discovered. If Teilhard were alive today and had available to him all that scientific discovery has currently made available to us—the existence of countless galaxies, the continued expansion of the universe, etc.—I wonder how he might wish to refashion his reflections.

Still, even in the mid-twentieth century, Teilhard was not speaking only of a physical end of things. His view was holistic. He understood that even if we solved all the outstanding questions of the physical world, human knowledge would still be left hopelessly incomplete. In his words, "The difficulties we still encounter in trying to hold together spirit and matter in a reasonable perspective are nowhere more harshly revealed. Nowhere either is the need more urgent of building a bridge between the two banks of our existence—the physical and the moral—if we wish the material and spiritual sides of our activities to be mutually enlivened."[4]

---

[3] Pierre Teilhard de Chardin, *The Phenomenon of Man*, trans. Bernard Wall (New York: Harper Perennial Modern Thought, 2008).

[4] Teilhard de Chardin, *Phenomenon of Man*, 62.

Closer to our own times, John Polkinghorne, who seemed to find Teilhard a bit too optimistic for his taste, approached the question of the end time in this way:

> I do not think that the eventual futility of the universe, over a timescale of tens of billions of years, is very different in the theological problems that it poses, from the eventual futility of ourselves, over a timescale of tens of years. Cosmic death and human death pose equivalent questions of what is God's intention for his creation. What is at issue is the faithfulness of God, the everlasting seriousness with which he regards his creatures.[5]

Citing Mark 12:26–27 (Jesus's discussion of the Resurrection with the Sadducees), he concludes: "In other words, the faithful God is not one who abandons the patriarchs once they have served his purpose, but he has an eternal destiny for them."[6] Dark energy notwithstanding, each of us, all of us, and whoever else comes to be included in "us" must deal faithfully with our own mortal "completion," trusting in the all-embracing mercy of God. For now, we may leave it at that.

Black Holes, Holograms, and Hidden Information

One of the most fascinating and, I might add, terrifying phenomena in the universe is the *black hole*. Because of movies and television, we probably think we know more about black holes, their makeup, and how they work than anything else beyond our solar system. Our imaginations and those of science fiction writers have provided us with rich and exciting plots that have, in the process, taught us something about cosmology, even though we hope we will never need the information in order to survive. A black hole is created when the gravitational interaction produced by a concentration of mass, as might occur in a collapsing star, becomes so great that nothing, not even light, can escape its core. Instead, the gravitational pull begins to attract anything that comes near it, pulling apart and compressing whatever passes near the black hole's opening, called the *event horizon*.

Scientifically, black holes are hard to study, as you might expect, because they emit no light. First theorized in 1916, they remained

---

[5] John Polkinghorne, *The Faith of a Physicist: Reflections of a Bottom-Up Thinker* (Minneapolis: Fortress Press, 1994), 163.
[6] Polkinghorne, *Faith of a Physicist*, 163.

undetectable for most of the century. Even now, they can only be identified by the gravitational distortions that surround them. Of the numerous descriptions in scientific literature of what life in a black hole would be like, they are all very depressing (there is absolutely no social life). I do not think it will serve us well here to spend too much time and space on such reflections.

As we peer over the edge of our perceptions, however, studies of black holes begun in the 1970s have opened new doors through which many fascinating theories and possibilities have emerged. It begins with our old friend *entropy* (disorder). Quite apart from expectations that black holes would have very low entropy, since everything would be compressed together into one gravitational mush, physicists began to wonder if there were a way that the original higher entropy of the unfortunate lost material could possibly be reclaimed. To put it a little more bluntly, if a black hole sucked in my aunt's antique Tiffany lamp, is it gone forever? (An absurd example, but it demonstrates the gist of the issue.)

The very complex studies of black holes in this regard—investigations much more intricate than the scope of our work here permits—reflect some breakthrough research and theorizing by physicists Stephen Hawking and Roger Penrose, among many others.[7] Hawking and the others first grappled with the question of whether a black hole would last forever. Surprisingly, through a process now known as *Hawking radiation*, they concluded that a black hole would eventually evaporate away over a very (very) long period of time. That raised further questions. How might this newly freed energy look? How might it relate to the original material that was lost to the black hole in the first place?

Further research led to a startling and important discovery. In black holes, the original engulfed material is believed to be stored in two different ways. Sucked to the center of the black hole, the matter and energy are crushed, pulverized, and compacted in three-dimensional space. With no movement, and therefore no heat, the outcome remains in the lowest possible entropy. But not everything goes into the center of the black hole. The material's *information* remains at the event horizon,

---

[7] For those who may wish to pursue this area more fully, I offer two sources: Sean Carroll, *From Eternity to Here: The Quest for the Ultimate Theory of Time* (New York: Plume, 2010), particularly chap. 12, and Brian Greene, *The Hidden Reality: Parallel Universes and the Deep Laws of the Cosmos* (New York: Vintage Books, 2011), particularly chap. 9.

stored in two-dimensional space. The amount of material and the amount of information always remains proportional—the more material that is drawn into the black hole, the larger the event horizon becomes. When the eventual evaporation occurs, both the material and the information would be proportionately lessened. It seems that there continues to be a clear connection between the two.

What could possibly begin to explain this strange phenomenon? Holography, the same principle put forward by David Bohm in presenting his theories of the implicate order, has been suggested as a worthy answer. This might seem a bit surprising, that these great physicists would invest their theories in something that appears in some science fiction as not much more than some kind of trick photography. This is, however, how Sean Carroll describes the holographic principle:

> An ordinary hologram displays what appears to be a three-dimensional image by scattering light off of a special two-dimensional surface. The holographic principle says that the universe is like that, on a fundamental level: Everything you think is happening in three-dimensional space is secretly encoded in a two-dimensional surface's worth of information. The three-dimensional space in which we live and breathe could (again, in principle) be reconstructed from a much more compact description.[8]

We have already seen that the holographic principle, in some way, presumes nonlocality. Bohm's formulation of the implicate order understood that the whole is contained in each of its parts at some enfolded place or level. In the theories drawn from studying black holes, by comparison, all of reality is in two "places" at once. What we see around us in *four*-dimensional spacetime is a projection of sorts from "somewhere else" where it is stored in some different dimensional way. The material in these two places is not entangled; it is the same material held in two separate ways. It is, if you will, the same reality held in two parallel "universes," identical in content, although different in form.

If humans, and presumably all other living and aware entities, experience *one* of these universes while still mysteriously fully present in the other as well, what do we make of the contents there? What is this *information*? It is obviously different from what we think of when we hear

---

[8] Carroll, *From Eternity to Here*, 280–81.

someone say that we are living in an "age of information." This phrase usually means that we live with easy access to vast amounts of factual data through search engines and databases. If we look at the studies about black holes, the information stored at the event horizon entails the sum of what could be called material identity, everything that could possibly be necessary to actually *substantiate* rather than merely replicate everything held within.

Such a universe would, likely, function completely systemically. Systems rely on information to function, and, in such a universe, information is not so much knowledge but *process*. Particularly, information is how systems—from molecules to galaxies—conform to constitutive processes. This kind of universe could contain all of the information in which you and I subsist, including our DNA, vital statistics, stored treasuries of events and relationships, and how all of these would fit together and function as a whole.

In the four-dimensional reality of our everyday experience, the constitutive material of our bodies is temporary and is largely replaced every seven years or so. Everything in us materially is on loan, shared with the rest of creation, and reused again and again. That may not be how our *informational* universe would work. Perhaps, there, our information is stored permanently in a variety of dimensions and continues to maintain our substantial identity through the vicissitudes of spacetime. Would we, at some point, be able to find and reclaim the full sum of our lived experiences? So much of our lives seems to pass us by, and we may wonder if it is then lost to us forever, a mere fraction held tenuously by our fickle memories. If this more complete informational universe could be unlocked, however or whenever this happens, we may at first be advised to enter its chambers with circumspection. Perhaps we should enter such a universe, not seeking to fill in the lost gaps of our self-knowledge, but to assess fully the wisdom we may have holistically attained.

Hyperspace and Strings

In a black hole's event horizon, information of what was three-dimensional material is conceivably stored in two-dimensional space, like a geometric plane or the face of a sheet of paper. So, it would seem that reality can exist in fewer than three or, including time, four dimensions. Can it exist in *more* than four? Can it exist in five, six, or who knows how many dimensions? Scientists have actually considered this possibility since the mid-nineteenth century. In the quantum age, nonlocality, understandably, raises questions as to what might lie beyond the four dimensions we perceive and in which we generally function well. We have already seen this in several areas.

We have also somewhat explored the limitations of our four dimensions and have considered how we are neurologically bound by our four-dimensional perceptions. Our brains have evolved to apprehend these dimensions through our senses, but our brains can also see that we seem to be missing something going on around us on occasion. If, in fact, what we seem to be missing may lie in additional hidden dimensions, how would we go about finding them? Is that even possible? Additional dimensions beyond the common four are often termed hyperspace. Presumably, the answer to nonlocality would likely lie here in some fashion. What are we to make of dimensions we cannot perceive?

String theory is an area of contemporary quantum physics that requires additional dimensions. String theory has been presented as a possible solution to the perplexing search for the Theory of Everything, attempting to unite all four known physical interactions into one consistent theory. The original quantum theory did not provide for two factors that are necessary for the Theory of Everything: multi-dimensionality beyond four dimensions and size.

For string theory to work in terms of mathematical formalism, many more dimensions than our current four need to exist. How many more dimensions we need is an ongoing question as string theory itself evolves.[9] The "basic" theory indicates a total number of ten (nine spatial and one time dimension), but there may be eleven or possibly twice that number. If we can neither observe these dimensions nor even know how many there may be, how do we arrive at an indication that they could be there to begin with? For now, the indication lies solely in the mathematics. Certain numbers of dimensions would produce a formalism that would be necessary to fit what we know of electromagnetism, the strong and weak nuclear interactions, and gravity.

Of course, one immediate question that would spring to mind would be to ask where all these dimensions are. Why do we not see them or even experience them? Where might we look for them? Are they "too

---

[9] For those interested in exploring string theory further, I suggest Brian Greene, *The Elegant Universe: Superstrings, Hidden Dimensions, and the Quest for the Ultimate Theory* (New York: Vintage Books, 2000).

small" to be observed, as has been proposed? Furthermore, if they are very, very small, are we still not involved with three-dimensional space? The Kaluza-Klein theoretical model, originally proposed in the early decades of the twentieth century, and later adapted as string theory developed, proposes answers to some of these perplexing questions, envisioning many dimensions enfolded or curled up in complex loop shapes. It offers a concept that, in some ways, seems highly reminiscent of David Bohm's implicate order, although I have not seen that being suggested.

You will recall from Chapter 2 that scientific investigation involves three aspects: creative and reflective theory, mathematical formalism, and observable replicable experimentation. By its general nature, quantum physics remains incomplete to some degree. In many ways, we can chalk that up to the Uncertainty Principle, but quantum theory is upheld by extensive experimentation. String theory still must make its case that it is more than a mathematical formalism that can resolve the basic and enduring scientific problem of incompatibility between quantum physics and general relativity. Some indirect findings may contribute to its support, but clear observation seems to be a long way off. The four dimensions we have around us affect our lives completely and constantly. That these new dimensions don't seem to affect us in any way raises a question in my mind that needs to be addressed. String theory, however, will probably remain uncertain for a long time to come, for there is no clear path to experimentation and observation at the necessary level of strings.

The second factor that string theory introduced to further the search for the Theory of Everything had to do with size. The effects of string theory are not observable at our macroscopic level of existence. String theory is describing a level of reality that lies at a profoundly smaller degree, presuming that entities existing at the most basic level of reality would have to be much, much smaller than quarks or electrons. To unite all four known forces, including gravity, we must be able to go to this much smaller level, with sizes that are astronomically—billions of billions of times—smaller than anything we can now or may ever be able to see or measure. If string theory is correct, the basic structures of reality consist of one-dimensional strings that vibrate in certain ways at this infinitesimal level.

In string theory, everything in reality vibrates. Superseding what we have come to understand about the basic structures of reality, such as quarks, electrons, or the other subatomic particles, these one-dimensional filaments, and how they vibrate, constitute the essential aspects of reality, including ourselves and our experiences. Every element of nature depends on the variation of the vibrations emitted by strings. Could reality, at its core, "simply" be vibration? What an intriguing thought. And what amazing spiritual implications would then apply. Vibrating strings, in effect, ground the universe in a core of silent music. It would be a music that neither you nor I could hear, far beyond or beneath our physical capacity and yet a music in which we are continuously participating. Perhaps it would be a music only God could hear or a song that only God could sing.

If you had asked me what the goal of this human journey was all about some years ago, I might have said something like the integration of life. Perhaps, closer to our reality, a better response would be resonance, a spiritual vibration, like a choir or a symphony coming together, each voice, each instrument, blending in harmonic amplification. Perhaps God is the conductor. As anyone who has ever sung in a choir understands, when we all come into resonance, it is clearly noticeable, just as our discordance is noticeable. We will explore this idea in the chapters ahead.

Hidden Interactions

You may recall that in Chapter 4 I said *interaction* (force) is what influences things to move. Through this book, we have identified four physical forces that account for all physical movement. I also indicated, however, that this number is not necessarily a closed set. Recent possibilities of a new force have been reported, something that seems to influence a small subatomic particle called a muon in an unexplained way.[10] If this is eventually confirmed, could this indicate that there may be forces that affect even smaller entities? Could there be forces that empower something the size of strings?

Or could it be that we are perceiving only a range of interactions, with unnoticed forces beyond the range at either end? Gravity affects things that have mass across the universe. Could there be forces that affect even greater things, like the whole universe at any given time, forces that are so large, universal, and enduring that we "just don't see them"? Such speculation would obviously make some in the scientific community anxious, because some of the names that may be associated with such forces—love, for instance, or faith, grace, or karma—could not possibly

---

[10] Pallab Ghosh, "Muons: 'Strong' Evidence Found for a New Force of Nature," *BBC News: Science* online, April 7, 2021.

be treated quantitatively. They would exist as propositions that would only make sense in qualitative investigation.

As a *force*, love, for instance, could be more extensive and permeable than the other four, completely overlaying our four-dimensional perspective. What would such a love-force be like? Of course, we experience love at a personal and interpersonal level, where it is most strongly noticeable as an essential part of our emotional life. We see another form of love through the lens of religion and spirituality. At these levels, love certainly has its energies and produces distinct results, but despite innumerable sociological, psychological, and religious studies and surveys, it would still lack the kind of experimental verification that materialistic science would want.

Love as an interaction would also need to prove itself as more than an anthropocentric or biological phenomenon. It would have to stretch across spacetime, and probably beyond. Could it do this? Perhaps, of all the forces we have in our sight here, love possesses the possibility of generating the movement of the universe itself, a movement into existence. But can we say that love in some way moves gases, rocks, planets, and solar systems? Is love a force of evolution? It is certainly not for the reductionist, who only sees things like fields and particles. For physicists and theologians alike who see more to our universe than things to quantify, however, love has a power and dynamism that demands our reckoning.

Teilhard de Chardin explored such a wider understanding of love in his writings. In his principal evolutionary work, written in the 1940s, Teilhard called love an *energy*, reflecting that only two of the four acknowledged physical interactions had been identified and named by that point in his lifetime. From a more contemporary vantage point, *energy* may not be sufficiently comprehensive in itself to encompass the role that love can play. While the physical forces possess their energies—electromagnetic energy, gravitational energy, etc.—the energy arises from the interaction, and not the other way around.[11] Teilhard speaks of what he calls the *within* of love.

---

[11] In her extensive treatment on Teilhard's works, Ilia Delio rightly recognizes the *force/energy* nature of his thought, speaking on his understanding of love as the cosmological force that energizes and integrates the evolutionary process of the universe. See, for instance, Ilia Delio, *The Unbearable Wholeness of Being: God, Evolution, and the Power of Love* (Maryknoll, NY: Orbis Books, 2013), 43–46.

Considered in its full biological reality, love—that is to say, the affinity of being with being—is not peculiar to man. It is a general property of all life and as such it embraces, in its varieties and degrees, all the forms successively adopted by organized matter. . . . Farther off, that is to say lower down on the tree of life, analogies are more obscure until they become so faint as to be imperceptible. But this is the place to repeat what I said earlier when we were discussing the "*within* of things." If there were no real propensity to unite, even at the prodigiously rudimentary level—indeed in the molecule itself—it would be physically impossible for love to appear higher up, with us, in "hominised" form.[12]

In its inchoate and primordial sense, love could be understood as generative "from the beginning." It could also be propelling evolution itself *toward* something. In this way, reality might not be worked out in its details but may be pulled, lured, or enticed forward in response to some broad intention or purpose, a directional nudging that, despite our irrepressible human tendencies to recklessly assume control of the entire enterprise, keeps us humble and vulnerable. This purpose is with us for the long term, its intention seen only partially and, even then, mostly in a developmental sense. Along this line, we might think of Martin Luther King Jr.'s attention to a moral universe. He said, "The arc of the moral universe is long but it bends toward justice."[13] Is love forceful enough to bend the moral universe? If so, it would indeed be a long-bending one that only clarifies through an extended fashion.

Beyond the Edge

Are there dragons beyond the edge of our known world? Yes, there probably are, and everyone's dragons look a little different. But are they really dangerous?

We have seen throughout this book that we must learn to deal with the incompleteness of our perceptions and the limits of our knowledge. It should be recognized by now that each one of us, scientists and theologians included, are consigned to interpretive choices at some point. The choice of how we understand our experiences and investigations

---

[12] Teilhard de Chardin, *The Phenomenon of Man*, 264.

[13] Dr. Martin Luther King Jr., "Remaining Awake through a Great Revolution." Speech given at the National Cathedral, March 31, 1968.

will, somehow, be highly influenced by our "faith" systems. What are we willing to believe about reality? What personal investment lies behind our affirmations and denials?

By the end of the nineteenth century, when it came to the physical world, it seemed as if the nature of physical reality was pretty well understood. Inconsistencies in our experiences and investigations then began to wear away the veneer of the world around us (the *macrocosm*). By the mid-1930s, all the moorings had been dislodged, and questions and contradictions abounded.[14] As a result, objectivity—the Holy Grail of scientific method—was seen as standing on shaky quantum ground. It was being questioned on anything that related to physical, psychological, or spiritual investigation. Uncertainty was being affirmed. A more subjective way of viewing physical reality was coming into its own. Did quantum theory prove there is no longer pure objectivity? *Is true objectivity even possible?* And if it is not, what is real?

Our need for metaphors, of which I spoke in the beginning, points to an awareness that much of reality is imprecise. Recognizing that all of our knowledge is limited is disturbing for some of us at times. Our knowledge is not only limited. It is frequently *conditioned*. What we know, or think we know, often has underlying layers of presumptions, at least some of which are unconscious. We recognize that this is true in our individual reasoning and systemically, as in our families, our politics, and our business and social choices. But is it true for our religious beliefs? Our scientific discoveries? Does it even challenge what we understand as truth?

Holding for a moment on how theologies and spiritualities must respond, how could science ever go forward if much of reality is imprecise? At first look, it seems this might not be a major problem for science. Theoretical reflection is always close at hand. Some popular physics books offer considerable theoretical "possibilities" about the future, for humans and for reality in general. These are often presented as being highly doable in time, although sometimes not so quickly. When we are finally able to move freely beyond our planet, beyond our solar system, beyond our galaxy, this is what we will be able to accomplish or even what we will have become.

---

[14] By 1935, the well-known "Schrödinger's Cat" thought experiment had been proposed, and the Einstein-Podolsky-Rosen (EPR) challenge to Bohr and Heisenberg had been fully articulated.

It might be good to keep in mind that theoretical reflection and hypothesis will always be able to outstrip our ability to verify our theories by experiments and observation. Scientific experimentation requires that data be received, analyzed, and stored in four-dimensional spacetime, and this has always presented us with some substantial challenges not easily overcome. It has been estimated, for instance, that we would need a particle accelerator the size of the solar system to adequately test for string theory.

To some degree, mathematical formulation has been able to provide some aid here. Mathematics, quite literally, offers a world of possibilities. It is able to go where even theoretical reflection has difficulties reaching. The formalism of the dimensions of string theory is a good example of this, but mathematical formalism is not the same as verification. While we can theorize many possibilities and use the tools offered by mathematics, our ability to translate theory and formulation into practical, verifiable data remains severely limited.

Scientific method may also suffer the consequences of its distaste for one simple question. In the framework of the Enlightenment, there are many questions that can and must be asked: who, what, where, and when. "Why?", though, is tricky. For some in science, the *why* question can be quite problematic, if not unapproachable. When science uses *why*, it frequently means *how does this happen?* or *how does this work the way it does?* But there is a deeper *why* that continues to beckon us. For most people in the course of everyday investigation, the question *why* means something different. It often presents questions about meaning and purpose.

Within a system, *why* is usually seeking further information— clarification, logical conclusions, deeper appreciation, and *motivation*. At the edges of a system and beyond, *why* is a motivational question with which science, since the rationalism of the Enlightenment, seems uncomfortable. It rings of philosophy and metaphysics: for example, why is there something rather than nothing? Why, for instance, does the universe work the way it does, on some very exact constants that have no explanation in themselves, that have been discovered (really stumbled into) and not invented? Why would slight variations this way or that render our entire physical project of the cosmos unworkable?

Another self-imposed limitation of physical science deals with what kind of information it is willing to accept. As I have mentioned, the kind of verification the rational science of the Enlightenment feels most confident in is what comes from hard, factual, analyzed data, verified and replicable in four-dimensional spacetime. This means that, by and large, science has not accepted or has been very slow to acknowledge the kind of information and feedback that come from anecdotal data of personal experience. This kind of information is considered to reside in stories or neural images—possibly even delusional thinking—that can be neither tested nor replicated in spacetime. Anecdotal information and any potential value it might have are generally considered to lie beyond testable and measurable data. But does that make it inconsequential?

In what could be a boundless realm of nonlocality, lying outside of physical data, a potentially vast frontier remains uncharted. How do we begin to unlock it if not through anecdotal collection? It will not submit to rationalistic materialism. Thinking once again of his foundation metaphor, we will recall that John Polkinghorne understood physics as constraining metaphysics, but not determining it.[15] We may want to consider that this could also apply to anything beyond our rational limitations. Known physics may constrain anecdotal information (such as information that would want to contradict the unity of electricity and magnetism), but it would not determine it (such as by saying that forces that *appear to defy* electromagnetism cannot possibly exist).

Probably the biggest concern rational materialism would register toward anecdotal information is that it is inherently subjective and resistive to criticism. The "true believer," once committed to the cause, seems to be blind to seeing any fallacy in the system. The dangers in this are unfortunately often too real. This does not mean, however, that we are inevitably bound to reckless speculation, illogical and magical thinking, or much less to charlatanism. Instead, we still have at our disposal some well-founded spiritual tools of discernment—personal, communal, and societal. I like to use the phrase *Holy Suspicion*, which we bring to anecdotal information, not automatically closing ourselves to what is set before us but weighing it with an open mind and an accepting spirit.

If we dare to peer over the edge of four-dimensional perception, what do we see? Are there other dimensions at the edge of our knowledge, or just beyond the horizon? Is there new information, or are new possibilities lying over the edge that may be accessible in some way? A good example of what lies at the point of the mind's horizon is the brain function of

---

[15] John Polkinghorne, *Quantum Theory: A Very Short Introduction* (Oxford: Oxford University Press, 2002), 90.

intuition. Daniel Siegel identifies it as one of nine functions that take place in the brain's middle prefrontal cortex, but it also relies on neural information that is gathered and integrated from the wider neural interior of the body as a whole, forming something of a "heartfelt sense" toward life's experiences.[16] Yet intuition is usually outer-directed as well toward a heartfelt sense of something out there, beyond the body to which the body's mind/brain senses a connection. How does that happen, and how will we ever know unless we are open to studying it experientially?

Questions about extrasensory perception (ESP), including such reported experiences as precognition, clairvoyance, and telepathy, also lie just beyond the horizon of our four-dimensional senses. This involves an area of investigation that is certainly not black and white, most often cluttered with many varying shades of gray. Some of these shades point to highly questionable or even dismissible reports, while others possess degrees of verifiability that defy explanation.

Perhaps a bit more traditional (just a bit) is the witness of religious experience, an area that embraces such phenomena as miracles, healings, visions, locutions, and mystical experiences. We may also want to place life-after-death experiences somewhere in this general framework. The interrelatedness of spirituality/theology and scientific investigation, while forming the general focus of this book, is by no means confined to it. The common ground between the two has been treated in many other works, in both popular fashion and much more technical formats.[17] Here, we engage with phenomena that have roots much older than anything rationalistic materialism can offer. Even more than with instances of ESP, we must sift through a vast collection of reports and experiences that include clearly pious tales that challenge gullibility, including historically documented events and scientifically evaluated yet unexplained occurrences.

All these areas of investigation, and others besides, lie in that borderline territory I have been referring to as the Edge of the "Known World,"

---

[16] Siegel, *Mindsight*, 29.

[17] Through the years leading up to the millennium, for instance, a joint project between the Vatican Observatory and the Center for Theology and the Natural Sciences in Berkeley, California, produced through a series of conferences five volumes on the theme of "Scientific Perspectives on Divine Action." The last volume, the focus of which was quantum mechanics, has been quoted and referenced in this book. Volumes included other topics on chaos theory, evolutionary and molecular biology, and neuroscience.

moving now closer to the safe harbor of materialistic science and then veering off toward more *dangerous* limits. Seasoned sailors of these choppy waters come eventually to understand that paradoxical or nondualistic thinking becomes the essential navigational tool for the journey.

The Paradoxical Journey

We are considering the possibility of additional dimensions that are hidden to us. One place to look for such dimensions could be four-dimensional spacetime itself. Is it possible that there are dimensions around us that, to some degree, are noticeable but, for whatever reason, have been overlooked, misunderstood, or incomplete? One such possible "hidden" dimension we may wish to consider is what is referred to as nondualism or paradoxical structure. While strict rationalism, at least rational science prior to quantum physics, may feel uncomfortable with such a topic, paradoxical structure has been a well-known commodity in the spiritual life essentially since its inception.

Many experiences in our daily lives have two energies or two manifestations that strike us as more or less overtly contradictory. Such contradictions are not just in reference to things but also to processes, attributes, and so on. Centuries ago, the biblical author of Ecclesiastes (Qoheleth) identified this universal quality of life and our perplexity with it. He writes of divergent times, a time for birth and a time for death, a time to mourn and a time to dance, a time to love and a time to hate, and so on. He acknowledges that God "has made everything suitable for its time; moreover he has put a sense of past and future into their minds, yet they cannot find out what God has done from the beginning to the end" (Eccl 3:1–11).

Why does such uncertainty seem to be worked into the very structures of reality? Why does life continue to look so contradictory? Years ago, I explored the nuances of contradiction and paradox, writing generally from a spiritual point of view.[18] Without rehashing too much of that here, contradiction and paradox, as I describe them, are not the same. Contradiction leads to immobility and futility. If there isn't a way to tie these "contradictory elements" together, they will eventually end up in conflict. Today, we speak of this sort of dualistic thinking as polarized thinking—not dipolar, but *bipolar*, fractured, disjunctive, a cognitive dissonance.

---

[18] Bernard Tickerhoof, *Paradox: The Spiritual Path to Transformation* (Mystic, CT: Twenty-Third Publications, 2002).

In the quantum world, what had previously been seen as *either/or* is now widely accepted as *both/and*. Many aspects in physics, such as the wave/particle ambiguity, seem to have a dualism (a dipolarity) that might seem contradictory. As Niels Bohr suggested, however, the polarities actually *complement* each other. Both, therefore, have to be taken equally into account. Such dualities are common factors in quantum mechanics (for instance, the pairing of observables, such as momentum and position).

This same kind of dualism plays a role in other fields of study, including psychology, sociology, philosophy, and spirituality. The Gurdjieff School, for example, refers to such perceptions as *affirming* or *negating* (also referred to as first and second forces). Hegel formed his philosophy around another language, the process of thesis and antithesis. In Eastern spirituality since antiquity, this same kind of awareness is found in the life principles of *yang* (active) and *yin* (receptive). Examples of such expressions of dipolarity go on and on. This kind of paradoxical, or nondualistic, apperception in spirituality is freeing and transformative, not disjunctive or fractured. The difference, however, is not so much a matter of two different kinds of reality but with two distinct kinds of *perception*.

The models of faith developed by James Fowler can help us understand the difference.[19] Fowler presents the individual's journey of faith in six stages through the life cycle, ranging from infancy, which he terms *undifferentiated faith* (stage 1), to full human maturity, which he terms *universalizing faith* (stage 6). The dualities of life that we have been observing first show up in Fowler's model in stage 4, *individuative-reflective faith*. Prior to this, in the earlier stages, faith has been a matter of degrees of conformity to beliefs the individual has either imagined or been handed by others. In stage 4, however, the individual begins to see there is another way of looking at reality, a view of life that is different, even opposite, from what he or she has held or accepted. This new perception, however, is characterized in either/or terms. Which view is right; which is wrong? Do I accept what society, or my parents, or the Church says, or do I reject and turn from them?

Moving into stage 5 (*conjunctive faith*), the dipolarities are viewed with much more complexity. The individual begins to see that each opposing view has something to offer. There are important values on every

---

[19] James W. Fowler, *Stages of Faith: The Psychology of Human Development and the Quest for Meaning* (San Francisco: HarperCollins, 1981). Fowler's descriptions of these stages is laid out in Part IV of the book, chaps. 15 through 21.

side of the question. No longer an either/or matter; it has become a both/ and amalgamation. As Fowler expresses it:

> The phrase "dialectical knowing" comes close to describing Stage 5's style, yet the term is too methodologically controlling. Better, I think, to speak of *dialogical* knowing. In dialogical knowing the known is invited to speak its own word in its own language. In dialogical knowing the multiplex structure of the world is invited to disclose itself. In a mutual "speaking" and "hearing," knower and known converse in an I-Thou relationship. The knower seeks to accommodate her or his knowing to the structure of that which is being known before imposing her or his own categories upon it.[20]

The final stage of faith, *universalizing faith*, brings this process to its full completion, or perhaps better to say its full resolution. In this stage, the complex differentiations of life are overcome. Fowler does not imply that life ceases to be problematic in universalizing faith. Quite the contrary.

> Persons best described by Stage 6 typically exhibit qualities that shake our usual criteria of normalcy.... In their devotion to universalizing compassion they may offend our parochial perceptions of justice. In their penetration through the obsession with survival, security, and significance they threaten our measured standards of righteousness and goodness and prudence.[21]

The world is seen as a whole, with differences becoming only surface impressions of a deeper unity at the heart of everything.

These characterizing stages presented in Fowler's model are descriptions of developmental processes and, in themselves, speak most directly to various individuals' stages of maturation and, we might say, wisdom. This developmental schema may be of greater interest in the coming chapters. Here, however, we are more concerned with the kind of perceptions of life that these individuals experience along their faith journeys. To see and understand a world where opposites are experienced and then reconciled into a kind of oneness, where, finally, reality is not actually divided, polarized, or fragmented but in some way transformed— this itself could be an important spatial dimension that is quite different from our common perceptions.

---

[20] Fowler, *Stages of Faith*, 185.
[21] Fowler, *Stages of Faith*, 200.

In the history of spiritual development, this transforming experiencing was felt to be the sole domain of those in the mystical state. Fowler's theory suggests that the human brain possesses the kind of plasticity that enables us to grow into such a perceptive frame of reference. Although doing so may not be easy, and it may not be attainable by everyone, perhaps we stand on the verge of expanding our parameters and experiencing this paradoxical dimension.

Not to have considered dipolarity as a dimension of its own seems rather surprising given how noticeable it is in the context of the interactions of nature. The movement to identify the *Grand Unified Theory* (GUT) came about in theoretical science, to a great extent, in response to the dipolarity of electromagnetism. The strong force and the weak force, as well, were so apparently dipolar, even if they and their relationship were not easily understood. Somehow, it was felt, they just have to fit together. Even gravity, while not dipolar per se in relativistic theory (the gravitational force actually following a straight line through curved spacetime) does not totally escape dipolar influences completely. It does have a repulsive effect in regard to still-mysterious dark energy. The jury, apparently, will be out for some time to come on that investigation.

What about love? If we are making a case for considering love as a "hidden" interaction, is it dipolar? Yes, decidedly so.[22] Like the forces of electromagnetism and the nuclear forces, love is thoroughly dipolar, possessing attraction and repulsion. In his first letter to the Corinthians, the Apostle Paul says that love is patient, kind, and not jealous, but we know in certain circumstances love can be extremely impatient, heartless, and callous. Jealousy may be a well-known experience. I have said elsewhere that love in action is the continuous discernment between truth and compassion. These are both admirable qualities, but sometimes, when it comes to "showing love," truth can be *ruthless* (without pity) and compassion can be dishonest.

In all of this reflection on dipolarity and paradox as an additional dimension, we need to keep in mind that this new dimension does not mean that the world is caught in contradiction. That has been obvious for eons. The new dimension comes in apprehending the two poles of reality as coalescing or transforming into a new oneness. Paradox, in my understanding, is *not* living with or coming to terms with contradiction

---

[22] This paradoxical nature of love is pursued in greater detail in my earlier book (*Paradox: The Spiritual Path to Transformation*, 146–50). Again, I am choosing not to repeat the bulk of that material in this work due to its substantially different focus.

or even balancing or complementing the two contradictory poles. Paradox is *the ability to fully embrace contrary or divergent experiences*, in some way surrendering to them, in order to see them dissolved (transformed) into something new. This is, as Fowler suggests, a rare occurrence.

Freedom and Determinism?

With this paradoxical dimension in mind, we can revisit the tension between determinism and freedom that emerged in Chapter 2. This question usually devolves into polarized positions. Is freedom an illusion, or wishful thinking, allowing us to evade our own final impotence? Is determinism the ultimate fabrication of valueless materialistic existence, what Ken Wilber calls Flatland?[23] And is there any way out of this dilemma? Is there a path for pursuing a transformed understanding? Can reality be both determined *and* free? That would be truly paradoxical.

A series of questions arise around freedom. How free is the universe (creation)? How free are humans? Do we make choices or only appear to? And how free is God?

What about determinism? As I said earlier, the "advantage" of determinism is primarily its *predictability*, but at what cost? Classical (Newtonian) physics historically seems to have had some vested interest in reality not being free, as freedom, here, is interpreted as unreasonable. Determinism was able to be built around rational conclusions from experimental data, therefore seen in classical physics as the preferred stance.

At the beginning of the nineteenth century, classical physics had more or less settled on the certainty of causal determinism. The introduction of quantum theory by itself seemed to hurl physical science into the midst of a whirlpool of uncertainty. Discoveries from that point until now have led our scientific understanding into shifting movements from feeling rational invincibility to experiencing ever-expanding horizons.

With quantum physics, are we once again free? Are we actually compelled to be free, thrown into freedom by the very structures of the universe? Classical determinism was shaken by quantum theory, but that does not mean it was scrapped. There are physicists who advocate a form of quantum determinism, noting that probabilistic uncertainties are small and likely do not greatly affect outcomes. These same physicists may also claim, though, that such small uncertainties play a vital role in other circumstances.

---

[23] Ken Wilber, *A Brief History of Everything* (Boston: Shambhala, 2007), 370ff.

When we look at our universe from an evolutionary point of view, it would seem that determinism holds a winning hand. From what we know of evolutionary development, a reductionist-like process can easily be imagined. We do not even seem to have a likely scenario of anything approaching freedom until biological life begins to have some form of mobility. If freedom is somewhere in the picture, it would seem to be, to use Teilhard's term, deep in the *within*. That may very well be the case, however. If it is, that would seem to suggest some correlation with the interaction of love. Freedom could be our compass in the movement from rational predictability to cooperative wonder.

When freedom is inserted into the picture, the mixture quickly gets stirred up. Things become unpredictable, therefore uncertain, and potentially chaotic or random. Freedom introduces the tricky terrain of causality. Where did all this come from, and *why*? Are humans free because God loves humans more than anything else? If that's true, God has an interesting way of showing it. If not, are we witnessing the fall of anthropocentrism, the position long held throughout religious and philosophical tradition that humans are the primary focus of creation? A holistic understanding might see God as immersed in a continuous evolutionary creation. But if that is so, is God also free to withhold? Can love be withheld? What if withholding is the loving thing to do? Does God disturb the rational order on occasion? If that is the case, to what extent? And for what reasons?

Stepping back from our collective mind's wrestling with all the implications of this determinism/freedom dialectic, we may wonder where we go from here. The issue, it would seem, lies in how we interpret several aspects of our human existence. What do we understand by the brain? What do we understand by the mind? What do we understand by consciousness? What are the nondualistic implications of accepting God's freedom, and do we dare permit it? All of this moves us toward an immersion into our last major consideration, exploring the frontiers of consciousness.

Reflections on Prayer #4:
Prayer as Knowing and Not Knowing

In this final reflection on prayer, we may now have sufficient perspective to look more fully at the definition of prayer I have been using. Prayer, I said, is *an attempt, with some degree of consciousness (at least in desire and intention), to encounter God in mutual presence and invited union.* You will remember that, in first introducing this definition, I said that no prayer is totally *conscious* (not fully comprehending what is taking place) or totally *unconscious*, the pray-er at least having consciousness of *desire* (longing to encounter God) and *intention* (the motivation of the moment).

Now, as we are considering the vastness of our hidden reality, we may wonder how much—of prayer, of reality, of life—we don't or perhaps can't know. As we have considered the array of things the universe has likely withheld from us—things like dark matter, hidden dimensions, unknown forces, and so on—it may not seem surprising that so much of prayer remains beyond our reach. This is not surprising, but it is still mysterious.

And, of course, the most mysterious aspect of prayer has always been God. In prayer, our desire for God always leaves us hungering all the more for a deeper encounter with God. The well of our thirst seems endlessly deep. In the Gospel of John, the Samaritan woman asks Jesus for the living water he is offering her so she will not need to keep returning to her community well (Jn 4:15), but our experience tells us that, not only will we need to return to the well of prayer, we will always desire to do so.

Contemporary science, we have already seen, understands that we live in a reality that is in continuous motion. In the last chapter, we were introduced to the theory of vibrating strings, which may comprise the most elemental foundations of existence. When we sit silently in prayer, in whatever fashion we choose, we are scarcely aware of any of this activity. In fact, we may be attempting to move as little as possible, even while knowing that our conscious efforts to still our muscles and quiet our minds leave the rest of ourselves mostly unaffected, blood pumping, digestive juices flowing, not to mention the interior atomic restlessness continuing unabated—and infinitely small strings vibrating, resonating some unheard sacred music.

What immeasurable incomprehension! Beneath our mental attention, well below our physical awareness, deeper than our emotional searching, God's Spirit and our own vibrational resonance may be caught up in a mystical dance of faith, trust, and freedom, governed by an interaction of love so strong that it is continuously reshaping the very fibers of our consciousness. We cannot know this; we can only experience its fruits over time.

There are so many movements, transitions, and changes that take place in our prayer moments. Some are transitory, as with periodic changes in our prayer forms. There are, however, also permanent changes related to our deepening spiritual journey. Do we see them? Do we take note of them, reflect on them, or do they pass us by as strangers on the street, noticed but seldom attended to?

In the mystical tradition, *not knowing* has always been presumed, but, for the most part, it has pertained to the unknowability of God. Perhaps now we must also take into account the unknowability of ourselves. In what parallel universe somewhere are the hopes and longings, the fears and uncertainties, the heartfelt commitments and the questioning discernments of our prayer held in store for us? Are they alive somewhere in our unconscious? Or is *unconscious* even the correct term? Perhaps they are in some kind of suspended consciousness, as in the event horizon of a black hole, patiently held in waiting for a time to be reunited with their unperceiving owners?

If so, it is then God's Spirit that tenderly cares for them, so that nothing will be lost. "And even the hairs of your head are all counted" (Mt 10:30). And what more besides?

PART III

SPIRITUALITY AND CONSCIOUSNESS

7

Mystery

Mystery Imposes Itself upon Us

For more than thirteen billion years, following the original singularity, the universe has been expanding and evolving. In the process, systems and systems within systems have organized, diversified, entangled, amplified, declined, and expired. New systems have emerged and have begun this general process anew, over and over again. Countless holistic systems have unfolded in a natural evolutionary process. Within all of these systems, interconnected elementary material has constituted the substantial relationships that have provided the power and information to allow the systems to develop and function. Motion has been generated, change has occurred, spectacular events have transpired, unseen by human eyes. But, mostly, the motion and change have been uneventful and subtle, systemic interactions undergoing natural functions, unseen, unheard, and, apparently, unattended.

On this planet, the only one of which we yet have good firsthand experience, something started to happen. Things began to move and change in such a way that new kinds of physical structures started to emerge. Writing in the 1940s and '50s, Pierre Teilhard de Chardin referred to this emergence as the *biosphere*. Life-forms began to appear on the Earth, and they continued to develop and evolve. These bacterial, botanical, and zoological forms generally thrived, diversifying into ever more complex systems—systems within systems. What or who brought about this evolutionary process has been fiercely debated in the last two centuries in both science and religion/spirituality. The changes that subsequently took place in these living systems, the changes that were successful and that endured, took place slowly and with no perceivable administration.

There are, however, two questions now to be explored as life on Earth continues its journey. First, "Why?" A little more specifically, why has all of this happened, and what does it mean that it continues to do so? Second, is there a point where a system can decide *for itself* to move and change (evolve)? Asking or daring to ask this second question, perhaps proposed in the biblical Garden of Eden, enters new investigative territories of *consciousness*. We briefly engage the first question here. The second question will be addressed in some greater detail in the chapters ahead.

How we answer the first question, of course, greatly depends on how we articulate our positions of faith. How we each understand a belief in God—although for many that is not nearly as simple a position as some might suppose—is central to this articulation. As we know, there are many who speak of a power that would encompass what has traditionally been referred to as God under many other names. What is meant by any of those names could vary substantially. In this chapter's title, I refer to God as Mystery not because I feel particularly uneasy speaking of God, but more because I wish to respect those who have very ambivalent feelings around this name. In the kind of open dialogue I envision here, it is better to stand in awe before Mystery than to stand in ambivalence or even something worse before a "God" who elicits feelings of anger, judgment, or shame.

What I am calling Mystery, therefore, is what has stood behind, under, over, or throughout the evolutionary process I have been describing. For right or wrong, however, the presentations of "God" in the long journey of Western civilization have taken on a certain particle-like atmosphere. The articulation of ideas about who or what God is have tended to identify something that can be imagined as *being somewhere*, and at least metaphorically can have a kind of spatial and sometimes even temporal location. Eastern spirituality, in contrast, seems to present "God" as much less a person or a thing and more a process, a Way, or a philosophical backdrop to reality. But does that metaphoric process then suggest something more aloof or passive or even disinterested? Could we consider it to be both in some way? Yes, certainly! This Mystery is understood as presenting a full spectrum of metaphoric conceptualizations.

Whatever or whoever this is, one thing is certain. It will not leave us alone. Mystery impinges on us, sometimes seeping in, sometimes hitting us with full force. Most often, perhaps, it seems to arrive in our midst as a gentle breeze of compassion and concern. It also leaves the clear impression that it is foundational to everything we have and are, foundational to reality itself. In short, we seem to be deeply cared for, but why?

Mystery Revealing Itself

Let us return to an image used in Chapter 1: the finger pointing at the moon. There, the message was relatively simple. We should not allow intermediate metaphors to distract us and lose our focus on deeper realities. Yet this or any metaphor only has validity if, in fact, there is something to point to in the first place. Furthermore, I can only point to what allows itself to be seen in some way. What is it that draws us to move beyond our own established limits? Are we hard-wired to pursue what we cannot know but what still seems, to some degree, reachable?

To engage these questions, we must consider *revelation* as a basic concept. The word suggests the pulling away of a veil that is keeping something hidden or the manifestation of something that is, to this point, unseen. When Mystery unveils itself, however, and it still remains Mystery, then we understand that we have moved to a deeper metaphor.

Returning, then, to one of our original questions in the book, what do we think it means to say that we are made in the *image and likeness of God* (Gen 1:26)? In Chapter 1, when this question was first presented, we posited that this was an indication that *we ourselves* are metaphoric. We are living metaphors, possessing aspects of what we believe God has in greater depth or reach. While this may be true, it also carries serious risks. For centuries, common folk, if not always their theological educators, more or less presumed that God was like humans, only a lot bigger. God was all the things that humans thought they themselves should have or be, only God was all—all-powerful, all-knowing, all-merciful, and so on. This, in turn, may have seriously compromised a necessary understanding of God's otherness.

At the same time, in the Christian tradition, this revelation of God from the beginning was also recognized as more complex, to say the least. The earliest Christians, though steeped in monotheism through their Judaic roots, came to some kind of understanding within their first generation that, in fact, God was different. *God was in some way systemic.* Without having that word available to them, they were soon calling God a *Trinity.* They did not really know how to define it. They knew their faith

fully embraced the God of Abraham, of Moses, and of the prophets, the
One who Jesus called Abba. They sensed, however, that it also embraced
Jesus, whom they believe to be the Christ, the Messiah, the Redeemer and
Savior, and they were clear that Abba and Jesus were not interchangeable.
Their experientially based belief further included the One whom Jesus
promised to send, the Spirit, the Advocate, who would remain with
them always. This was the understanding of God to and about which
the apostles of Jesus attested, preached, and wrote. It took the Christian
communities a further three centuries, however, to arrive at what they
considered an adequate expression of this, one at that point they could
all agree to—a relationship of the "persons" of the Trinity, with some
philosophical concepts attempting to express how they all fit together.
After all of that, they arrived at ... Mystery, and they let that suffice.

We must say that God is *systemic* only in a metaphoric sense, because
a system is a created concept that is only meaningful to the extent that
it attempts to aid our understanding of the universe around us. When
it comes to understanding the Trinity, or any other effort to wrap our
minds around God, we would be well-advised to follow Paul the Apostle's
proclamation at the end of his theological treatise on justification in
his Letter to the Romans: "O the depth of the riches and wisdom and
knowledge of God! How unsearchable are his judgments and how
inscrutable his ways! For who has known the mind of the Lord? Or who
has been his counselor?" (Rom 11:33–34).

If, however, we would still want to venture down that metaphoric path,
considering the possibility that humans (and everything else) are systemic
as a reflection of how we experience God (made, as we are, in the *image
and likeness*), then we would have to recognize our connection to a basic
belief about the Trinity: *God exists in relationship*. Since Christians do not
fully understand the relational aspects of Trinity, we have struggled over
the centuries to explain this. We should not be surprised that most of our
efforts to do so have been historically shaped, and, therefore over time, have
lost much of their immediate meaning. In Scholastic theology, for instance,
the Trinity's relationships are understood through the concept of *processions*.
The Son *proceeds* from the Father; the Spirit proceeds from their bonding.
Today, our holistic understanding of relationship may help us emerge into
a new appreciation of the Trinity and its relationality, but only to a degree.

Furthermore, we surely need some rethinking around some simplistic
misperceptions of Trinity. For instance, the Trinity doesn't work like

a board meeting, where everyone is operating out of their own job assignments and reporting back to the whole board. Nor is the Trinity like a team that happens to execute all its plays perfectly. And, with apologies to St. Patrick, a shamrock is a poor demonstration of what Trinity tries to express. Actually, we should presume that the relational interactions of a Trinitarian God are fully beyond our reach. All we can hope to know about the Trinity is constrained, and our knowledge only touches God's interaction with creation. We cannot hope to fathom the workings of the Trinity unto itself.

Franciscan friar/priest Richard Rohr says, "Like probably nothing else, all authentic knowledge of God is *participatory knowledge*."[1] Rohr goes on to say,

> In other words, God (and uniquely the Trinity) cannot be known as we know any other object—such as a machine, an objective idea, or a tree—which we are able to "objectify." We look at objects, and we judge them from a distance through our normal intelligence, parsing over their varying parts, separating this from that, presuming that to understand the parts is always to be able to understand the whole. But divine things can never be objectified in this way; they can only be "subjectified" by becoming one with them! *When neither yourself nor the other is treated as a mere object, but both rest in an I-Thou of mutual admiration, you have spiritual knowing.* Some of us call this contemplative knowing.[2]

Knowledge of God, we may then conclude, comes in pursuit of God, not in speculations about God.

When discussing the overall topic of God's revelation, we must recognize that other faiths and other traditions of belief have arrived at considerably different paradigms of divinity. This is a significant addendum. Even many people who otherwise would consider themselves Christians find a revelation of Trinity a large hurdle to get beyond. At least from the twentieth century onward, this has not stopped interfaith dialogues from moving forward. Most parties believe that there is more to be accomplished by continuing a dialogic process than by setting up

---

[1] Richard Rohr, *The Divine Dance* (New Kensington, PA: Whitaker House, 2016), 49.

[2] Rohr, *The Divine Dance*, 50–51.

roadblocks. Honest and respectful interchange concerning the differences in our faiths has produced wonderful results, leading to deeper insights and greater mutual respect—far greater results than would the ending of discussion, putting a halt to further dialogue, and saying in effect, "Well, we can't arrive at the same conclusion, and so I have no reason to pursue this question any further."

This is true even when the discussion about belief includes those who apparently have none. In other words, when it comes to exploring the dynamics of faith, conversations involving atheism also have potential. From my understanding, commitment to a stance of atheism requires that one has assumed a position of faith, and real atheists are true believers in their cause. Knowing why and how someone has arrived at the conviction that God is absent can be very helpful in understanding why I have, in turn, arrived at the opposite conviction.

This can be significantly different from someone who may claim to be agnostic (although labels are only labels). The agnostic is someone who says, "I don't know," or "I can't know." But for many who use this label, it may mean "I don't care," or "I'm not interested enough to pursue this topic." That may lead to the question, "Well, what then are you interested in?" Their answer may be a career, wealth, fame, knowledge, pleasure, fashion, likability, or any number of other things. Their answer may also be deeply influenced by surviving serious hurt or trauma, for which, to some degree, they blamed God. Their answer may be the outcome of finding life just too bewildering, relieving themselves of that pressure by assuming a position of indifference. This becomes their faith stance, such as it is, even though such an agnostic may not use that designation. It is a kind of practical atheism, bordering on apathy. In life, it behooves us to move from such a position.

One sort of agnostic position could be termed *the idle speculator*: I could spend my life investigating things in which I find some residual interest or perceived controversy, but I have no real interest in arriving at a point where such investigations would produce something within that could actually be called meaningful for life. Instead, my speculations are surrounded by criticism and judgment. Perhaps the idle speculator has given up on meaning or purpose, or has been disillusioned when an initial search produced disappointment or failure. Perhaps disillusionment is feeding the cause, and the speculator relishes, to some degree, a pleasure arising from debunking or unmasking the illusions of others. The idle speculator could settle one's focus on a range of topics, from politics to the arts, but God is certainly a favorite topic for many. Debunking God can truly stir up negative reserves of energy in others, and there is, we would suppose, some payoff for that. But underneath such speculation lies a deep well of self-disillusionment. The ability to be in the one place where belief in God could actually be empowering, with the strength that is found in *commitment*, is missing from such a worldview. Such speculation has nothing at hand to which the speculator can give one's life, no priceless treasure discovered in a field.

From Agnostic Speculation to Holistic Surrender

While we are speaking of a worldview (or better, a view of the universe), how does my faith bring me to an understanding of any role we may assign to God in regard to all the things we see around us (the universe)? Did God bring all this about? How, in other words, did this universe come to be as it is? In some quarters, a speculative view of evolution would answer that it is all a matter of *chance*. In the course of things, things happen. When they don't work out, they fall apart or disappear. This could happen over and over, just meaningless iterations lost in futility. When by chance something works out, however, it survives, and, in its survival, it begins to replicate. Nothing succeeds like success. In this form of speculation, we are here because we presently stand at the end of a who-knows-how-long line of successful and unsuccessful iterations. We are the hacked accomplishment of something like a cosmic computer bot spinning out an endlessly random series of algorithmic variables. The bot has no creator, nor does it know or care what it does. It just does what it does, and you and I have eventually appeared. Within that truly exciting possibility, what role would God have at all?

In the words of Marilynne Robinson, this is the crucial difference between *accident* and *intention*.

> In the course of my reading, I have come to the conclusion that the random, the accidental, have a strong attraction for many writers because they simplify by delimiting. Why is there something rather than nothing? Accident. Accident narrows the range of appropriate strategies of interpretation, while intention very much broadens it. Accident closes on itself, while intention implies that, in and beyond any particular fact or circumstance,

there is vastly more to be understood. Intention is implicitly communicative, because an actor is described in any intentional act. Why is the human brain the most complex object known to exist in the universe? Because the elaborations of the mammalian brain that promoted the survival of the organism overshot the mark in our case. Or because it is intrinsic to our role in the universe as thinkers and perceivers, participants in a singular capacity for wonder as well as for comprehension.[3]

If we feel we do not want to settle for accident or chance and instead feel more drawn to intention or wonderment, then the evolutionary process opens us up to something vastly more imaginative. We are invited on a journey that knows no certain itinerary. Much like the central metaphor of our previous chapter, the unknown seas lying beyond our familiar perceptual maps beckon us, as they have so many voyagers before us.

"I do not know what I may appear to the world, but to myself I seem to have been only like a boy playing on the sea-shore, and diverting myself in now and then finding a smoother pebble or a prettier shell than ordinary, whilst the great ocean of truth lay all undiscovered before me," Sir Isaac Newton said.[4] How much have the findings of such shoreline wayfarers benefited the expanse of our human knowledge? How much more lies in the ocean depths before us?

As stated at the beginning of Chapter 2, this imaginative journey of wonderment has proved itself to lead through the seas of mathematics, which really should not surprise us. Mathematics is, as you will remember, one of the essential pillars upon which scientific investigation rests. This is also where many nonscientific folks turn and run for the hills. If any of you are tempted to make a break for it, first consider that when we speak of mathematical formalism and its importance, we speak of science's *discoveries*, not science's inventions.

Mathematics, as Sir Isaac would attest, is essential for verifying what we may have suspected is already there. Max Planck, for instance, spent

---

[3] Marilynne Robinson, *Absence of Mind: The Dispelling of Inwardness from the Modern Myth of the Self* (New Haven, CT: Yale University Press, 2010), 71–72.

[4] David Brewster, *Memoirs of the Life, Writings, and Discoveries of Sir Isaac Newton*, vol. 2 (Edinburgh: T. Constable, 1855), chap. 27.

one evening in 1900 manipulating mathematical equations after the departure of a dinner guest who was baffled by his work with radiation. Eventually, Planck said that he arrived "by lucky guess-work" at what came to be called Planck's constant (6.626×10^{-34} joules-seconds, or h, as it appears in most formulas). This discovery, a number so small that it is practically zero, opened the scientific world to quantum physics. Who knew that an evening of *beachcombing* (as Newton may have put it) would find the key that would unlock the quantum world?

There are underlying questions in all of this, of course, such as *Why do such mathematical constants exist in the first place? How did they get there? Who or what fixed or established the systemic processes they generate?* Such questions ultimately lead to another question: *Does all of this point to something still to come?* In other words, is all of the reality we experience around us a part of something that has a plan or purpose to it? Are we moving with direction toward something, or are we only moving? If there is a greater plan at work, what plan (and whose plan) would that be?

For reductionists and materialists, there is no plan, because nothing lies ahead offering direction. The universe is solely a bottom-up experience, generated from the atoms, molecules, and, yes, mathematical constants already in existence. We have no need to question how such things got there; we just work with what we find. There is evolution, to be sure, but it has no intentional movement. Perhaps we can, or even should, add some intentional planning, thanks to our "accidental," recently emerged-from-below intellectual prowess, but there is nothing else walking with us. And there are no limits to what we should do, no ethical wisdom to hold our focus other than what we ourselves agree to.

This is not the evolutionary process that I and countless others perceive. In regard to creation (the universe), we believe that Something has some long-standing intention and provides some direction, even if it is not always obvious or apparent. I and many others name this Something "God" (or your preferred expression that fulfills the job description). We believe this God stands both within and beyond our evolutionary processes.

From this perspective there is a plan, a Great Plan, at work, a plan that has always been at work. It is a plan that works from the bottom up, the top down, side to side, and outside to inside. It is a plan that has been in place, guided by a Consciousness we are always only beginning to perceive and acknowledge. Due to our own emerging consciousness, it is a plan in which we are invited to participate—in the true Franciscan sense—not as its masters but as its servants. "And we were simple and subject to all."[5]

Jesus called this unfolding plan the Reign of God. The Reign is present and pervasive, a spiritual field theory, if you will, and it is still coming into its fullness (theologically, often paradoxically framed as *now and not yet*). The sense we get from scripture is that it is not so much like a kingdom but much more like a sovereignty. Kingdoms have boundaries, but the Reign of God is boundless. Spacetime will not be able to contain it. It is generated and charged by the interaction of Love. Jesus didn't define it any further, but he did tell many stories about it—what it might look like, where you could find it, how you could pass it on.

In Christian theology, God's emergence within natural reality has traditionally been called Providence. As expressed in the Catholic framework, "The universe was created 'in a state of journeying' (*in statu viae*) toward an ultimate perfection yet to be attained, to which God has destined it."[6] This Providence is an aspect of the outpouring of God's love. God is the master of the plan of creation, but to carry it out, God also makes use of creation's cooperation.[7] In other words, Catholic theology has long understood humanity and all of reality as having a cooperative role in the plan's unfolding.

If we at least have the capacity to be in cooperative alignment with God, what will be the outcome of this great adventure? What will it look like when this whole process is completed? Will there ever be a time when we (or whoever or whatever is around at that point) will know it all? We explored that ever so briefly in Chapter 4 when we considered the two different metaphysical views of time, the *block universe* and *flowing time*. Some four-dimensional models, you will remember, simply predicted a not-so-exciting ending of the universe as everything reaches the total stasis of entropy.

The Great Plan that Jesus seems to envision, however, doesn't look much like that. At his crucifixion, Jesus says to the criminal next to him,

---

[5] From the *Testament* of St. Francis in Regis J. Armstrong, J. A. Wayne Hellmann, and William J. Short, eds., *Francis of Assisi: Early Documents*, vol. 1 (New York: New City Press, 1999–2001), 125.

[6] Catechism of the Catholic Church, 2nd ed., #302, English trans. (Washington, DC: USCC, 1994), 80.

[7] Catechism of the Catholic Church, #306, 81.

"Truly I tell you, today you will be with me in Paradise" (Lk 23:43). This would necessitate something quite outside of the four-dimensional point of view. Jesus and most of the Western spiritual tradition envision an outcome quite distinct, at a different level of reality. But how much of this lies beyond our evolutionary track? The "advances" that we see around us—biologically, technologically, intellectually, etc.—and all those yet to come, can we see them as part of God's Great Plan, or are they simply the tedious and distractive circumstances we put up with until we die and the real stuff starts? Some within the Western spiritual tradition, it is true, have taken such a position. The purpose of the journey is to get through it with a passing grade so the real benefits of salvation can at last begin. Without saying that there are no benefits beyond our perceived human life, I believe we can whole-heartedly claim that this life is worth living, and the evolutionary track provides us with present and ongoing benefits of great value. Western spirituality heralds the goodness of physical life, yet that doesn't mean we can ignore or downplay its challenges.

The Eastern spiritual tradition, or at least a substantial part of it, however, looks at the physical world I have been investigating in the past chapters as ultimately an illusion. In many forms of Eastern spirituality, the endless changes of form in physical existence are simply to be let go of. Upon death, the self will return to something quite different, and individuality will be dissolved. There are, of course, many variations of this general framework, but Western spirituality seems to fundamentally follow a different track. In my own tradition, we would not be so quick to write off created reality or the permanence of the whole individual.

Teilhard de Chardin is a good twentieth-century representative of a holistic and evolutionary Christian spiritual viewpoint. Teilhard understood the created universe as being in evolutionary movement toward what he called an Omega Point. He was not simply tracking an evolution through time and space, but also a movement of convergence, powered by Love as an energy, and leading to a point of Personalization. In regard to the culmination of the Omega Point, he writes:

> Thus it would be mistaken to represent Omega to ourselves simply as a centre born of the fusion of elements which it collects, or annihilating them in itself. By its structure Omega, in its ultimate principle, can only be a distinct centre radiating at the core of a system of centres; a grouping in which personalisation of the

> All and personalisations of the elements reach their maximum,
> simultaneously and without merging, under the influence of a
> supremely autonomous focus of union.[8]

Teilhard understood that this process, in the end, would escape the threats
imposed by the forces of entropy, and, in turn, Omega would also escape
from time and space.

> But . . . we now see ahead of us a psychical centre of universal drift,
> transcending time and space and thus essentially extra-planetary,
> to sustain and equilibrate the surge of consciousness. The idea is
> that of noogenesis ascending irreversibly towards Omega through
> the strictly limited cycle of a geogenesis. At a given moment in the
> future, under some influence exerted by one or the other of these
> curves or of both together, it is inevitable that the two branches
> should separate. However convergent it be, evolution cannot attain
> to fulfillment on earth except through a point of dissociation.[9]

The evolutionary process he envisioned here, Teilhard admits, escapes our
imagination. While he continues to reflect on some presumed parameters
of what may come, in the end, we still find ourselves back, standing before
Mystery, holding solidly to our faith.

However, now we must understand that this mystery is not simply a
metaphor for God. Although that has been my focus in this chapter, we
now must consider it a mystery that includes us as well. In the last chapter,
I invited some reflection on the dipolarity found in our paradoxical
perceptions. Mystery involves paradox, and, as I have suggested, we and
all reality have a paradoxical mystery of our own.

We struggle daily with perceptual unknowns that we will not be able
to overcome. They are part of the makeup of human experience. We
would only need to reflect on the presence of human suffering. Why can
life take on such tragic proportions so quickly? How do we place such
suffering and tragedy into our faith in a loving and merciful God? What
does it mean to see suffering in the context of freedom? We long for happy
positive outcomes, but instead, at best, we are invited to live with a kind
of transformed vitality, touched with a pervasive sadness. Why is this so?

---

[8] Pierre Teilhard de Chardin, *The Phenomenon of Man*, trans. Bernard Wall
(New York: Harper Perennial Modern Thought, 2008), 262–63.

[9] Teilhard de Chardin, *Phenomenon of Man*, 273.

At some point, as I have tried to suggest, in practically every turn of quantum theory, reality as we can understand and perceive it moves to the unknown, to Mystery. This persistent mystery defies our desire for control and satisfaction. We know so much more than the ancients who struggled to explain the world around them. Our knowledge has far surpassed the medieval philosophers who sought to explain the nature of human reason. We know vastly more than the scientists of the Enlightenment. And we are learning more with each passing year. Yet, what do we know? Not nearly as much as we desire. In keeping with the gospel's understanding, the ongoing development of the Reign of God—the great unfolding plan at work in the universe—will always escape our desire for certitude. In this, Mystery asks us for *holistic surrender*. We will not master it nor, in time, control it. This call to surrender, in whatever language we may choose to express it, is the deepest and the most transforming feature of prayer, and the most significant aspect of our spiritual journey as a whole.

8

The Brain and the Mind

We stand at an *edge of knowledge*. Our journey through the past chapters has, time and again, led us to the limits of our perception. At this boundary of available information about our universe, space and time, the Mystery of God, and ourselves, we don't know where to go. Our curiosity is not yet satisfied, and we want to go further.

At the edge of perception, we could have concluded that there is nothing else to learn or just that there is nothing more out there at all. This conclusion, however, has not been favored over the course of our collective human journey. Question marks have usually been met by determination to overcome them, to answer them. Whatever and wherever that determination might lead us, we encounter this further task most significantly at the point of something we call *consciousness*.

Consciousness is not easily defined. People have attempted to define it in different ways. In quantum theory, consciousness jumped into the mix almost from the very beginning. At the end of any verifiable quantum experiment is the conscious decision of the observer. Short of that last crucial step, the outcome of the measurement is left uncertain because the superposition of the wave function remains intact. That fact alone demonstrates the important role that consciousness plays.

Consciousness, however, is not just floating out in space. It happens in a particular arena of experience that we call the brain and/or the mind. But wait, brain *and* mind? Are we speaking about one thing or two? Scientists, philosophers, theologians, and religious people are divided on this point, and I'm sure that doesn't surprise you by this juncture in our journey. Where are we supposed to look to better understand consciousness? For a moment, let us consider both of these phenomena, brain and mind, to try to find some direction.

The Wonders of the Human Brain

The workings of God may be the most mysterious aspect of the universe. God, however, is not the only mystery to encounter. The human brain may very well be the second most mysterious thing in the universe. We each profoundly depend on it, but we understand it so little.

Our human brains didn't simply show up one day fully formed. As I said briefly in Chapter 3, the brain emerged through a long, cooperative evolutionary process with divine creativity that has extended from primordial life to the present. While this creative process is extraordinary, it is not magical. Life on Earth has evolved over eons as it has responded to environmental wonders of all kinds. The creative, evolutionary process has been a work of struggle for survival, growth, companionship, regeneration, meaning, excellence, and many things besides. In the process, there have been dead ends, tragedies, and a great deal of suffering. And there have been amazing developmental bursts of energy and advancement. As far as we know, the human brain can be understood as the current apex of cosmological and biological evolutionary existence. And still, the process is not complete.

Our brains have limits, however. We have not yet reached their limits, and we might not even know what it means to do so. Yet we recognize that, practically speaking, there are a host of things we cannot do with the brains we have now. As I have stressed throughout this book, one area of those limitations has to do with perception. By *perceive*, I mean the process of taking hold of and comprehending something. This is accomplished through education in all its forms. With it we can embrace and even master various parts of perception. Each of us have been in a learning process since we were born, and we remain learners in some capacity throughout the course of our lives. But the product of our learning, our knowledge, depends on our perception. Everything we understand, comprehend, and know—including events like experiencing, analyzing, knowing, remembering, thinking, acting, deciding, and recalling—comes from sensory and neuronal information that is processed by our brains.

How much can we rely on this information to be *real*? Conditions of reality like factual accuracy, true presence not merely seeming or fictitious imagination, and objectivity (all found in Webster's *New World Dictionary* first definition of real) all depend on the brain's processing of neural information. How can we verify our perceptions of this reality without calling into question the parameters that these perceptions accept as true? We believe our perceptions are sound and adequate to the task, looking for consensus, replicability, and logical consistency. If we are reaching for something we might term *absolute certitude*, however, none of these would completely fill the bill. These are some of the significant questions in what has been called the philosophy of mind, and following too far would lead us down avenues beyond the scope of this book.

The limits of our brain's perception can be demonstrated with tricks of the mind or optical illusions, and discarded physical and psychological theories that once were accepted as indisputable show how our learning moves us beyond limits at times. In addition to this, there are indications that some animals can perceive things totally off our perceptual scale. Recent studies are also upending our long-standing presumption that plants, which have been here on this planet much longer than any warm-blooded creature, have just been stuck in the ground on their own, growing and going nowhere. These studies, however, point to systemic intercommunication within the soil and root systems of plants, incorporating networks of fungi in communication systems that, it seems, we never completely noticed.

As our understanding of other animals and plants has increased, so has our knowledge of our own brains.[1] For most of human history, our brains were largely in the dark. Due to moral and ethical limitations, most of our knowledge of the brain came from postmortem examination. Thanks to modern technology, like the development of MRI, EEG, and other innovative breakthroughs, our knowledge of the brain and how it works has advanced exponentially. Today, we can view the brain in some degree of action, and our neurological science has made many of the brain's mysteries accessible.

Two main approaches to viewing the human brain are helping us understand ourselves: the *triune*, or vertical, view and the *bilateral*, or

---

[1] Many contemporary authors provide substantial detail of the human brain. Short of a few scattered images and examples, there is nothing particularly original in my reporting of their schemas. My overview description of the brain presented here is drawn primarily from the following works: Michio Kaku, *The Future of the Mind: The Scientific Quest to Understand, Enhance, and Empower the Mind* (New York: Anchor Books, 2015); Daniel J. Siegel, *Mindsight: The New Science of Personal Transformation* (New York: Bantam Books, 2011); Curt Thompson, *Anatomy of the Soul* (Carrollton, TX: Tyndale House Publishers, 2010); Evan Thompson, *Waking, Dreaming, Being* (New York: Columbia University Press, 2015).

horizontal, view. Both provide the information necessary to get even the most basic understanding of how the brain functions. The vertical approach focuses on development that begins with the brain stem. The horizontal approach focuses on the division of the brain into a right and a left hemisphere.

The *vertical* viewpoint could also be called the triune or evolutionary brain, for it lends itself to understanding how our brains evolved through the millions of years of zoological life on this planet. In an evolutionary sense, if we were to examine the brains of reptiles, for instance, we would see that the reptilian brain greatly resembles the lowest parts of our human brains, the brain stem, the cerebellum, and the basal ganglia. Reptiles know how to do basic survival things, like breathing, digestion, and heartbeat. They also understand fear and aggression. Lacking several brain functions that are necessary for emotional expression, they are not capable of forming deep, long-term emotional relationships.

That capacity, which we and some other mammals possess, requires an advancement in brain development. The limbic system surrounds the top of the brain stem and consists of the hippocampus, the amygdala, the thalamus, and the hypothalamus, enabling mammals to live in society, form relationships, and have an exciting emotional life. The limbic system does not necessarily make sure that our relationships are also well-ordered, intellectually meaningful, or intending to result in a successful life plan. The cerebral cortex forms the outer surface of the brain and is crucial for these developments. In humans, it is highly developed, allowing for the possibility of success for life plans. It also makes possible our thinking, imagining, calculating, creating, and a wide host of other things.

Four distinct areas of the cortex, four lobes, specialize in certain tasks. The frontal lobe deals with rational thought, evaluating information, and carrying out actions as a kind of "command center," or our control tower. It helps regulate the endless information that flows from other areas of the brain, to help decide what actions are to be taken. Daniel Siegel identifies nine functions performed by the prefrontal cortex: body regulation, attuned communication, emotional balance, response flexibility, fear modulation, empathy, insight, moral awareness, and intuition.[2] The parietal lobe deals with sensory attention and body image, and handling skilled movements. The occipital lobe is in the very back, controlling our

---

[2] Siegel, *Mindsight*, 26–30.

visual senses. The temporal lobe on the two sides of the cortex plays an important role in how we perceive the world around us and communicate with it.

The second view of the brain, the bilateral or *horizontal* view, considers the brain from the perspective of its two complementary hemispheres. For many years the language of "left brain and right brain" has been well-known parlance in contemporary spiritual writings, and many feel they have a general sense of what it refers to. In the past, it has been overstressed at times, seeming to hold the key to a complete understanding of how the human mind works. This bilateral view of the brain is real and important, but we do not want to lose track of the fact that the brain is complex, not simple. If there is a key to understanding it, we should focus on the idea of *integration* rather than simplistic explanation.

The two hemispheres perceive the world quite differently. The right hemisphere gets an early jump on the process, beginning a quicker development at birth or before. The left side starts to catch up when the person is around two years old. In addition to the pace of development, perceptions in the two hemispheres are quite distinct. The right hemisphere sees the world holistically, composed of one, interconnected fabric. There is no sense of a separate self. Communication is nonverbal, and social awareness is high. Attention is sustainable and seeks to view the bigger picture. The left hemisphere, by contrast, sees the world in its individuality, rapidly attuning to the logical and linguistic, following a path of linear processing. Its perception is focused, detailed, and generally utilitarian.

From the outside, so to speak, the two hemispheres would appear to be almost identical. When surgically or experimentally separated, they seem to function practically independently of each other, possessing what would appear to be almost a complete duality of consciousness. Of course, they were not meant to operate in that way. They were meant to be complementary. They are separated by a layer of tissue, the corpus callosum, but are continuously communicating back and forth. The left hemisphere, more analytical than the right, initially tends to dominate, passing information to the right hemisphere before it is processed and circulated to the prefrontal cortex for decision making.

Even with an understanding of the integration of these two fundamentally different representational approaches to the human brain (the triune and the bilateral), our brains are still significantly more complex. For one thing, our brains are completely *systemic*. Neural and biochemical circuits thoroughly connect different regions of the brain, continuously acquiring and circulating information provided by our neurological system running in multiple levels throughout the body. Neural patterns are quickly established and reinforced as information is sent and received back and forth. As these patterns follow the same circuitry over time, they form the habitual channels that bind our conditioning, perception, and judgment.

These patterns are forged through an elaborate mix of genetic proclivities handed to us upon our arrival in this world and the rich interconnected storehouses of experiences we have acquired over a lifetime. Yet even with this deeply wired circuitry, established over many years, the brain is still capable of forging new neural pathways as it responds to new information from new experiences of life. This kind of organic creativity in new experiences of life is called *neuroplasticity*. It is an open-ended process that, in adult life, often requires the aid of substantial direct and focused attention. Neuroplasticity has become an important tool for surviving and overcoming various forms of trauma and emotional difficulties that can affect human existence throughout the life cycle.

The neurological processing of emotions offers an excellent example of the systemic nature of brain circuitry. If you were sitting in a counselor's office or sharing an important conversation with a spouse or a good friend at the kitchen table, and you were asked, "What are you feeling right now?" whatever response you might provide as an answer, neurologically speaking, could well be considered "old news." In the nanoseconds it may take to formulate a response, even a "spontaneous" one, a lot of brain processing will have already taken place.

At the *primary emotional level*, the deeper parts of your brain gather data from throughout your entire nervous system—your heart rate, your blood pressure, and your vagus nerve transmit impressions from your throat, your stomach, your liver, your muscles, your spine, and so on. Through electrical neural firings, this information is transmitted to the brain's right hemisphere, registered there, and transmitted to the left hemisphere and throughout your brain. These primary sensations are compared to similar patterns of the past, preparing you to anticipate the range of emotions that your body has come to recognize. All of this takes place prior to any significant involvement of the brain's more rational and reflective components. Finally, with due awareness and reflection, we are able to report particular feelings, such as anger, joy, and shame, in what are termed *categorical emotions*.[3]

Our memories are another example of the systemic nature of the human brain and the entire neurological complex. The ability to remember what we have learned—whether it is for Friday's high school biology quiz or the sequence of movements in the long form of *tai chi chuan*, or simply recalling who starred in a movie seen twenty-five years ago—brings us to a quick realization that not all memories we seek have the same feel to them. Neuroscience speaks of two distinctly different kinds of memory, even though they frequently overlap in our experiences: implicit memory and explicit memory. The distinction between the two may help us understand how not all memories we seek to remember have the same feel to them.

Implicit memory is exercised "without thinking much about it." It is the memory our bodies know either from what was passed to us genetically—breathing, smiling, screaming, or the repetitive beating of our hearts—or from what our bodies learn over time—our mother's voice, the pain of a vaccination needle, or the skill of driving in a Northeastern snowstorm. Implicit memories are systemically stored in the brain stem, in the neurological pathways throughout our bodies, and in some parts of the limbic system. We could consider them as being on "automatic pilot." They are not the kind of memories that we think of when we are asked to recall a certain event that took place at some point in our lives.

Explicit memory describes memories of past events, including both episodic (autobiographical) and factual memories. Explicit memory emerges with the engagement of the region of the brain called the hippocampus. When we think of memory recall (What were you doing last Tuesday? Who served in George Washington's cabinet?), we may be tempted to think that there is a kind of memory library somewhere in our brain where all our knowledge is stored. Instead, the hippocampus is more like an electromagnetic search engine that draws information from many previously stored neural sources over a wide range of locations in the brain, then integrates and contextualizes the information before sending it on to the prefrontal cortex. There, the final memory report is

---

[3] For a more detailed description of the process, see Curt Thompson, *Anatomy of the Soul*, 91–96.

constructed. This process is important to grasp because it indicates that the neural firings of explicit memory are always a *present* experience—newly constructed information. The reliability of our explicit memory, therefore, is always something of an open question, because, over time, our neural information and how it is sorted can change. If Grandpa keeps retelling the family about his past fishing adventures, and the fish keeps getting bigger and the difficulty of hauling it in keeps increasing, it can become a social smile-worthy event. If Grandpa (or anyone else) has witnessed the committing of a crime, eyewitness reliability has much more serious implications.

Explicit memory constructs narratives based on episodes, which are linked and sorted through a time sequence along with relevant factual information. This process requires *conscious attention*. In the prefrontal cortex, there may also be the further construction of interpretations, and meaning can also be created or deepened. How that happens, however, is not so clear. This is where our investigation passes over to something we call the *mind*.

The Mysteries of the Mind

Whoever controls the definition of mind controls the definition of humankind itself, and culture, and history. There is something uniquely human in the fact that we can pose questions to ourselves about ourselves, and questions that actually matter, that actually change reality.[4]

What is the mind? Where is the mind? Modern technology has helped us explore many of the intricacies of the brain, but it has been much less forthcoming on revealing the mind. Though we can see through technological advancement where and when certain events are processed in the brain's various regions, we do not necessarily understand how those processes happen. Neither have these technological advances helped us understand how we give quality, depth, or richness to those events, much less how they lead us to understanding, meaning, and insight.

If we don't know those things now, however, will we come to clarity about these mental features, and more, in time? Will we in the future be able to technologically replicate all that the brain is and can do? The

[4] Marilynne Robinson, *Absence of Mind: The Dispelling of Inwardness from the Modern Myth of the Self* (New Haven, CT: Yale University Press, 2010), 32.

mushrooming artificial intelligence (AI) industry is banking that we will. While we still expect AI to make our lives more convenient, efficient, and dynamic, our further expectations of it continue to push its potential boundaries ever wider. Will we someday be able to technologically reproduce what we humans understand as the complete brain/mind? Or even further, can something comparable to human consciousness be assembled in a laboratory? Is such an enterprise even feasible?

Before we could ever answer such a question, however, we would first have to address whether the brain and mind are one thing or two. Are the mind and the brain the same? Many in the scientific community claim that they are. Those who embrace a purely materialistic understanding of reality would, without hesitation, claim that brain functioning is "all there is." Those who would further view the universe from a reductionist position would say that everything is ultimately manifested through particles, from the bottom up—subatomic to atomic to molecular, and so on. It all happens through a natural process of evolution. There is nothing we would find in the brain—nor would the mind add anything—that is not simply a reconfiguration and complication of what was already there.

Can everything be explained through neurons, synapses, and the complexity of neural pathways? Many scientists and scholars would reject such a premise, and others would radically modify it. While acknowledging that the brain and the mind are closely correlated, they would want to make a clear distinction between them. Roger Penrose, for instance, sees clear problems in seeking to artificially create conscious intelligence strictly through a process of computations. Penrose argues that the present binary system by which all current computers operate, quantitative computation, possesses insurmountable limitations for creating consciousness.[5] Philosophers of the mind such as Edward Feser and others point to the inability of artificial intelligence to solve the current problem of *qualia*. AI, they contend, has yet to overcome qualitative considerations beyond quantitative computations.[6]

Will future technological advancements enable the production of something that could pass for consciousness? Perhaps. However, working

---

[5] Roger Penrose, *Shadows of the Mind: A Search for the Missing Science of Consciousness* (Oxford: Oxford University Press, 1994).

[6] See, for instance, Edward Feser, *Philosophy of Mind: A Beginner's Guide* (London: Oneworld Publications, 2006).

from a starting point that the mind and the brain are distinct, some authors are more concerned about how we can utilize the synthesis of mind and brain to further enhance the human project. Daniel Siegel, introduced earlier in this book, is one such thinker. In the face of certain difficulties that have yet to be overcome in artificially producing consciousness, what are we to make of the expanding mind that is already revealing itself to us? Siegel offers a model of the mind and the process of its integration throughout our human journey that provides us with a good framework for understanding the connection between the brain, the mind, and their cooperative nature in our relational life. Siegel calls this framework the Triangle of Well-Being.[7]

Recalling Marilynne Robinson's attention to the relationship between a definition of mind and a definition of humankind itself, we should consider how Siegel defines the mind. He offers a simple definition that he sees as acceptable to a wide range of disciplines: *The human mind is a relational and embodied process, emerging from within and between brains, that regulates the flow of energy and information.*[8] Siegel's specific term *mindsight*, then, is the process that enables the monitoring and modification of this energy and information flow within the Triangle of Well-Being.

The key to this process lies in Siegel's understanding of *integration*. Integration brings about well-being, but it doesn't just happen, and it doesn't happen all at once. Integration is a process, and Siegel describes it through a rich metaphor: a *river* of integration. This river flows along a channel bound by two banks. One bank represents rigidity; the other bank chaos. We don't want to land on either bank, and we definitely don't want to *stay* on either one. We want to stay in the flow. Our journey along this river is open-ended, and its progress is assessed by the presence of FACES—qualities that are *flexible, adaptive, coherent, energized,* and *stable.*[9] Siegel identifies nine domains of integration:

> These domains do not necessarily develop in a linear fashion, and ... you'll see that they sometimes emerge in combination. How we experience a "sense of self"—a feeling of who we are over time and of the patterns of energy and information that unfold in our

---

[7] Siegel, *Mindsight*, 11.
[8] Siegel, *Mindsight*, 52–55.
[9] Siegel, *Mindsight*, 66–71.

inner lives—will be directly shaped by the degree of integration in these domains.[10]

Siegel identifies the following domains of integration:

- Integration of *Consciousness*: building skills that focus our attention and awareness. It is the foundation for integrating the other domains.
- *Horizontal* integration: integrating the two hemispheres of the brain.
- *Vertical* integration: integrating the triune (vertical) levels of the brain.
- *Memory* integration: bringing into integration implicit and explicit memory. This would include the integration of past traumatic experiences.
- *Narrative* integration: bringing sense and cohesiveness to our understanding of the story of our own lives.
- *State* integration: attaining an openness to the many "states" we find ourselves in, some of which can appear as self-contradictory, thus releasing ourselves from patterns of shame, terror, and so on.
- *Interpersonal* integration: understanding how past life adaptations affect our relationships, then choosing to open ourselves more freely to intimacy, while maintaining strong self-identity.
- *Temporal* integration: allowing us to live more comfortably with uncertainty, impermanence, and mortality.

As these domains continue to integrate over time, a final integration begins gradually to emerge: *Transpirational* integration, where we become aware we are part of a much greater whole.[11] Elaborating on this final integration, Siegel speaks of what he terms *expanding identity*:

The study of positive psychology suggests that being involved in something larger than a personal self creates a sense of meaning and well-being—an essential part of the experience of "happiness." ... Ironically, being personally happy requires that we greatly expand our narrowly defined individual preoccupations. We are

---

10 Siegel, *Mindsight*, 71.
11 Siegel, *Mindsight*, 71–76.

built to be a "we"—and enter a more fulfilling state, perhaps a more natural way of being, when we connect in meaningful ways with others. A living organism links its differentiated parts—and without this integration, it suffers and dies.[12]

Siegel's *Mindsight* model is supported through inspiring case studies, rich imaginative insight, and reflective depth. Even with its extensive and acclaimed approach and argument, we should still ask, "Is it complete? Does it also engage us with Mystery? Does it help us to look beyond our perceptual limits or invite us to encounter the darkness surrounding and lying beyond our 'known world'?" It is hard to say. *Mindsight* does not address spirituality or faith directly. Even though it utilizes well-known Eastern and Western spiritual practices that Siegel often refers to as *mindfulness*, it says very little concerning their historically spiritual roots. Human phenomena that have a significant place in Siegel's model, such as insight and intuition, are presented as functions arising from an integrated middle prefrontal cortex, and, therefore, seem to be completely explained. But could they also be more?

Mindsight does offer a possible point of transition into addressing what I will call the *mystagogic* dimension of life. Siegel assigns from the above list of the domains of integration a central role to the *integration of consciousness*.

With the integration of consciousness, we actually build the skills to stabilize attention so that we can harness the power of awareness to create choice and change. This is why the integration of consciousness is the foundation for the other domains. Creating what I'll call a "hub of awareness" enables us to acknowledge troubling states without being taken over by them, and to see things as they are, rather than being constrained by our expectations of how they "should be." It also opens us to the full range of our perceptions—to information from the external world, from our bodily states, from relationships, and from the mind itself.[13]

Consciousness invites us to lay aside preconceived expectations and to stand open to the full range of perceptions, even, I would add,

---

[12] Siegel, *Mindsight*, 259.
[13] Siegel, *Mindsight*, 71–72.

when they lead us into unanticipated terrain. Siegel's understanding of consciousness, then, fits well within the range of such definitions soon to come in this book.

Consciousness is the door that opens into Mystery, but it will be that only for those who are willing to entertain the possibility, who can move beyond their resistance, and who can trust enough to take up the adventure.

9

Consciousness

The Bumpy Landscape

For the moment, we may want to step back a bit and ask a few questions about where our journey has taken us. How did we ever get from microscopically tiny wave-like constructs at the subatomic level of reality to now addressing a consideration of the very nature of human consciousness? And why would we ever think that is important? And what does any of it have to do with spirituality?

The easiest question to answer is the first. We moved from subatomic wave functions to consciousness because of the measurement problem. When physicists first looked at the data of the experiments supporting quantum theory, questions immediately arose concerning the role of the observer in a quantum measurement. Is the experimenter's conscious expectation predetermining the experiment's outcome? That was the question that shook the previously unassailable presumption of scientific objectivity. The Uncertainty Principle then asked us to consider that our conscious observation was not somewhere outside of what we were observing. And it raised the nagging consideration that our conscious observation might actually be changing, or directing, what was being observed. As I have suggested throughout this book, questions about consciousness have never left our considerations of quantum theory.

In the last chapter, we considered the relationship between the brain and the mind. Some argue that they are one, the materialists and reductionists among us. Others disagree, holding that they are integrally connected rather than identical. Some argue that the mind is an open-ended process yet to be fully explored. This spectrum of opinions has been with us for a long time and will likely remain an unsettled question into the future. If the brain/mind questions could ever satisfactorily be answered, would we then, perhaps, be in a position to answer some of the equally elusive questions around consciousness?

The scientists and philosophers who study consciousness will tell you one thing: *no one agrees exactly on what consciousness is.* This is about the only thing they all hold in common. It is very clear that, while there is little agreement, just about everyone thinks that understanding consciousness is very important. This disagreement creates something of a problem. At the conclusion of the last chapter, I introduced Dan Siegel's description of consciousness as a "hub of awareness." Others, including thinkers we have already encountered in this book, have offered their own descriptions, definitions, and arguments.

John Polkinghorne: "Consciousness is the ill-understood but undeniable (except by certain philosophers) experience of the interface between the material and the mental."[1]

Michio Kaku: "Consciousness is the process of creating a model of the world using multiple feedback loops in various parameters (e.g., in temperature, space, time, and in relation to others), in order to accomplish a goal (e.g., find mates, food, shelter)."[2]

Pierre Teilhard de Chardin: "Here, and throughout this book, the term 'consciousness' is taken in its widest sense to indicate every kind of psychism, from the most rudimentary forms of interior perception imaginable to the human phenomenon of reflective thought."[3]

Ken Wilber: "[Consciousness] is not a thing, or a content, or a phenomenon. It has no description. It is not world views, it is not values, it is not morals, not cognition, not value-MEMEs, mathematico-logico structures, adaptive intelligences, or

---

[1] John Polkinghorne, *Quantum Theory: A Very Short Introduction* (Oxford: Oxford University Press, 2002), 51.

[2] Michio Kaku, *The Future of the Mind: The Scientific Quest to Understand, Enhance, and Empower the Mind* (New York: Anchor Books), 43.

[3] Pierre Teilhard de Chardin, *The Phenomenon of Man*, trans. Bernard Wall (New York: Harper Perennial Modern Thought, 2008), 57n.

multiple intelligences. In particular, consciousness is not itself a line among other lines, but the space in which lines arise. Consciousness is the emptiness, the openness, the clearing in which phenomena arise, and if those phenomena develop in stages, they constitute a developmental line (cognitive, moral, self, values, needs, memes, etc.)."[4]

David Chalmers: "What is central to consciousness, at least in the most interesting sense, is *experience*. But this is not definition. At best, it is clarification.... Trying to define conscious experience in terms of more primitive notions is fruitless. One might as well try to define *matter* or *space* in terms of something more fundamental. The best we can do is to give illustrations and characterizations that lie at the same level."[5]

Charles Tart: "To be more precise, in my systems approach to understanding altered states, I define a *discrete state of consciousness for a given individual* (individual differences are very important) as a unique *configuration* or *system* of psychological structures or subsystems. The parts or aspects of the mind that we can distinguish for analytical purposes (such as memory, evaluation processes, and the sense of identity function) are arranged in a certain kind of pattern or process."[6]

Roger Penrose: "[There] are both passive and active aspects to consciousness, but it is not always clear that there is a distinction between the two. The perception of the colour red, on the one hand, is something that certainly requires passive consciousness, as is the sensation of pain or the appreciation of a melody. Active consciousness is involved in the willed action to get up from one's bed, as it is in a deliberate decision to desist from some energetic activity. The bringing to mind of an early memory involves both active and passive aspects of consciousness. Consciousness, active

---

[4] Ken Wilber, *Integral Spirituality: A Startling New Role for Religion in the Modern and Postmodern World* (Boston: Integral Books, 2007), 68.

[5] David Chalmers, *The Conscious Mind: In Search of a Fundamental Theory* (New York: Oxford University Press, 1996), 3–4.

[6] Charles Tart, *Waking Up: Overcoming the Obstacles to Human Potential* (Boston: New Science Library, 1986), 4.

and passive, would also be normally involved ... in the type of mental activity ... encompassed in the word 'understanding.'"[7]

Evan Thompson: "Consciousness is that which is luminous, knowing, and reflective. Consciousness is that which makes manifest appearances, is able to apprehend them in one way or another, and in so doing is self-appearing and prereflectively self-aware."[8]

With so many approaches to understanding consciousness, how can we ever hope to arrive at anything that would resemble a common understanding? Definitions of consciousness frequently vary, confusing things all the more. When consciousness interfaces with such terms as understanding, intelligence, awareness, and mind, are definitions even helpful for our investigations? And what if we cannot arrive at a definition that avoids being so general or complex that it would offer no clarity at all? It seems we have two possible conclusions: we may be describing more than one thing that goes by the same name, or we may be describing one thing that changes, develops, or grows over time and experience. If we wish to step away from too hasty an acceptance of one alternative over the other, it is important to focus on some basic information that is crucial for approaching an understanding of consciousness.

Some Basics of Consciousness

What could be called "fundamental consciousness" is sometimes stated as simply knowing that I know, or self-awareness. Expanding that slightly, we could say that fundamental consciousness is the awareness of what is presently happening in and around an individual, including one's thoughts, feelings, impressions, and a cognizance of one's surroundings. Consciousness is understood, at least, to be an operation of the brain/mind. There is not, however, an agreement that the brain/mind is the source of consciousness. In this basic description, awareness forms the backdrop of the present moment, what I understand of my life at this time. Awareness is, however, more than a passive backdrop, a stage where life is acted out, for it is the way I participate in the present.

---

[7] Roger Penrose, *Shadows of the Mind: A Search for the Missing Science of Consciousness* (Oxford: Oxford University Press, 1994), 39–40.

[8] Evan Thompson, *Waking, Dreaming, Being* (New York: Columbia University Press, 2015), 18.

Such awareness has a long history in both Eastern and Western traditions of meditation. In today's neuroscience, the process of consciousness known as mindfulness is frequently used as a healing and relaxation technique. "Mindfulness" is a word borrowed from Eastern spiritual thought to generally describe a process of meditation using few or no words, employing techniques of breathing and posture, which aid the individual in deepening relaxation, lessening stress, and producing a feeling of well-being. It encourages the participant to live in the present moment, open to the Oneness. Western spiritualities, including Christianity, also have a long history with such experiences. Early Christian patristic writers, such as Evagrius Ponticus and Pseudo-Dionysius, described these meditative approaches as *theologia*, pure contemplation, or mystical theology. Today, the practice of centering prayer utilizes such practices in a more popular form.

Two different elements factor into our sense of awareness: *intention* and *attention*. In some ways, our awareness changes when our intention changes or when our attention shifts. The interactions that take place through intention, attention, and awareness are continuous and could be crucial in sorting out how consciousness "works."

Evan Thompson compares Eastern and Western views of consciousness, addressing intention. Thompson writes, "All consciousness is consciousness of something in one way or another. Phenomenologists call this feature of consciousness 'intentionality.'" Both Buddhism and Western phenomenology, he continues, agree "that intentionality, being directed toward an object, belongs to the nature or being of consciousness; it isn't something that gets added to consciousness from outside."[9] Intention is always involved in conscious activity, but it often goes unrecognized. If someone, including myself, were to question my behavior, "Why did you think that?" or "What was your purpose in doing that action?" I might not immediately know an answer. Sometimes, an answer may not be easily available for a considerable length of time.

Attention, however, is usually much more identifiable. I can tell when my attention has shifted, often even when the shift is unwanted or problematic. To pay attention requires a degree of focus. Thinking of awareness as that backdrop of the present moment in which I stand open to the range of my possible current experiences, I am, in effect, attending

---

[9] Thompson, *Waking, Dreaming, Being*, 36.

to nothing or perhaps everything at once. My open awareness places me in an advantageous position to be receptive to what the moment will offer. Life is happening around me, and I am letting it take place. There are meditation techniques that encourage this stance. As soon as something "catches my eye," however, my attention focuses on that. The fisherman stands by the stream all afternoon, allowing the stream, the clouds, and everything else to pass along, taking it all in. When a fish hooks on the line, the fisherman's attention focuses in on the task at hand. Consciousness lets most of the scene dissolve in order to deal with what has occurred in the present moment.

In everyday life, most moments are filled with a variety of elements that are continuously vying for attention. This does not just involve outside elements that are picked up by our senses. The various areas of the brain, from both hemispheres, are also constantly sending neural messages to the prefrontal cortex, demanding to be heard. The moment's attention will be managed in that control center of the brain. How well can our brains manage such complex operations? To some degree it depends on the person, but we should not be living in the illusion that we are capable of handling it all. Contemporary society's desire to reward "multitasking" comes with a risk of actually accomplishing very little if anything at all. In spiritual direction, I usually advise a directee, especially in times of meditation and prayer, that it is important to proceed with the operative maxim: "If I am trying to do more than one thing at a time, I am likely doing nothing."

Reflecting on the role the prefrontal cortex and the left and right hemispheres play in focusing attention raises a question: Is attention an aspect of consciousness or is it a function of brain activity? Can it be both? In her book on attention, Gay Watson quotes an interview of psychiatrist Iain McGilchrist, in which he states that attention "is an integral aspect of consciousness." He contrasts awareness as a disposition of consciousness in a particular situation with how minds and machines have been described with similar language. "In cognitive models of mind," he points out, "there are so many things that are made to sound like something a machine would do—like it could remember things—well of course it can't remember them but it can do a simulation, but it can't even simulate attention."[10] Attention, it seems, is significantly integral to consciousness.

---

[10] Gay Watson, *Attention: Beyond Mindfulness* (London: Reaktion Books, 2017), 75. McGilchrist is being quoted from an interview. Watson mentions two of

Seeing intention and attention as integral aspects of consciousness may not be disputed out of hand by some reductionists or materialists as long as it would be understood that consciousness itself was reducible. Such a position argues that consciousness is merely a complex reworking of the basic substructures of reality—subatomic particles, atoms, neurons, synapses, and so on. Functionally, consciousness is, then, a product of purely physical materiality. All we're working with here would be the physical constructs of the brain. Whatever consciousness is, it is right there in the brain (or brain and neurological system). Speaking of the mind as such would then largely be superfluous.

David Chalmers rejects this kind of reductionist conclusion. Chalmers argues that the reductionist understanding of consciousness "will ultimately be given in terms of the structural and dynamical properties of physical processes." This is a critical problem for Chalmers because "no matter how sophisticated such an account is, it will yield only more structure and dynamics" as part of the account. He is convinced that the problem of consciousness is about more than mere structures and that it functions on top of structures and functions. Though "there could eventually be a reductive explanatory technique that explained something other than structure and function," Chalmers thinks that such a technique might not even be possible "given that the laws of physics are ultimately cast in terms of structure and dynamics." For Chalmers, "the existence of consciousness will always be a further fact relative to structural and dynamic facts, and so will always be unexplained by a physical account."[11]

Evan Thompson agrees with Chalmers, emphasizing the further impossibility of charting consciousness by scientific method. *"Consciousness itself has not been and cannot be observed through the scientific method, because the scientific method gives us no direct and independent access to consciousness itself. So the scientific method cannot have the final say on matters concerning consciousness."*[12] Thompson further explains:

Perceptual observation, which is necessarily first-personal, and the intersubjective confirmation of perceptual experience, which necessarily presupposes empathy or the recognition of others as

---

McGilchrist's works, *The Divided Brain and the Search for Meaning* and *The Master and His Emissary*.

[11] Chalmers, *The Conscious Mind*, 121–22.

[12] Thompson, *Waking, Dreaming, Being*, 97; italics in original.

having the same kinds of experiences as oneself, are the bedrock of experimental science. In addition, the scientific method includes asking questions, formulating hypotheses, doing background research, analyzing data, and communicating results, none of which is possible or even intelligible as a human activity without consciousness. The upshot is that there's no way to stand outside consciousness and look at it, in order to see how it fits into the rest of reality.[13]

Thompson concludes that our direct experience of consciousness must be primary and scientific experience secondary. We have spent most of this book looking at and evaluating the experiences of science. What rewards, then, could lie open before us in exploring the experiences of consciousness as primary?

The Experience of Consciousness

States of Consciousness

Conscious experience always happens in the present. Memories of past experiences and projections of future events are just memories and projections. They are not the same as conscious experience. Each present moment of consciousness takes place in some kind of *state*. A state of consciousness is the set of conditions or attributes that characterize that particular moment, including how we perceive the mind as presently functioning.

As I noted above in my second reflection on prayer, we experience states of consciousness as temporary. We could say that every moment has its unique state of consciousness, but this sort of generality would make the term practically meaningless. States of consciousness usually refer to kinds or categories of conscious experiences. At its most general level, for instance, we could identify a waking state, a dreaming state, or a state of deep sleep. Each state could be described in more detail. Our waking state, for instance, could encompass a state of alertness, a state of noticeable stress, and a state of relaxation.

Obviously, states of consciousness can change. I am awake, then I go to sleep and begin to dream, and then I go into a deeper sleep, and then I wake up again. These states appear to change seamlessly. Patterns

---

[13] Thompson, *Waking, Dreaming, Being*, 99–100.

of thoughts can also change within a state. As I write these sentences, for instance, I am reflecting on my choice of word structure, exploring my own ideas of our current topic, and seeking some insight into how I can connect with a future reader—with what appears to be little change in my conscious state. Circumstances, however, can occur that substantially modify my brain functioning emotionally and chemically. We need only think of the effects from the influence of alcohol or a sudden, terrifying barrage of gunfire outside. Altered states of consciousness, which can also include experiences associated with meditation and other spiritual experiences, have become an important focus for the exploration of consciousness.

As altered states of consciousness can disorient the conscious mind, possibly challenging an individual to reevaluate certain presumptions about life and life's experiences, they provoke questions about the nature of conscious intention and attention itself. First, how "conscious" must consciousness be? And then, can I be aware of something but not be attending to it? Exploring answers to the first question moves us into consideration of what could be called *depth consciousness*.

This phrase, associated more with psychoanalytic therapy, stands in contrast to the general approaches to therapeutic techniques that are represented in cognitive therapy and in the behaviorist model that it has largely replaced. Both of these models focus on accessible human behavior, which can be recorded, studied, and functionally applied. What are the behavioral patterns in life that are causing difficulties for an individual? What are the circumstances that characterize these patterns? What is the history of these patterns, and so on? In the turn to recordable behavior, the question of consciousness is frequently ignored.

In exploring depth consciousness, we are looking for a further explanation beyond functionality, perhaps a motivational question or a track that takes us behind the surface appearances of behavior. Delving into depth consciousness does create some challenges. Language may be the most noticeable challenge. The conceptual language of depth consciousness has been developing through a wide variety of schools for over a century and, in some cases, is dependent on a spiritual language that goes centuries back. Depth consciousness speaks of conscious states in decreasing levels of awareness—from what is *conscious* to what is *preconscious* or to the *unconscious*. All of these levels intend to address, articulate, or uncover the *soul* or the *self* or the *true self* or *essence*.

Looking briefly at each of these levels, *conscious* generally keeps the meaning of the word we have been using throughout this chapter, the awareness of the present moment. *Preconscious*, however, is a new term that carries the sense of something lying just beyond the horizon, or under the surface, still out of reach but not far away. Think of the times (all too common for some of us who have been around for a while) when you were trying to remember the name of a famous person that you should know, but, for the moment, it escapes you. Or think of a task that lies before you tomorrow, but, at this moment, you are doubting your competence. It is on your mind as you go to sleep, but you wake up with "new insights" that now make you question why you were ever so anxious. "Allowing" the preconscious to come forward can manifest itself as a rewarding and self-affirming experience.

The *unconscious* may be the most confusing of the three terms. How can consciousness be unconscious? Is that not a contradiction of terms? Recognition of this inconsistency has led some to use the term *subconscious* in an attempt at providing a fix. *Unconscious*, however, has the honor of precedence as it is the term used by Freud, Jung, and others. In light of the many advances in comprehending the workings of the human brain/mind today, an understanding of the unconscious needs to be significantly reworked from how it might have been articulated in the last century. It may be truer to consider the unconscious as the *un-cognitive*, an important move going forward. Using a phrase that is often associated with the Jungian archetype the Shadow, we could say that the unconscious is generally understood as the unrecognized or unexplored aspects of myself. I have no current recognition or recollection of many parts of my accumulated life experiences. Some of this accumulation—for example, the present sensation in my left big toe that is available to me in an instant—is easily accessible, but many life experiences are not. With some, I may have an unrecognized resistance toward even considering such things. Maybe I am about to open a door, having knowledge that the person on the other side has been a past adversary. I may or may not have particular thoughts about what might transpire, but I am aware of a sense of anxiety or dread, even if it is only preconscious. There may not be anything "going on in my mind," but there is some sort of awareness that accompanies my opening the door.

The waking state of consciousness is often ill-prepared for dealing with this inaccessible material. Waking life largely focuses on events and relationships that are passing in and out of the moment. Perhaps in times of reflection, prayer, or meditation, some of the remaining material may come forward, but such times are usually not sufficient for the extent of preconscious or unconscious material to surface. Dreams, and to a degree some other altered states of consciousness, can fill in the gap. This is particularly true of the emotional dimension of our lives. Given the fact that just about every life experience we have contains one or more emotion of some measurable level of intensity, our consciousness searches for ways to process these valuable experiences. From general human experiences such as repression, denial, and projection, we know that if we do not find conscious methods of processing our experiences, the preconscious and the unconscious will find a way.

The Development of Consciousness

My life journey is not complete, and neither is yours. In different ways, we are still growing, and we will continue to do so until our deaths.[14] As our life continues to develop, our consciousness does as well. Investigations of psychological development came into focus in the middle of the twentieth century with the work of Erik Erikson. Erikson took Freud's early stages of psychological development and expanded them to cover the entire life cycle, identifying eight stages (which he termed *crises*) of human development. In the next several decades, a number of authors worked and reworked Erikson's basic framework. We have already looked at James Fowler's faith development, which is an example of this kind of paradigm.

Varieties of treatments concerning *spiritual* development are actually much older in the West. In the thirteenth century, the Franciscan St. Bonaventure provided a theological language that has continued for many centuries, identifying three "hierarchical ways" of pursuing spiritual development—purgation, illumination, and union—that lead the individual toward something termed perfection.[15] Neither Erikson nor

---

[14] What happens to consciousness beyond our death is relevant, although not something I intend to explore here. For those who are interested in a scientific exploration, I would recommend Pim van Lommel, *Consciousness beyond Life: The Science of the Near-Death Experience* (New York: Harper One, 2010). You would probably also want to explore an assessment of van Lommel's conclusions found in Thompson, *Waking, Dreaming, Being*, 299–314.

[15] Spiritual writers and theologians subsequent to Bonaventure took his terminology and largely treated it as referring to three successive and distinct stages, the

Bonaventure speak specifically about the development of consciousness, since exploring consciousness developmentally seems to be relatively new. Jesuit theologian Pierre Teilhard de Chardin was a pioneer in the field, formulating his theory of the noosphere in the mid-twentieth century. Teilhard's understanding of consciousness development is integrally bound to his holistic view of evolution. This approach seems to have become standard in exploring consciousness development. Human consciousness evolves as the universe evolves. Because Teilhard's focus does not explore the individual's development so much as it looks at human consciousness as one holistic fabric, we will return to Teilhard after a brief discussion that focuses on individual development.

Ken Wilber, through his proposal of the Integral Operating System, may be the current writer who most focuses on and systematizes consciousness development in the individual. Wilber does not ignore what we might call the corporate context of developing consciousness. In his quadrant model of integral development, the corporate or social aspects of reality are addressed in the lower two quadrants. The individual's integral development is presented in the top half of the IOS quadrants. Recall the basic difference between conscious *states* and conscious *stages* for Wilber. States are temporary, circumstantial to the present experience, while stages, are permanent. They represent, if you will, attained life achievements.

For Wilber's model, development has no specific end point. Consciousness is open-ended into the future. In addition to this distinctive view of the future, Wilber's model recognizes that evolution takes place within a holistic *process*. In the IOS system, everything evolves holistically through a process that is described as "transcend and include." In evolving, nothing is left behind. The current circumstances in which each of us live will, in time, become so confining or discomforting that impulses toward transcendence, toward something new and life-giving, will appear. This will bring about a new personal paradigm, but this new configuration does not disregard what already existed. Instead, the new configuration will, in some way, carry the former along, transforming it to fit into what has replaced it.[16]

---

lower leading to the higher, to achieve a final perfectionistic outcome. Bonaventure himself was much more subtle. The three "ways," as they are presented in *De Triplici Via*, are three hierarchical but concurrent movements that are proceeding through the entire spiritual life.

[16] For a general overview of Wilber's IOS system, see Ken Wilber, *A Brief History of Everything* (Boston: Shambhala, 2007).

Wilber's Integral Operating System is a complete, complex, and tidy framework. That is certainly helpful. Its inclusiveness and consistency have very tangible benefits. Yet it also strikes me as lacking a sense of the insolubility of some of life's most significant challenges. That is to say, the Integral Operating System seems to suffer in the face of Mystery and at the edge of logic. Because our consciousness expands as we grow, as we encounter this edge in all its uncertainty, an open-ended treatment of consciousness development will benefit us in accounting for the very real consciousness through which we are aware of our faith questions on the brink of the unknown or in the midst of the Unknowable.

In all of this talk of consciousness developing in an open-ended way, what is actually taking place? Development, after all, is not exactly the same as change. Things can change continuously without any development occurring. Traffic lights change from green to yellow to red, but there is no real development. Does the development of consciousness, therefore, have meaning or purpose? Is it moving in a significant direction? If it is moving with significance, toward what might it be moving? Consciousness, could be moving higher (or deeper, depending on how one constructs the metaphor), toward greater complexity. It could, however, also be moving in a different way, toward an *unspecified* boundary or some critical point. Let us consider each.

If human consciousness continued to develop in tandem with biological and neurological evolution, where would it go? Michio Kaku addresses these kinds of issues in *The Future of the Mind*. Written from a primarily materialistic point of view, Kaku interviewed a number of contemporary scientists working in fields such as artificial intelligence, neurological engineering, and human-robotic merging. Much of their work is geared to carrying the human species forward to whatever science seems to dictate. Kaku himself maintains an air of contingency in regard to a final outcome.[17] I suppose this would be the general course of wisdom moving from such a point of view, since human consciousness begins to look very fragile from this perspective.

The second movement of consciousness development would envision a boundary or critical point where consciousness transitions beyond where biological or even neurological development could take

---

[17] Michio Kaku, *The Future of the Mind*. See especially his Appendix, "Quantum Consciousness," 329–42, where he focuses on the role freedom would play in the conclusion.

it. Teilhard de Chardin, toward the end of his signature book *The Phenomenon of Man*, looked at where he saw the growth of human consciousness moving into the future, toward what he called the Omega Point. He envisioned that the biosphere and the noosphere would, inevitably, have to separate.

> The idea is that of noogenesis ascending irreversibly towards Omega through the strictly limited cycle of geogenesis. At a given moment in the future, under some influence exerted by one or the other of these curves or of both together, it is inevitable that the two branches should separate. However convergent it be, evolution cannot attain to fulfillment on earth except through a point of dissociation.... With this we are introduced to a fantastic and inevitable event which now begins to take shape in our perspective, the event which comes nearer with every day that passes: the end of all life on our globe, the death of the planet, the ultimate phase of the phenomenon of man.[18]

Both of these possibilities, however, look at consciousness development as something that implies or utilizes *temporal* movement. Will science drag human consciousness along with it, or, given the general perspective of a universe ultimately growing cold and lifeless, will consciousness break free of the physical universe at some point prior to the universe's inevitable calcification or termination in the future? Is that how we must understand the development of consciousness now, in the present? Could human consciousness perhaps be presently transitioning through this boundary or critical point in another kind of crossing, such as a crossing from our current limitation of perception into the realm of the imperceptible? That is a startling prospect indeed.

Consciousness Crossing Over

In his book, *The Soul's Code*, James Hillman presented the Swedish folktale of Huldra.

> Swedes tell a folktale of the forests. The lumberjacks of northern pine, fir, and spruce used to work pretty much alone, felling trees, lopping branches. They drank, too, in the short days of white cold. Coffee. *Snaps* ... Sometimes Huldra would appear. She

---

[18] Teilhard de Chardin, *The Phenomenon of Man*, 273.

was an exquisitely formed creature, delicate, enchanting, and irresistible. Sometimes, a woodcutter would stop his work, even drop his ax to follow her beckoning farther into the woods. As he approached, she turned her back—and vanished. Once Huldra turned her smiling face away, there was nothing. She had no back, or her back was invisible. And he, drawn too deeply into the forest, unable to find familiar markings or get back to a clearing, lost his bearings and froze.[19]

In breaking open this tale of the siren or wood nymph, Hillman passes over various Jungian archetypal interpretations of male/female roles, the loss of soul to fantasy projections, and nature's revenge upon human destructiveness. He wants to go back to the tale itself and confront the nature of *invisibility*. As attractive and enticing as Huldra is, she has no back. Mythic structure and metaphoric symbolism inevitably pull us into mystery. Hillman writes:

Invisibility perplexes American common sense and American psychology, which hold as a major governing principle that whatever exists, exists in some quantity and therefore can be measured. If an image in your heart that calls you to your fate exists, and may be strong and long-lasting, has it measurable dimensions? A passion to cage the invisible by visible methods continues to motivate the science of psychology, even though that science has given up the century-long search for the soul in various body parts and systems. When the searchers failed to find the soul in the places where they were looking, scientific psychology gave up also on the idea of soul.[20]

I have related several times through the chapters of this book the importance of metaphoric structure in our efforts to bridge the gap between what we know and what lies just beyond our knowledge. When Hillman relates this folktale, in which he intends to emphasize the nature of mystery lying just beyond our rational, intellectual reach, he is utilizing the kind of metaphoric structure we call *myth*. In common parlance, myth is usually understood as something untrue, something made up to answer

---

[19] James Hillman, *The Soul's Code: In Search of Character and Calling* (New York: Random House, 1996), 92–93.

[20] Hillman, *The Soul's Code*, 92.

complicated questions of life for those looking for simple or childish solutions. Weren't myths simply offering inadequate explanations to a primitive humanity?

That is not, however, what the anthropological and theological communities understand a myth to be. Myths are, instead, *foundational belief statements*. They deal with how cultures, religions, communities, and individuals make sense of the world that surrounds them. They speak to a level of insight beyond rational thought. Hillman links them to intuition. "Intuitions occur; we do not make them. They come to us as a sudden idea, a definite judgment, a grasped meaning. They come with an event as if brought by it or inherent in it. You say something and I 'get it,' just like that."[21]

All myths are metaphoric. They are extended metaphors, utilizing a more complex metaphoric construction than any single metaphor offers. They tell a story. If we take the mythic story as fact or history, we have missed the essential point. The role of mythic structure, and symbolism in general, is to articulate what literalism is incapable of producing. To make myth history is to attempt trapping mystery into a manageable intellectual confinement. In the process, we make myth unintelligible.

Metaphor and myth are not unreasonable, for they reside within a particular kind of reasoning. *Metaphoric reasoning* is not the reasoning of mathematics (which actually can be very imaginative), reasoning that lives within the realm of an equation (=). Mathematics understands $ab = ba$. It is simple. Everything on one side of the equation turns out to be the same value as everything on the other. Metaphoric reasoning is different. It looks more like this:

KNOWN REALITY > ~ ~ *metaphoric distance* ~ ~ < IMPERCEPTIBLE REALITY

In this reasoning, the distance between what is known and what is imperceptible is not always the same. Metaphoric closeness is not the same as identity. The distance of our comparisons can vary. The metaphor may be very strong (close) or faint (distant).

In Hillman's story, I noted that he briefly passed over several possible applications that would fit, to some degree, into a Jungian context (male/female roles, etc.). These would all be appropriate uses of this myth. In

---

[21] Hillman, *The Soul's Code*, 98.

applying the story to each, the myth of Huldra would take on something of a different meaning. It would possibly have a stronger fit for one application than for another, but none would be wrong.

With each application, our attention would shift a bit, and our awareness would take on a different intentionality. It may lead to deeper insight. It may touch some original intuitive level. We may actually consider the story *inspiring*. It may (or may not) touch some level of experience that we never have reached before, somewhere we might term *mystagogic*, that which can open us to a spiritual and religious level. Consciousness crossing the boundary to the imperceptible does not come with guarantees, only possibilities, but the possibilities are real. In spiritual experience, it seems that we meet the symbolic and mystagogic most powerfully at the *edges* of our consciousness.

But not so fast. Doesn't the myth say that following Huldra into the woods could lead to death? That sounds dangerous. It does say that, and it is dangerous. If you were planning on escaping death, you may not want to go any farther. But then, how realistic is that? Where are you expecting to end up? In Chapter 6, I suggested that our journey over the edge of our perception would be a journey of paradox, and death is like that. If you follow Huldra into the woods, you will die in some way. But if you *consciously* follow her into the woods, what dies in you will likely offer you some benefit. It may be necessary or even *life-giving*. If you don't, you may be sentencing yourself to a different kind of death, at least the death of a lost opportunity.

Because embracing the mythic lies beneath or beyond our usual intellectual activity, we may expect to see it appear in indirect or unfamiliar ways. It may be *much like* (metaphor alert) electrons passing through a double slit—the impact they leave does not look like what we would have anticipated. Once we understand the wave nature of the electrons, though, we see that the whole experiment has a pattern to it. When we understand that electrons have dual natures, a particle nature and a wave nature, paradoxical as it seems, electrons seem to have been tamed, if not controlled. In much the same way, metaphor and myth provide us with a kind of diffused pattern. It allows consciousness a greater awareness, but consciousness will continue to remain mysterious. Huldra's back is still invisible. If we cannot, or choose not to, befriend her, she will still remain dangerous.

The mythic diffusion of our consciousness is the playground of our dreams.[22] Dreaming, one of the identified general states of consciousness, has neurological functionality. Daniel Siegel describes the brain's activity that brings dreams about. "They occur when cortical inhibition is released enough to allow our subcortical limbic and brainstem regions to have a heyday with imagination and feeling."[23] The expression of preconscious or unconscious emotions is central to dreaming, and imagination (symbolic creativity using spontaneous images) is their primary language. The question is, do they mean anything of significance?

For many people, including some brain researchers, dreams don't have much significance. For others, including myself, they do. Working with retreatants and spiritual directees over many years has led me to a deep belief in the benefit and power of dreams. In this work, I have helped individuals and groups creatively work with their dreams, and I work with my own in my personal practice.

Yet even if the dreams of the night are haphazard, random, and hold no particular significant meaning, the experience of actively working with their images and emotions can be rewarding, enlightening, and freeing. The images we dream are *our* images, chosen from somewhere deep in the brain, and the active work with our imagination itself can lead us through the boundary area of our perception into what has previously been unknown to us. In the presence of others who honor these experiences, intentional consideration of dreams can be a life-giving practice of meaning-making.

Dream images, which for the most part arise from our preconscious and unconscious, appear to us and respond quite differently than the concepts and images we have in our day life, which are more resourced from our brain's left hemisphere and managed from our cerebral cortex. Dream imagery is largely metaphoric and, being somewhat free of cortical supervision, seems more willing to venture into areas otherwise guarded by rational conceptual thought. Dreams may explore areas considered taboo or fantastic, and they may enter into what is unexplainable or extrasensory.

---

[22] I have treated my approach to dreamwork in somewhat greater detail in *Paradox: The Spiritual Path to Transformation*, (Mystic, CT: Twenty-Third Publications, 2002), 173–82. I do not intend to repeat much of that here.

[23] Daniel J. Siegel, *Mindsight: The New Science of Personal Transformation* (New York: Bantam Books, 2011), 141.

Dreams can be visited by rational consciousness, the experience known as *lucid dreaming*. Here we become consciously aware in the dream that we are dreaming, and the conscious state can once again take over management of the dream. Is this a good thing? Some who study and work with dreams favor training and further development along the line of lucid dreaming. This is particularly true in some areas of Eastern spirituality, where lucid dreaming represents a significant deepening of meditation.[24] It can also be seen as an opportunity to actively pursue dreamwork from within the dream itself. From this point of view, the dreamer can become something like one's own director in a dream-scenario psychodrama. This could have benefits; conceivably, it could also have risks.

Another way of looking at lucid dreaming, however, could see in it a missed opportunity. The preconscious and the unconscious deserve their say, and they're not likely to get it from waking consciousness. I like to call a dream the "minority report." A healthy society listens to its minority voices, even if, after a full discernment, other voices will prevail. Giving the unconscious a sounding board provides our consciousness with the fuller picture. It also offers the unconscious an alternative to acting out of repression, denial, and so forth.

Dreaming, of course, is not the only way our consciousness can enter into the uncharted boundary areas of life. Conscious waking life provides many opportunities for opening to the unknown in what one of my teachers referred to as the *interstices of life*—the spaces, however small, that exist between those parts of life we usually call "normal." These spaces— times of prayer, meditation, retreat periods, hiking, exercising, reflective manual work, and opportunities for writing, painting, and so on—should make up some sizable percentage of our lives. If they do not, we may need to make conscious choices to consistently create them. These are the spaces where we are open to the unusual, the unexpected, and the unencumbered. These are the spaces where Huldra, or something like her, can find us.

In such spaces, we need to resist the temptation to fill them up with practical and useful—even spiritually useful—things to do. We need to learn how to let go of agendas and future plans. The spaces should largely be *spaces*, with substantial unplanned time, where we can receive *inspiration*, opportunities to be influenced, stimulated, prompted,

---

[24] See Thompson, *Waking, Dreaming, Being*, particularly 139–65.

or impelled to creative manifestation. Inspired by what? Inspired by whatever grace (favor) is sent our way. Consciousness can be influenced from outside.

In thus allowing consciousness the opportunity to cross through the boundaries of our current perception, we will need to remain attentive to how our consciousness is changing (being changed) through ongoing time and experience. This is an open-ended process that requires continuing discernment. In discernment, the spiritual traveler, you and I, must be led by *obedience*. In this context, obedience does not mean doing what you are told to do. The root meaning of the word is to *listen for* (*ob audire*). Inner obedience attunes me more to seeking questions than to looking for answers. Here, entertaining questions is better than seeking immediate answers, for, if there were any such answers, they only stop the processes of consciousness. This discernment involves me with a plethora of difficult questions, such as:

- What keeps me from owning my story (my narrative of the memories that have given shape to my present)?
- What in my past can't I let go of?
- What is my awareness of who I am and what I am doing?
- Where are the challenges of growth for me now?
- What choices are being laid out before me now?
- Where is the opposition in them? True choice involves me in the mystery of paradox.
- What apprehensions or anxieties are currently standing in the way before me?

This is not an exhaustive list. Discerning such questions requires bringing every part of myself—my prayer, my reflection on experience, my cognitive intelligence, my emotions, my intuitions and gut feelings, and my dreams and images—to bear on these questions and others. It implies what scripture calls *endurance* (Rom 5:4) because these questions do not resolve themselves quickly. It also implies that this listening is done with a surrendering heart, a willingness to allow appropriate changes to come into my life.

In the end (which at that time will be the present), as my ongoing journey has continued to evolve, the full context of my personal understanding of my own consciousness will lie before me. In the best-case scenario (no guarantees on that here, of course), my life's journey will lie open for my assessment. I hope that what I see would reveal a great blessing to myself and others. It would, however, consist of my own self-imposed limitations as to how far I had been willing to allow consciousness to fully develop under God's grace.

Shared Consciousness

If we are living in the kind of holistic universe that quantum theory strongly suggests, it would be quite understandable that one would ask whether my unique experience of consciousness can interact with or embrace consciousness beyond me. Can my consciousness touch others? Of course, we interact with others all the time, in our bodies, in our language and communication, between minds. Daniel Siegel maintains that the mind is a *relational* reality, "a relational and embodied process, emerging from within and between brains, that regulates the flow of energy and information." In this flow of energy and information, like you and I are doing now through the words and ideas expressed in the pages of this book, minds can touch and interact. This is, of course, relevant to the fact that both of us are conscious beings whose individual consciousnesses are presumably enhanced by our sharing of these important human features. But can our individual consciousnesses touch everything?

The relatedness of our minds is different from our having a fully *shared* consciousness. Such an experience would probably need to include some kind of open access, where part or all of my present awareness would be open to you, or to someone, and vice versa. This would be the kind of access we would expect to have with God, at least in one direction, for God would always remain somewhat unknowable from our end (Rom 11:33–34 again).

The very idea of having some kind of shared consciousness would likely raise all sorts of questions. How much access to my consciousness would be entailed? Are we speaking of some sort of mind reading? What kind of permissions and safeguards would be in place? And why would we want this in the first place? The details of such arrangements could get very complex without ever beginning to approach a fundamental divergence between Eastern and Western thought regarding the continuance of a unique personal consciousness beyond death. Is individuality real or is it only an illusion? Would we be seeking to share something that may not be real in the first place?

Before we get too bogged down, let's look at what is being proposed. When we are speaking about human consciousness moving toward a shared or even universal consciousness, we are again speaking about an evolutionary process. I mentioned above that Pierre Teilhard de Chardin saw the evolution of the noosphere toward Omega as, primarily, a holistic movement affecting the entire species rather than the process of individuals as such. Ilia Delio, who has researched and written extensively on Teilhard's ideas, states, "The noosphere is a level of shared consciousness that transcends boundaries of religion, culture and ethnicity. It is a sphere of collective consciousness, a new interior consciousness that is showing itself in the way culture is organizing itself around social networks."[25] She continues,

> Hence, the noosphere is a super-convergence of psychic energy, a higher form of complexity in which the human person does not become obsolete but rather acquires more being through interconnectivity with others. In this respect the noosphere is not the realm of the impersonal but the realm of the *deeply personal* through *convergence* or the bringing together of diverse elements, organisms, and even the currents of human thought—a medium of collective consciousness that enhances more being.[26]

If shared or collective consciousness lies in our future and is following an evolutionary track, however, a question of origin arises. From where did consciousness come? The evolutionary track is usually seen as beginning with the Great Singularity and has been evolving into ever greater complexity throughout the historical course of the universe. Was the capacity for consciousness something that was there, in some way, from the beginning? That seems to have been Teilhard's understanding. Evolution, for Teilhard, is present in the *within*. Something imperceptible is already there that finally emerges, first in the biosphere; then, with growing self-awareness, into the noosphere; and continues to follow a path of convergence toward shared consciousness and ultimately toward Omega.

It could be noted that this is not totally out of keeping with a reductionist view of evolution, with, of course, some major exceptions.

---

[25] Ilia Delio, *The Unbearable Wholeness of Being: God, Evolution, and the Power of Love* (Maryknoll, NY: Orbis Books, 2013), 170.

[26] Delio, *The Unbearable Wholeness of Being*, 171.

Consciousness, from a reductionist and materialist point of view, would be seen as arising through an evolutionary process from elemental material, through the emergence of certain amino acids, then to living organisms, and then onward, but purely from trial and error and self-generated from *chance*. From Teilhard's point of view, or actually from just about any position of religious faith, human consciousness and further developments toward shared consciousness emerge from some kind of *disposition*, or from some emerging *plan*, even if that plan had extensive possibilities for permutation. Such an approach implies the presence of a greater Consciousness, one that *accompanies* the development but is not subject to it—a Consciousness that is influencing or motivating its development.

We may now be able to return to some questions I raised toward the end of Chapter 6 concerning the *interaction of love*. There I spoke of love as the force that could be, in the words of Martin Luther King Jr., bending the moral universe. I was then primarily speaking of the role this love-force has played over the course of the universe's development. Now, however, we may wish to entertain the possibility of love as an interaction that is driving the continued unfolding and deepening of consciousness. As it may now or soon be coming forth in some animals, consciousness began in humans as the simple awareness of self, the knowing that I know. Presently, we are the substantial evidence that consciousness continues to move toward ever greater personalization. Consciousness does not simply stay self-awareness. It deepens as systemic relational consciousness, an emerging *integral intimacy*, bearing the potential to further motivate reality toward greater meaning and purpose.

Certainly, we cannot achieve such consciousness solely on our own initiative and power. The track record of human "progress" is convincing testimony to our tendency to drag our deepest faults along with our greatest accomplishments. That we continue, even with the clear awareness of the danger, to walk precariously along the edge of self-destruction should produce some desire to foster *humility*, reminding ourselves that we are still "of the earth." It should call us to look beyond ourselves for a greater and deeper Help, a Higher Power.

This Helping Consciousness, God, if you will, invites our participation in an unfolding Plan. The invitation is freely and unconditionally offered, at every moment, in every circumstance. The invitation is offered again and again, continuously, and is never withheld. It is not, nor has it ever been, presented with preconditions—preliminary steps to take, intentions to prove, forms to complete. It is the amazing gratuitousness and mercy of God, whose sun rises on the bad and the good (Mt 5:45).

But wait! There is one other thing. ("I knew it!" you say.)

The invitation is continuously *extended*, but it is never *imposed*. It is ours to accept or let pass, which we often do, perhaps even most of the time. That it will come again, and then again, doesn't seem to help. We still let it pass, even as we protest that we want it and are desperately waiting for it. The invitation into the deeper plan of consciousness is offered *freely*, but it can only be accepted and integrated, in turn, with our *free* response.

Consciousness and Freedom

You will recall that part of my definition of prayer from past chapters is the seeking of a relationship of mutual presence, consciousness meeting Consciousness. Such a development of consciousness, at the level in which we now find ourselves, requires the presence of free and mutual responses. God's response is always free, and God is totally loving. As we continue to strive to bring our consciousness into relationship with God's invitation, we must seek to deepen and integrate our free and loving response in our uneven but developing way. That is the work at hand.

As I indicated above, however, it probably didn't start that way. When our distant ancestors first emerged into consciousness, they passed more or less "unknowingly" from the biosphere (to use Teilhard's terms) into the noosphere. The Genesis story has them among the rest of living things, but not clearly cognizant of the power they were already exercising. When humans did cross the critical point into consciousness, they brought the divine giftedness with them, as well as the selfishness, the competitiveness, and the tendency to dominate and subjugate, present to some degree in most if not all species. Did humanity slip a fast one by God? Not in the least; it was to be expected. That is the paradoxical nature of the whole project. Everything possesses two energies, held together as tightly as the dipolar particles of the atom. And the nature of the developmental process, to transcend and include, anticipated that was how it would be, and still is.

Now, however, as humans have continued to grow and evolve through thousands and thousands of years of experience, we have come to the belief, partially true, that we have, to a large degree, mastered many of the forces of nature. If we want to unleash our power over electromagnetism, for instance, we only need to turn on a switch. This can put the lights on, and in turn can give us extensive power to overcome many other limitations, including the natural limits faced in gravity, enabling humans to drive fast, fly often, and pull up from the earth what we have come to convince ourselves to be an unlimited supply of fossil fuel. We can do all of this, so we say, for the benefit of the common good. We are slowly coming to realize, however, that our exercise of power touches all of humanity very unevenly. If we think of the *common* good as what is good for everything on our planet, then our exercise of power may be much more at its expense than for its benefit.

The interaction of love has been there from the beginning, and it is the force that can correct this dangerous imbalance. Love has the power to exercise a wide range of decisions and actions that can reshape ourselves and the environment around us—actions guided by such energies as tolerance, humility, empathy, foresight, discernment, generosity, wisdom, and so many others. God, who possesses all these powers in an abundance of love, exercises them for the full common good, as God always has, not magically but progressively, through the unfolding of creation. God will continue to do this. Of late, say in the last few tens of thousands of years, we have come to a place of development where we can begin to see that we could share in this great work. Our consciousness now has the capacity to cooperate in this task locally, by which I mean the shaping, administering, and enhancing of our little planet.

The energies of love are all empowered by faith and trust, as I have been suggesting from the beginning. This is not the faith of doctrine or creedal beliefs, which has its significant part to play. Instead, it is primarily the faith of decision, commitment, investment, fortitude, and so on. The capacity for this kind of faith lies more within our consciousness than in our intellectual powers, technological capabilities, or creative innovations. We must tend to our consciousness to fully experience this faith within our spirit, our soul, the depth of our integrity, our desire for meaning and purpose, the store of goodness, and in concern for what is beyond ourselves. None of these is present and deepening in our lives *automatically*. They have all been placed there in their nascent form by our early formation, if we were fortunate enough to have had such beginnings. Whether we had such opportunities or not, we still all have the capacity for these things. With the proper aid, we can incorporate and integrate them into our lives if we choose to do so. Freedom to make such choices is therefore to be seen a *constitutive aspect* of love.

The ironic thing here is that many materialists who study the brain and its functioning often deny that humans have real freedom. They point out that some studies of the past few decades clearly indicate that what we call free will, the ability to make a free choice, is an illusion. Our "choice" was already chosen by unconscious activity in parts of the brain's deeper functioning in the milliseconds prior to the final indication of our course of action. What we think is our free choice is actually our falling back on what we have learned from previous experiences. In short, our "choice" was not free, but rather, predetermined.

Closer scrutiny, however, points out some discrepancies in such a line of thinking. First of all, it presumes a faulty comparison. Freedom is not the true opposite of determinism. The opposite of determinism is spontaneity. The materialist position seems to confuse freedom with spontaneous action. Someone throws a punch at me, and I make a swing back. Was that a free choice on my part? No, it was an automatic conditioned response based on deeply held fears and past threats lying somewhere in my reptilian brain. It was spontaneous, but it wasn't free. Freedom comes when I can put such a reaction on temporary hold, process it with other information from aspects of my emotional experiences, draw upon my reflection on other choices I have made, and pull all this together while taking into account what I see as the higher ideals for which I am striving in life. In other words, I have the opportunity to *discern* the best choice of action and follow that. Real freedom consists of this. In the moment, do I always have such time to fully complete this process? No, not always. But, over time, my reflexive tendencies learn to be more fluid and tempered with my discernment. Freedom leads me to assert more conscious mastery over my conditioned reflexes.

A second discrepancy in the materialist outlook deals with what could be called an inappropriate disjunction. The materialist view betrays its own sense of systemic wholeness. When I say, "I did not choose that. My unconscious brain already made the decision," when did my unconscious brain become disconnected from who "I" am? If my unconscious brain made the decision, who is the "I" who is falsely claiming responsibility? My prefrontal cortex? Then my brain has become split, and I am split. I am no longer whole. Freedom, however, ultimately must witness to my wholeness.

A third problem with the materialist view lies with what is termed our *motivational system*. Freedom, free choice, if it exists, has to do with motivation, what I want or desire to do. In some of the studies linked to the materialist position, the subject is instructed to choose at random when to do a simple action such as moving a finger while looking at a clock. Following this on an EEG scan, a clear lag can be recognized between when the unconscious brain "makes a decision" and when the action is performed. But is that how motivation in humans usually works? Hardly. Motivation is systemic. In making most decisions, there is a great deal of activity going on in the brain. The prefrontal cortex is receiving neurological information from many parts of the brain—the nervous system, the brain stem, the limbic system, and so on. From all these elements, the cortex constructs its response. Often, our free choice is a work in process. I may change my mind later, with fuller discernment. Instead of a betrayal of freedom, such an episode is its reinforcement.

If we can thus establish the actuality of freedom, how do consciousness and freedom relate to each other? Conscious action requires free choosing, and genuine free choice is not usually spontaneous. This may surprise us because we have been led to expect it to be so. Real freedom is not impulsive. That doesn't mean that free choice is slow, belabored, or indecisive. It does mean, however, that free choice is deliberate. In clarifying what I usually call *practiced mastery*, there is something habitual at work. I distinguish between what is "habitual"—achieved with consciously repeated practice, how one might come to master a sport or skill—from what is "conditioned"—behaviorally modified and encoded. Though these concepts, habituation and conditioning, may seem to be close at face value, they are miles apart in reality. The first represents a systemic process of conscious choosing, and the second consists of predetermined calcified programming.

The various definitions of consciousness that opened this chapter were all helpful in laying out the landscape, but there were none that I wholeheartedly embraced. I am understandably hesitant, therefore, at the end of this part of our conversation, to now offer my own definition. Of those initial definitions, I find Ken Wilber's to be the most intriguing because it was more of a non-definition, focusing mostly on what consciousness was not, while hinting at what it had to be. Wilber called it *space*, ... an emptiness, an openness, a clearing in which phenomena arise and develop. When I attach this to my own understanding of spirituality (my life lived in faith), it brings me close to my belief (my *trust*) that focusing on consciousness is absolutely essential to understanding what the spiritual journey is all about.

While we may not be able to adequately define it, we can recognize that consciousness is "where" mind is integrated, intention and awareness are entertained, relationship is encountered, and the interaction of love is manifested in presence, freedom, and empowerment. Consciousness is what we carry forward. It is the lasting corollary we bear with us as we move into our examination of the spiritual journey.

10

Spirituality in a Holistic-Systemic Quantum World

Holistic Spirituality and Spiritual Integration

Though it may seem that our pursuit of neuroscience and consciousness in the last three chapters has drifted far from quantum fields and superposition, remember that quantum theory is a pursuit of understanding the makeup of reality. In these latter chapters, our investigations have focused on an essential component of the quantum experience: the nature and disposition of the *conscious observer*. In a general sense, the only reason humans know anything at all about subatomic and cosmological reality is because our collective consciousness has led us to observe it and to seek understanding of what we have observed.

In these chapters, we situated our exploration of quantum theory toward a view of God/Mystery, toward the Primal Observer,[1] if you will, and of the human brain, mind, and consciousness. Having spent the greater part of the book on securing a basic understanding of quantum theory within our story's interplay of science and the spiritual journey,

---

[1] It is understandable that some readers might raise protests, perhaps even alarms, against references to God as an Observer. God is, after all, an *actor*, not an observer. Portraying God as an observer seems to be a fallback onto Deistic divine passivity. God is engaged with reality, not merely watching it mechanistically unfold. But God as Primal Observer *is consistent with* the quantum metaphor I am presenting. In the Copenhagen model of Bohr and Heisenberg, the conscious observer is not passive. In fact, the observer is the *generator* of the outcome, without whose conscious intention the outcome (the measurement) would not take place at all. The understanding of God as Primal Observer honors the fact that the universe was 13.7 billion years old before human (or likely any other kind of) conscious observation came along.

we now turn to a more systematic discussion of spirituality. We begin our systematic investigation with *systems*, that is, with a look at the nature of spirituality from the view of systemic wholeness.

I have written this book in a language called English. Because of historical circumstances through the centuries familiar to most of us, it is a language known to and spoken by a wide range of people around the world. It has some roots in Greek, Latin, and early French, but it is mostly rooted in the language spoken by two Germanic tribes who came to dwell in the British Isles. The Anglo-Saxon tongue is the direct linguistic ancestor of today's English. Obviously, the language has changed quite a bit. Mostly, it has become vastly more complicated as we have had centuries of experiences, backed by a great deal of nuanced writing, thinking, inventing, and dramatizing. Where one word initially represented to an early population a general experiential concept, eventually new forms and structures were needed to represent its finer linguistic details.

So it was with the Anglo-Saxon word *hāl*. Over the centuries, forms of this word's initial concept (the sense of being sound, hale, uninjured, vital) have broken into three directional variations within modern English. Today we speak of someone possessing *health* (healthy, healing), being *holy* (holiness) and *whole* (wholesome, holism). Mental health, social health, physical health, and spiritual health have developed from the unfolding of a common objective. *Holistic spirituality* could be seen as a move to reconnect these concepts once again, a spirituality that is vital, sacred, and complete, a spirituality that is *integral*.

From the outset of this book, I have described spirituality as a holistic enterprise, touching every aspect of our lives, something that contains what is most vital and complete. That is also why I have defined spirituality as *my life lived in faith*. This definition embraces the conviction that everything we do and everything that happens to us is affected by what we put faith in. And in turn, all our experiences influence our faith, either deepening its conviction or causing doubt or uncertainty, making life a bit more precarious.

What I put faith in depends on what I trust. In the Greek of the New Testament, they are the same word. Faith and trust (Greek: *pistis*, the noun, and *pisteuō*, the verb) convey the sense of decision and commitment, to have confidence, to entrust. I see this kind of trust as the fundamental spiritual attitude. In what do I trust? The structures of the universe? Friends and loved ones? My own life efforts and successes? Nothing? This attitude, and where I focus it, gives shape to my entire life.

Whatever I cannot trust—and it seems that life offers us many possibilities—I will learn to fear. Fear is also a foundational spiritual attitude, and for all the wrong reasons. Trust and fear are inversely proportionate attitudes. The deeper my trust, the less I fear; the less I trust, the more my life is ruled by fear. For each of us, these two attitudes guide our approach to living more than anything else, whether we know it or not. As our life journey goes forward, the shape of your spirituality and mine depend essentially on which of these two predominates.

This kind of fear is different from *primordial* fear (our instinct for self-preservation; fight or flight; something responding automatically from our reptilian brain) and certainly different from *awe* (what scripture calls "fear of the Lord"). This kind of fear, instead, is the rooted attitude that life and everything about life is basically untrustworthy and should, therefore, be guarded against. From a religious point of view, we have not always focused our spirituality in this way. These attitudes lie beneath our creedal beliefs and doctrines. Creedal belief and atheism are largely irrelevant at this foundational level.

Throughout the early chapters of this book, we reflected on freedom, often in contrast to materialistic science's challenges. It is essential that we can affirm our freedom with confidence, and this was a significant point in the previous chapter. Since both trust and fear are within us, often instilled there by outside voices and early experiences, we must have the capacity to freely choose to deepen trust and move away from a fear-dominated life. Doing so is no easy task. Whether we take that option or not is largely in our own hands.

How we take that option, of course, is a crucial part of the role of consciousness in our lives. Identifying the presence of these two attitudes in our spiritual lives requires reflection and conscious examination. Our fears hide under numerous respectable guises. Yet our choice to move away from disabling fear is only one of many aspects that the spiritual life assigns to consciousness. Its overall importance is reflected in the process of integration presented by Daniel Siegel, where consciousness has a foundational role in the overall development of mindsight. Even more so, consciousness is our primary means for accessing the deepening awareness of the relational interchange that we are promised with the Ultimate Power that lies beyond us.

In this chapter, therefore, I invite you to view, however briefly, the spiritual journey of consciousness as it makes its way toward God and all of creation. I present two related-but-different movements in holistic spirituality: the *journey onward* and the *journey inward*. Although both of these journeys entail reflection on the accumulation of our life experiences in different ways, it is important to keep focused on the fact that consciousness involves the present moment. We may reflect on memories of stored experiences, but we always do this in the here and now.

The first, the journey onward, describes a developmental movement through the human life cycle. This is a movement of time, and, in various ways, this journey has been our focus since Chapter 4, our introduction to temporal motion. Here, we elaborate on the spiritual integration process that has emerged from our tour of the brain/mind and the development of consciousness in our most recent chapters.

The second, the journey inward, describes a parallel journey accompanying the first. Instead of being concerned with the passing of time, this journey is focused on movements of space. On this journey, we attend to the inner space traveled by consciousness as it deepens and develops. It is a movement that follows no particular clock. The journey moves through a series of experiences, reflections, meditations, and integrations. These two movements ultimately come together in what I call *transforming resonance*.

The Journey Onward

The onward journey is a movement through spacetime that can be identified in its four-dimensional coordinates, by the *where, when,* and *what* of an event. Where did I move? When did I move? What took place there? We can each track this journey in different ways. Some people keep careful track in journals. Some record this past year's movements in annual retreat diaries of one sort or the other. Some occasionally do exercises similar to the Steppingstone process suggested by the Progoff Intensive Journal.[2] Some just seek to hold it in memory. Does it matter how we record our journey? Different people offer different answers to that question.

Of the diverse ways to approach and explain the journey onward, I like to begin with an explanation of *formation* and *transformation*. My

---

[2] The basic work is Ira Progoff, *At a Journal Workshop: The Basic Text and Guide for Using the Intensive Journal* (New York: Dialogue House Library, 1975).

life in faith, spirituality, can be understood as the continuous interaction between these two aspects of experience. Taken together, they are leading us toward inter-communion with God, others, and everything that we seek in faith.

We are not born with a blank slate. Far from it. At our birth, much of who we are and will be is genetically handed to us. However, as we move through our life experiences, we also become the product of those experiences, as we are likewise a product of our perceptions of them and the actions we have taken because of them. In the complex of these factors, what is our formation? Formation is the sum of all the ingredients that make us who we are—our culture, our family (nuclear and extended), our education, our political and social structures, and so on. I have been formed by how the events of life have acted on my language, worldview, relationships, and character. Furthermore, my decisions in response to all of it—my history, structures, rituals, etc.—contribute to my formation. Formation, however, is not the accumulation of mere factual information. It is holistic, not merely cognitive. It is what we repetitively perceive, internalize, and encode in our brains—for better or worse. Every day, we participate in our formation process. We cannot choose to do otherwise. As our brains take in our experiences, they process the material they receive, in one form or another, and store it where what is important can be retrieved.

Transformation, though, suggests something to do with change, particularly changing one thing to something else. Transformation, however, does not necessarily refer to the changes we choose to bring about in our lives. We are always changing from one thing to another. We change our minds; we change our politics; we change our perspectives on life as we age. Are any of these *transformations*? In the sense in which I am using this word, they are not. For our investigation here, I am focused on a certain kind of change. Transformation is the sort of change that brings about new meaning, new insight, what brings about inspiration. This kind of transformation originates somewhere outside of me, and it represents a kind of invitation that I receive.

Real transformation gives evidence to an action beyond us with which we are invited to cooperate. Transformation is a work of God's initiative, the interaction of *initiating love*. In the Christian Trinitarian framework, it is an action attributed to the Spirit. This initiating love, which we are free to accept or not, leads us to choose to be fashioned into a new creation. It is a gift that will be offered, and it is one that I must choose in order to keep. An event of transformation—one thing becoming something else—is not a development or an outgrowth. Although our contemporary religious art may, on occasion use butterflies and rainbows as images, neither of these are real transformations. Rainbows are a matter of reflected spectrums of light, and caterpillars have no choice but to undergo the process that will lead to their becoming butterflies. These are natural processes that require no conscious choosing. Furthermore, though transformational events can come from such experiences, a transformation experience is not merely something that I feel good about or associate with positive emotions such as talking to a friend or walking in nature.

Formation and transformation are tied to our brain/mind reality. In formation, our minds play a much more active role by simply participating in life and being involved in life's activities. The acquisition of culture is a good example. As we grow up in our family circumstances, we acquire a felt sense of what belonging to our ethnic background, our family lifestyle, and our neighborhood activities is all about. We do not think, "Now I am choosing to participate in my culture." My activity, as unreflective as it may be, is still being processed by my brain and, to some degree, being retained and encoded.

In the experiences of transformation, our brains are more receptive. We may be undergoing the same experiences and participating in the same kinds of activities, but the insights, the emotional impact, and the noticeable gut reactions give us pause. There is the sense of new ground being broken, and we recognize the necessity of becoming reflective, taking a mental step back, and assuming an open stance toward the experience. While we are more receptive, we also recognize that further action on our part will likely be required.

The journey onward can easily be viewed as a temporal journey through the years of our life cycle. It could, therefore, be presented in a format similar to how developmental theorists chart their systemic models, as James Fowler, for example, charted the stages of faith. The onward journey, however, is not a theoretical journey. It is the actual way that your life and mine unfold. Rather than a theoretical model, our onward journey looks more like a developing story, a tale of adventure we each are creating through the integration of our experiences and perceptions. That is why it is often referred to as a spiritual narrative.

As I mentioned above, exploring this spiritual narrative is always a present experience, even though it is dealing with things that have already happened. Memory is a complex brain operation that reconstructs for the present moment neural material that it pulls together from what it has stored away from past events. These constructions consist of remembered material that affected my life enough to have been encoded in the brain. These memories are interpreted to some degree in light of my current life and are shaped to provide meaningful and enriching continuity as I seek understanding of what is currently taking place through my ongoing spiritual journey. Experiences of transformation in my life may particularly stand out as important guideposts along the way of my journey.

Because of the nature of this process, however, we may expect our spiritual narrative to change somewhat over the course of time. How I remember my life journey as a young adult will look different from how I recall it during midlife and later. Also, the ongoing events of life affect my narrative. New relationships, traumatic experiences, accomplishments, failures, and the grief of significant losses can all change or redirect my interpretation of the past. Emotions provide an extremely important element to the mix, greatly influencing how I interpret all the events of my past. They continuously interact with the other neural information our brains provide. It is all significant. In forming my spiritual narrative, nothing should be considered irrelevant or unimportant, and nothing should be discounted. On the spiritual journey, we must learn holistically from our experiences.

My spiritual narrative is a story or adventure that I come to know so well. Though it may or may not be written, it must still be accessible to my consciousness. Humans have always attempted to relate (not explain) transformation through stories. The imaginative and symbolic language of a story is more capable of carrying mystery than simple biography. In stories, ugly frogs become princes; servant girls are transformed into princesses. In stories, evil is bigger than life, and goodness is achieved through gallantry, often after excruciating suffering. In many stories, "they all live *happily ever after.*" In real life, however, happily ever after doesn't exist. Our real-life stories are not yet complete, and many of our stories are not particularly happy ones.

But how can this be? Are we not created for happiness? How can it be that so many people live out such sad and tragic lives? How can this happen in God's good universe guided by the interaction of love? The good news and the bad news about this are related to consciousness. With the appearance of consciousness and its companion, freedom, we must deal with paradox. The force of love and the love of God ultimately envision a world transformed, but the process of transformation happens as we live through our present incomplete world of good and bad, our world of both triumph and tragedy.

All this being said, many people live their lives believing their spiritual narrative reveals only their darker side, to the degree that they would choose not even to look. What, they think, will looking back at the past tell me? It will only confirm how weak, shameful, and hopeless I feel. I'll just go from here, making my futile efforts toward the flawless perfection that I feel I must achieve in order to please God and make it possible for me to get into heaven. This inner narrative, I hope you can see, will not produce a story line in keeping with belief in the infinite mercy and love of God. It produces one that is far out of touch with the reality of our giftedness and capacity for transformation.

Transformation doesn't presume that our lives up to this point have been miserable. Transformation presumes that they have been a complex amalgam of positive and negative experiences, filled with joys and sorrows, triumphs and defeats. It does not try to eliminate the sorrows or increase the joys. It seeks to transform them all. In the process, transformations are openings to new life experiences guided by a new, conscious vision.

We are going to tell our story. We always do. We can't hide it. It will be told by our words and our actions even when we don't want it to be. It will be seen in our defense mechanisms—our repressions, denials, or projections. It will be revealed in our addictions—to drugs and alcohol, to food abuses, to consumerism, to the need for acceptance or approval, or to the vast array of our un-freedoms. It will be revealed in the memories of past traumas that we have endured and with which we and others have dealt. It will be seen in all the baggage we carry around with us, the regrets and self-judgments we never learned to release. When our baggage becomes so heavy that we can no longer function freely, we must face the reality that we may need help to sort it all out and move forward in the process of consciously leaving it behind.

This is where the transforming power of that ancient word, *hāl*, can manifest itself in our lives, if we allow it. These are the places where we may need to find the aid available in a healing process, spiritually, physically, emotionally, and, possibly, medically. The kind of healing that we need depends on the nature of what we have dragged with us or what continues to haunt us. Whatever it is, we can presume that we will be entering into a *process*, and we must be open to providing the time necessary to allow the process to work. Some processes have very clear time frames; some are more extended. For some people, the necessary process may represent a lifestyle change that is permanent. This is frequently the case with addictions.

Many types of healing involve more than one person. In a healing process, it is very unlikely that a single person would be the only one touched. Sometimes the healing required is relational, between individuals. Sometimes it involves families, communities, denominations, or even nations. Sometimes it involves individuals or groups to whom I am no longer present—people who are deceased, far away, or even unknown to me. Often, such healings are called *reconciliation*. In such cases, there are certain attitudes and experiences we may presume will be part of the process: trust (of God, of myself, of others, of the process), then honesty, empathy and compassion, resilience, and forgiveness.

For the individual, or even groups, who go through a healing process, it often leads to something called *reframing*. With an understanding of how memory works, I may have a sense of how I have come to look at some events in the past in a certain way. Perhaps the healing process I have been in has led me to the conclusion that there may be another way to interpret those memories, another way to frame them. Am I open to seeing things in a different way? Seeing a new story? Receiving new information? Can I change the script?

The transformation process has gone by other names in the course of spiritual theological development—conversion, redemption, sanctification, etc. All of these lay out the process of how the interaction of love draws the conflictual nature of our consciousness toward something new, a new and vibrant life, a new creation. For *all of us*, letting go of our baggage is a lifetime project. In general, spirituality can be seen as the gradual unfolding of my life narrative, of my story. Entering into this story invites *transcendence* as my story opens me up to God.

The Journey Inward

Integration could be the goal of the journey onward. Integrating the pieces of life is perhaps a bit more tangible than how I have used transformation. Integration itself is open-ended. I am only integrated to the degree I continue to integrate. Life keeps moving on, and what seems to have worked for me up to now may not do so tomorrow.

The desire for life integration requires another process to be at play as well. It requires a journey inward, bringing consciousness to a deepening awareness of mutual presence and a bonding (union) with God. The journey inward, here, replaces the traditional *journey upward* (purgation, illumination, perfection). There is nothing wrong or incorrect with these expressions, and they have been in use since the early centuries of the Christian experience. Yet there is often a trap involved with how these concepts are perceived. The trap of the journey *upward* is that it has often been seen as something I must achieve, a "self-accomplishment," gained through my ascetical and perfectionistic performance. This is actually the last thing consciousness needs or could find useful.

The journey inward is a journey of "imperfection," where consciousness seeks self-healing, compassion, reconciliation, and the ability to extend these things to others.[3] This journey of imperfection recognizes and values my successes, but it also acknowledges my failures. The journey inward makes me aware that my journey onward has not been a smooth coasting at even speed to date. It has been bumpy and uneven, with some roadblocks and detours along the way. It is also a journey in which I have not been self-sufficient. I have had to rely on others, who have helped me out on many occasions. And I have had to rely on God, my Higher Power.

For the journey inward, Jeremiah 18:1–6 is a tremendously helpful text. God sends the prophet Jeremiah to a potter's house to watch the potter work for a while. The potter is a master artisan, but he still doesn't get his creation-in-process the way he wants it on the first try. He tries again, and perhaps again. The word that comes to Jeremiah is that this is how God is and how God works. God is still working with us. We are constantly being shaped and reshaped by God's hand. Unlike how things are at the potter's house, however, on the human journey *we get to help*.

We have a cooperative role to play here. Spirituality is not about "letting God do it all." Such an attitude can deaden the journey of consciousness. We must understand, therefore, that we ought to not politely step aside because God knows best. Our role is to be *co-operative*. God is always operative in our lives, and we also have our hand on some of the controls. Because of our freedom, our conscious choices *matter*. In

---

[3] To get a sense of this kind of spiritual journey, I recommend Ernest Kurtz and Katherine Ketcham, *The Spirituality of Imperfection: Storytelling and the Journey to Wholeness* (New York: Bantam Books, 1992).

our successes, we succeed; in our failures, we fail, and there are no erasers on this journey. God continues the work of the Great Plan, and we are encouraged to get up and carry on alongside.

The inward journey, therefore, is a long one. We have our whole life to do the work, for as long as we get. As we are cognizant of the onward journey developing year by year, the inward journey reveals who we are one piece or one layer at a time. The whole process involves prayer, solitude, community and relationships, ministry and service, spiritual direction, a lot of body work (nutrition, exercise, and sexual integration), and much self-reflection. It also involves *soul-making* and *discipline*.

Soul-making is not just another area of life, like the ones in the preceding paragraph, that becomes a focus of the inward journey. Soul-making is directly tied to the process itself. It plays a role in the way consciousness explores and integrates prayer, solitude, community, and relationships. The term was created by James Hillman, the maverick Jungian therapist whom we encountered in the last chapter. Hillman's ideas on soul-making have been widely popularized by Thomas Moore.[4] In using their term, I am generally following their line of thinking, although my application is meant to fit into the framework of this chapter.

Soul-making has to do with depth. It would be distinguished, therefore, from pursuing *spirit*, which has the sense of seeking to go higher, echoing all the "dangers" of the upward journey I have already suggested. Soul-making relates to deepening values, personal substance, unknown treasures, and, in the process, recognizing the lurking inner guardians who might be inclined to resist our search. It is, as you can tell, more the way of imagination than of conceptualization. Soul-making enriches us through any channel in which we are brought into touch with the depths of our consciousness. It is, therefore, a highly holistic process. Yes, dreams come into play here. So, too, does the process Jung called active imagination, as well as various forms of creativity like creative writing, poetry, painting, sculpting, song, dance, and photography. What is on your list?

---

[4] James Hillman wrote numerous books. An anthology of his writings, edited by Thomas Moore, is titled *A Blue Fire: Selected Writings by James Hillman* (New York: Harper Perennial, 1989). Thomas Moore's best-known work is *Care of the Soul: A Guide for Cultivating Depth and Sacredness in Everyday Life* (New York: Harper Perennial, 2016).

Many of us are not very comfortable speaking of the riches of our consciousness. Many people seem to ignore or avoid looking at what lies beneath the surface of their lives. "I don't have the time." "I'm not into that stuff." "I'm afraid of what I'll find there." We may not say that last one very often, but it is probably the truer statement. We fear, and therefore underestimate, our own depth. It is all unfortunate. Images, symbolic expression, and soul-making in general are all excellent ways of pursuing the deeper awareness of who we really are. They produce important moments when we get in touch with our wholeness, our health, and our holiness. They enrich and shape the meaning of our lives. The most profound and intense inspirations and manifestations of sacred life have always tended to be metaphoric and symbolic (analogical) rather than literal and intellectual (analytical). The deepest and most insightful theological works of Bonaventure and Duns Scotus never quite make it up to what we find in Francis of Assisi's poetic *Canticle of the Sun*.

Why are we not more trusting of our inner lives? Do we believe that what we find there will be out of our control? Do we believe that we will meet inner complexes of energy that present dangers to us? Our unconscious certainly contains powerful energies, but what are these powers? For the most part, they are defenses that we ourselves, or those who formed us, have placed there. When we meet them, we incorrectly believe them to be bigger than we are. Taken together, Jungian psychology refers to them as the Shadow. They are strangers to us, and we perceive them to be enemies.

They are not, however. Our unrecognized self—unrecognized by our current self-awareness—resides in the Shadow. These Shadow elements are often threatening to our self-image. They may seem ugly, cruel, or deformed. The conscious movement toward wholeness and holiness, however, envisions our meeting of this Shadow self. It is usually necessary to do this one step at a time, facing each unknown aspect of ourselves, befriending it (not trying to destroy it, which wouldn't work anyhow), and integrating it into our conscious awareness. We can speak of this as an extended inner healing process. It is one of the most important aspects of soul-making. Uncovering the Shadow, facing it, and befriending it takes a lifetime. Rather than a journey of triumph, it is a journey that requires humility, patience, and self-honesty. Having a sense of humor helps, too. And, significantly, it is a self-purification process that requires *discipline*.

The lifelong process of soul-making on the journey inward is accompanied and enhanced by *discipline*. The root Latin word here, as with the word *disciple*, has to do with one being in a learning process. That is exactly what is happening in the journey inward; we are learning about life, about ourselves, and about how one fits into the other. Spiritual traditions are full of stories concerning individuals who want to learn about holiness and wisdom. They seek out teachers and spiritual masters, ask them to accept them as disciples, and these teachers bring them under their discipline, which could mean many things. In the journey inward, you might say we are seeking what we can learn from our own inner teacher. No one can complete the journey inward with self-knowledge alone, but there is still much to learn from our own experiences and our reflections on them.

Discipline has a more traditional name, *asceticism*. It can be a scary word that many of us may shy away from using, but I like it. It brings forth all sorts of ideas about harsh denials of pleasures, self-punishment, meaningless routines, and perfectionist self-judgments. This is obviously not the kind of asceticism I wish to encourage. In Matthew's Gospel (9:14–17), some disciples of John the Baptist come to Jesus. They have obviously been paying attention to how Jesus is instructing his disciples. They notice that Jesus is not requiring the kinds of intense fasting that they and the disciples of the Pharisees are expected to undergo. They wonder why not. Jesus answers their question in two ways. First, he places fasting in a relative context. It should fit the circumstances. His current presence among his disciples should lead to celebration and enrichment because of who he is. Their fasting will have to wait for another time, which will come.

Second, such fasting as they are describing is incomplete. It is leading them through behaviors that cannot in themselves bring them to where they want to go. This is a cautionary remark that should alert any of us who are planning on an array of ascetical practices, thinking that doing them in and of themselves must be beneficial. Jesus refers to the danger of pouring new wine into old wineskins. In the context of the gospel story, the new wine of Jesus's teachings must be placed into containers that will allow for its expansiveness. Trying to place a new teaching into an old framework that is rigid and unyielding could be disastrous. In a general spiritual context, the image also suggests that our ascetical activity must not be piecemeal or compartmental. Our ascetical practices must be holistic. The quality of the wine and the quality of the skins cannot be disconnected, or the holistic fabric is lost and the benefits are destroyed.

Our discipline, therefore, must be strategic. The best ascetical practices are those we plan for and execute. They are designed to achieve desired ends. Discipline is work, even if it is enjoyable work, which it should often be. What kind of work? There are several appropriate categories. First, there is work on oneself. Such discipline includes our journey of self-knowledge and self-awareness and can be practiced in keeping with the patterns of many different spiritual schools. Self-observation and Self-remembering, connected to the Gurdjieff school, are two examples.[5] Second, there is the work we direct toward deepening our relationships and the many social systems to which we belong, such as our family, church, or business. Third, there is the work that we are called to direct toward society as a whole, considering issues of justice, fairness, equality, and mercy. This work also includes our attention to the well-being of creation within which we are interrelated. Finally, and most centrally, although it is present throughout, there is work on the relationship of presence into which we are being called with the Mystery (God). From this perspective, prayer is work. The Reflections on Prayer at the end of earlier chapters showed how expansive this work can be, and I invite you to return to these reflections again, enriched with your growing journey.

Discipline, strategic design, conscious work—to some, these words may all seem terribly dry and uninteresting. That depends totally on your attitude and creativity. Discipline, strategic design, and working consciously can also describe the human experience we call *playfulness*. Whether we are speaking of softball, charades, poker, or chess, all the elements of discipline and strategy are present. Playfulness can remind us that the best kinds of strategy and work also rely on the presence of freedom and wholeness. Ascetical practices without holistic restructuring can be problematic, possibly dangerous, as with new wine and old wineskins. If real freedom is not present, the choice of even the most heroic of disciplines can be risky business.

---

[5] There are many introductory works that could be referenced here. One, that I have already cited is Charles Tart, *Waking Up: Overcoming the Obstacles to Human Potential* (Boston: New Science Library, 1986). In regard to these specific terms, Self-observation and Self-remembering, you may wish to refer to the topical index at the end of that book.

Consciousness and Transforming Resonance

Through this chapter, we have been on a dual journey, onward and inward, a spiritual journey of consciousness as it progresses toward God, others, self, and all of creation. I have called it a spiritual narrative, a story of creativity and imagination. It is a Love Story, yours, mine, and everyone's. It is a story about freedom and faith, revealing our wholeness and interconnectedness, inviting the recognition of our capacity to experience wonder, meaning, and purpose. This story is a journey of Transforming Resonance.

In my own story, I came upon the word *resonance* while exploring quantum theory and attempting to integrate my learning with my life. Though I had preferred *integration* to describe the life process that we are considering, subsequent reflection has led me to a growing appreciation of the nuances of resonance in the context of our overarching theme of spirituality and quantum theory.

Resonance is rooted in Latin and early French words that mean *to sound again*, or, if you will, to *reverberate*. Vibration, of course, has everything to do with hearing. You and I hear because sound waves strike our eardrums, causing them to vibrate, sending the brain electrical impulses that our brain then interprets as sounds. When various sound waves combine and vibrate in precise tones, the result, called harmony, is sound that is pleasing and complete. Thinking about vibrations and reverberations may be a familiar focus from our earlier explorations of quantum theory.

First, let's remind ourselves of what has been said about quantum field theory. All reality exists primarily in wave-like form. Because reality is wave-like, it presents itself as having qualities of a field, which does not designate a particular location but rather an area of influence. Everything is in superposition, potentially wave or particle, unless it has been measured or observed. When it is measured or observed, it collapses into either one or the other form, depending on how the observation takes place. Even then, however, its underlying nature remains wave-like. Even though everything around us, including us, seems to be relatively stable, all reality is in constant motion. Visible particles are still understood as essentially vibrational waves occurring in particular locations at particular times.

Resonance is fundamental to string theory. String theory, you will recall, seeks to synthesize a workable Theory of Everything, uniting quantum theory with general relativity. It maintains that everything in reality consists of infinitesimal one-dimensional strings billions and billions of times smaller than anything we can now observe, all of them vibrating in certain ways. Everything in reality vibrates. These vibrating strings theoretically present a picture of the universe that, at its core, is resonant, infinitesimally musical, each small part participating literally in a universal resonance, a spiritual symphony inaudible to the human ear.

Unlike resonance, integration is not a relevant concept in quantum theory. It is a construction of our cerebral cortex. Even so, it could be conceptually useful in a musical context, as for when we desire to provide a proper musical balance to an orchestral ensemble. Siegel himself introduces his model of integration with an illustration of how a spontaneously assembled choir can, with some ease, discover its hidden capabilities for harmony. Transforming resonance does not replace integration but seeks to represent more fully and richly the emergence of consciousness as a basic spiritual framework. This is a nuanced difference.

If we explore the concept of integration, we recognize that it is work. It is a lifetime work that doesn't end because we are always having new experiences that are yet to be integrated. Although it is true that early successes at life's integration usually make later integrations easier, unexpected transitions can come along. Just when we think that we more or less have our life journey all figured out, these transitions can make us feel like we're starting all over again.

Resonance, in contrast, is not a project. We cannot think or plan our way to resonance. It happens upon us almost spontaneously. If we wish to view it is a product, it is a product of the present experience. Continuing the metaphoric connection with music, more-seasoned choirs, of course, can become more adept at producing harmonics, but resonance itself always seems surprisingly satisfactory and almost gift-like. That is because resonance is always produced in the moment. It is always new and fresh. It can be extended, but it cannot be saved.

Integration can, at times, seem puzzle-like. We integrate our lives piece by piece. Sometimes we are not really sure that we have the right piece until we try to make it fit. If it doesn't fit, we may have to set it aside and try another piece or a different approach. If it does fit, we may have a minor moment of celebration, but more missing pieces still need to be found and integrated.

Resonance doesn't come in pieces. Things don't just fit in. Resonance is, well, wave-like. It has no boundaries; it simply fills the entire field as music fills the room. Though resonance is in harmony with the moment, it is not a matter of emotions or attitudes. It is not the result of feeling good or having everything go well, nor does it show up simply by "looking on the bright side." This is because resonance is an experience of consciousness. If not intrinsically emotional, it is decidedly attentive and intentional. It requires focus. Neither resonance nor integration, however, respond well to perfectionistic tendencies, and both resist forced manipulation, which is not sustainable through the life journey.

Integration is mine to do. It is not the job of parents or caregivers. I cannot blame teachers, authorities, the government, or the Church. Certainly, all these factors have affected me. They have been major components of my formation, and I carry their scars with me as I carry their gifts. The task of getting beyond the scars and the damage can be huge. I may need help, perhaps a lot of help, and there is frequently help available in a variety of forms. But as my life progresses, no one can live it for me. Even God's boundless mercy and grace will leave a part of the process to me. The force of love is always extended, but it is never coerced. We must be co-operative.

Resonance is also a matter of cooperation but of a different kind. Resonance is systemic, unsatisfied with personal achievement or success. Transforming resonance is ultimately meant for the whole. Turning again to our musical metaphor, complete experiences of harmonic resonance in the performing arts are the result of the full ensemble of the musicians. While each may have his or her part, the variety of parts blend together to produce a sense of fulfillment. Ultimately, God intends for spiritual resonance within the Great Plan to reverberate across the universe.

Yes, there are nuanced distinctions between integration and resonance, but we see that each has its place. We don't want to lose or ignore integration any more than we would want to focus exclusively on waves and disregard particle reality. Integration is particularly important to the journey onward. As our lives move forward, each new experience must be integrated into what is already there—transcend and include, as Ken Wilber wisely reminds. We could, therefore, imagine resonance and integration as two takes on one reality. Perhaps we could imagine them as existing in a kind of superposition to each other, resonance and integration becoming metaphoric descriptions of our process toward holistic and universal consciousness.

This metaphor extends to our relationship with God and the spiritual life, our life in faith. It extends to our prayer journey and all the aspects that our spiritual life embraces—our relationships, our work, our Church involvement, our moral development, and our formative process. Each is upheld and enhanced, supported and embraced by resonance and integration. As our metaphor also suggests, however, even as reality existing in superposition is essentially wave-like, the adventure of holistic consciousness is essentially resonant. Our spiritual life, our life in faith, *essentially* involves our systemic union with Mystery, and that exists in an eternally present moment. Our spiritual life journey could therefore be summed up as you and I, and everyone and everything together, seeking transformative resonance with the Mystery of God.

This transformation is essentially interpersonal and systemic. Our consciousness is expansive, continuously moving from an isolated individualism to a dynamic interconnectedness, driven by the interaction of love. We have explored the evolutionary character of this expansive consciousness, moving with love and freedom toward ever greater personalization, beyond simple self-awareness, into a deepening system of related consciousnesses, an emerging *integral and resonant intimacy.* This is a cooperative unfolding of efforts between ourselves, our extended creation, and the Great Plan, the will and intention of God.

We must keep in mind, however, that the unfolding efforts that can move us to transforming resonance will be powered by the same processes that have gotten us this far. The non-dualist outcomes we envision here will first emerge by being led through dark dualistic valleys of contradiction, uncertainty, and occasional failure. An outcome of increasingly cooperative and integral consciousness will not exempt us from life's basic paradoxical dynamics, sprung from the by-products of conscious freedom in the first place. This will mean, among other things, that the stakes will likely continue to get higher. The choices we will need to make will require concerted discernment and steadfast determination. The advantage we will have, however, lies in our ability to work interpersonally and systemically, relying cooperatively on the Spirit of God, who is ever at work.

If there is reason to embrace this idea of an evolving universal consciousness, enhanced by deepening resonance, what does it do *now* for the world we experience around us every day? How can we heal our present disjunctions and prepare to meet those troubles we will likely meet in the near future? How can we creatively and wisely make choices to positively and cooperatively—with God's Spirit—not only benefit our world, but further the process of transforming it? How could our current action plan enable us to contribute to the Great Plan that continues to unfold around us?

This human and earthly action plan has many pieces that will need to be harmonized with each other. Science, politics, and faith communities are three vital pieces that lay before us. They are also significantly related to our present story.

Science, of course, has played a major role in this book. The scientific community understands the need to continue its activity into the future. It embraces the evolving mission that lies before it and, as in the past, is more than ready to take on its role for the future. It may, at times, however, see itself as the *only* necessary element. Here is a great danger. The sciences will not be capable of doing it all, and it would be a profound, and possibly disastrous, hubris for science and humanity to think otherwise.

By *politics*, I mean the accumulated body of governmental structures in the world. While they theoretically see their role in this mission, currently they seem woefully incapable of harmonizing enough to be effective in any major way to this point in our story. Even so, the role of policy and governance cannot be circumvented. The political world must provide the means to effectively contribute to the future. That they have been unable to do so should be a primary concern for everybody.

Faith communities must contribute what their name proclaims, the *faith*. By now, I hope you understand why this part of the mission is so crucial. They must provide the meaning, purpose, guidance, and discernment for where we are going. Faith must continue to deepen and resonate. Even though many faith communities do not see the development of our Earth, or our universe, as their only or highest mission, there is still what the Christian communities might call an *incarnational principle* at work. We may not be "of this world," but we are certainly in it and have a moral responsibility for it. Currently, many faith communities have not yet found their way to harmony among themselves, although they are probably doing better now through ecumenism and interfaith work than they ever have been (which in itself is a sad commentary).

Fully exploring the possibilities for the overall mission of these global communities as our planet continues to evolve is beyond the scope of this book. How science, politics, and religion are being called forth to interact with one another for the good of all produces a completely new subject to explore. As our present journey nears its end, I do want to speak a bit more about some aspects of this mission, particularly in relation to Christian denominations and my own Roman Catholic community. These thoughts are part of my concluding reflections in the following chapter, where I hope to give some vision of where Christian spirituality could find a beneficial interaction with contemporary science.

11

Religion and Theology
in a Quantum Universe

Is Common Engagement Possible?

We have made a huge linguistic leap as we have moved through our overview of quantum theory to consciousness studies, all from the point of view of holistic spirituality. We have encountered quarks, wave functions, and holograms in the maze of quantum terminology. We have considered the prefrontal cortex, hippocampus, and brain stem in the developments of neuroscience. We have reflected on altered states and lucid dreaming associated with the study of consciousness. We have followed consciousness through journeys onward and inward in holistic spirituality. The question remains: Are we there yet?

Our itinerary has certainly not had the familiar ring of what many would consider a traditional devotional and spiritual language. We have not mentioned the Day of Salvation or Redemption from sin. We didn't speak of the glory of the Cross, or the Kingdom of God, or amazing grace. From a specifically "high church" point of view—Catholic, Anglican, Orthodox, and the like—we didn't discuss the seven sacraments, or liturgical seasons like Lent or Advent. Most importantly, we have made no attempts at apologetics, critiquing quantum theory through doctrinal belief.

Even if the time and space were available for such an immense undertaking, the truth of the matter is that doing so would be profoundly premature. Even though quantum theory is a century old, we would find few who were in *complete* agreement as to what it actually entails. While a complete assessment of quantum theory in relation to Christian doctrine might be helpful, and possibly necessary, to do sometime in the future, no

181

solid defense could be made now. Until such a time, we are left only with questions and preliminary reflections.[1]

The last chapter ended with a desire for bringing about an evolutionary movement in our world toward a deepening system of universal consciousness, a cooperative unfolding of an effort between humans, creation as a whole, and the Great Plan, the emerging intention of God. Along with science and the coordinated involvement of governments, faith communities must step up to do their part. The faith communities of the world, East and West, cannot be absent. We must make wise and creative choices that benefit our world and further the process of earthly transformation. Our Christian communities, including our Catholic community, have a significant role to play.

While governments frequently get bogged down in political standoffs, partisan infighting, and bureaucratic quagmires, contemporary science is having a major impact on our world. The accomplishments of technological and medical advances, discoveries in the area of cosmology, the environment, and new forms of energy (to name only a few), have contemporary audiences intently focused on scientific issues. World communities increasingly look to science for direction and guidance for the future. This also coincides with a time when many people show little interest in their churches and synagogues, worship services and liturgies, and religious belief in general. Many, particularly in younger generations, seem to feel that faith communities have stepped to the sidelines or have become increasingly antiquated or irrelevant.

To the extent that this perception is true, our concerted movement forward proceeds precariously. Science, as we are seeing, continues to propose, experiment on, and develop new technologies, medicines, chemicals, and weapons, with largely blind discernment and no structures for evaluating attempts at ethical norms. In some cases, science presses its ability to do what is possible without also asking questions such as "Is it good we do this? Is it right we do this? Are we considering the implications of our actions?" This raises concerns as to the benefit, viability, and ethical value of the outcomes that may be imposed upon the human community and upon the wider creation we inhabit.

---

[1] For those who may wish to get a head start, I recommend John Polkinghorne, *The Faith of a Physicist: Reflections of a Bottom-Up Thinker* (Minneapolis: Fortress Press, 1996).

In the last chapter, I suggested that faith communities need to provide meaning, purpose, guidance, and discernment to the process that leads toward a universal resonance and integration of consciousness. Despite our limitations and failures, the churches, denominations, and religions have been the custodians of humanity's store of charity, belonging, and prophetic witness. In ways that science and government never can, communities of faith have provided the place where love and freedom reside in the world we have built and need to be present in the world we are now building.

To be effective in this mission, science, government, and faith communities will have to make greater efforts to form alliances that can work together with respect and efficiency. I have set aside the political world for the purposes of this book and focused on paving a pathway that could offer a context of how science and faith can work more closely in their common goal. To integrate the valuable contributions of both, we must find a way to restore the partnership that existed in previous eras.

Both science and religion bear the responsibility for the fractured state we see around us. Many of the fractures have arisen from the tendency of both to form calcified positions that will not yield to dialogue or pliability, forming absolutist positions that disregard the values and gifts of the other. Both science and religion are governed, if you will, by their own unique "Uncertainty Principle" that both pretend not to see. In this chapter, dealing with communities of religion and spirituality, at least to some degree, I look beyond this impasse. I reflect on our survey of quantum theory and the development of consciousness in previous chapters and suggest contributions that a deepening dialogue between spirituality and the quantum world can offer to communities of faith.[2] The primary questions of this chapter are, "Does quantum theory

---

[2] It is important to mention that some of the religious and spiritual traditions of the East come to this present moment possessing a longer track record of dialogue with contemporary science. It would be beyond the scope of this book, however, to attempt even a survey of this material, and it would lead us away from my focus on Western, and particularly Christian, spirituality. For those who would want to follow up on this aspect, I will mention some works previously cited as a good place to start: Evan Thompson, *Waking, Dreaming, Being* (New York: Columbia University Press, 2015), and Gay Watson, *Attention: Beyond Mindfulness* (London: Reaktion Books, 2017). Both of these works come from primarily a Buddhist perspective.

have anything of value to offer the Christian communities, and if so, where would that lie?" and second, "What might hinder the Christian denominations in general and the Roman Catholic community in particular from harvesting these benefits?"

The first part of the first question can be answered quickly: yes. The second part of the first question is the broader focus of this last chapter of the book. The second question, then, must be dealt with before we can fully dive into the implications of the first.

What might hinder our harvesting of the benefits contained in the earlier chapters? The short answer to that question is: ingrained skeptical attitudes that keep many of us from an openness to anything that is presumed to be new, unfamiliar, a little complicated, and "probably dangerous." Of course, if you have made it this far in the book, you realize that much of this hindrance lies within the fearful attitudes that reside somewhere beneath the brain's cognitive processing and could well keep us from trusting our own gifts and our capabilities of discernment. We need not revisit all of that now. Rather, I simply encourage anyone who might be experiencing uncertainties to take the risk, not just with what I have to say in this chapter or in the book as a whole, but with your life. It's the only one you have, and who would want to miss the opportunity?

When we think of the things that might be a little complicated and "probably dangerous," theologically speaking, we can turn straight to the heart of Christianity. Christians have struggled and fought over a particular area of concern since our earliest centuries. In each encounter with emerging philosophical or psychological systems, Christians contend with this topic. Expressed in the terms of this book's focus on quantum theory, we should ask: How would quantum theory treat the person of Jesus Christ?

Of First Importance:
The Eternal Word, Jesus Messiah

A theology of Jesus Christ, a complete Christology, would be the most essential challenge faced by a possible full correlation of Christian theology with the theories of quantum mechanics. In Christian theology, the Person of Jesus Christ is the unique point of meeting/union between God and creation. We would have to begin with the premise that, however we understand quantum theory's relationship to Christology, our best hope lies in metaphors. Realizing and accepting that God cannot be fully contained within creation, our turning to metaphor and metaphoric reasoning is a methodological necessity.

I have spoken of metaphoric structure throughout this book, introducing in Chapter 9 the concept of metaphoric reasoning as being fundamentally different from mathematical reasoning. Mathematical reasoning structures the evaluation of things around an equation, where one side is equal, and perhaps identical, to the other. Metaphoric reasoning articulates in a deeper way what cannot be fully equated—for instance, the description of Mystery, which is only somewhat knowable, with what could, in theory, be completely knowable, physical reality. Metaphoric reasoning, you will recall, looks like this:

KNOWN REALITY > ~ ~ *metaphoric distance* ~ ~ < IMPERCEPTIBLE REALITY

In this reasoning, the distance between what is known and what is imperceptible can vary. The metaphoric distance that separates the two realities can be strong (close) or faint (distant). Metaphoric strength is not the same as identity. A distant metaphor can still be useful, but it will have less of an impact. In what ways, then, might certain aspects of quantum theory serve as a metaphoric context for arriving at a deeper understanding of the Christian theology of Jesus Christ?

At the beginning of the Christian experience, the early Christians of the first century of the common era (CE) had an immediate need to find some common understanding of who this person, Jesus of Nazareth, actually was. The collection of the gospels and other writings of what came to be called the New Testament affirm the significant role of communal reflection and discussion in their attempts to do this. They were a small but growing community of people who had some common experience of him. Either before or after his death by crucifixion, he had changed their lives, but they didn't have the means at hand to arrive at a total consensus of who or what he was. He had called them to a way of life, which he said was good news (gospel) and which they were commissioned to spread. They believed that Jesus had been raised from the dead, and, while still present in their midst, would soon come again in glory. They believed they were being led by the Spirit of God to assemble a new community (*ekklēsia*—an assembly> church) based on love and service. Most of their time was spent building and spreading that community, while fending off outside forces that wished to destroy it.

Turning to what they had available—their prayerful reflection on the substantial body of Jewish sacred literature and a deepening assessment of Greek and Roman philosophical thought—there were still questions and differing opinions that remained as to who this Jesus was. While the New Testament gives evidence that belief in Jesus's divinity was widely present from the beginning, it was not until a couple of centuries had passed that the Church, still facing inconsistent theories of Christ, felt it needed to thoroughly evaluate and articulate exactly who it believed Jesus to be. It was a messy and confusing process, made all the more complex due to the ever-present influences, or should we say interferences, of the politics of the Roman Empire. The councils that shaped the final doctrinal product used the Greek and Latin philosophical categories of their day, forming them into creedal statements that have continued to provide the basic foundations of Christology, even though some of that philosophical language is no longer in use or fully understood in our contemporary context.

Along the way to the present, some other beliefs and teachings have developed or emerged from these foundations. Keeping quantum theory in mind as we look at these creedal beliefs, we believe a list of theological areas that are related to the identity of Jesus Christ as defined or believed by the Catholic Church would necessarily have to include:

- The pre-existence (prior to physical creation) of the Eternal Word (the God-nature of Jesus Christ).
- The identification of the historical Jesus Messiah (Christ) with the Eternal Word.
- The human and divine natures of Jesus Christ eternally existing in one Person.
- The physical Resurrection of Jesus Christ.
- The Mystical Body of Christ residing in and concurrent with the totality of all believers.
- The mystical presence of Christ in scripture and the sacraments as a whole.
- And specifically, the real presence of Christ in the Eucharistic sacrament.

Other aspects that emerge from these may also prove to be necessary along the way.

Without prematurely assuming the staggering task of thoroughly establishing a metaphoric correlation between aspects of quantum theory and these doctrinal beliefs, I invite us to briefly reflect on some elements of quantum theory here that may hold promise in the future.

The ***holistic and systemic nature*** of contemporary physics has been a frequent topic in this book. A holistic view of reality, as we have seen, presumes that everything in the physical universe is connected and is interacting, even though it is stretched out over the fullness of time and space. This fact itself points directly to the systemic nature of the universe. It leads to the belief that what will work in one part of the universe will work elsewhere in the same way. Carbon atoms act like carbon atoms wherever you meet them.

Christian theology holds that, as the fullness of God is present to and interacts with all of creation, so it is with the Eternal Word, the second person of the Trinity. While the historical Jesus is located in space and time, this human being is still fully united with the Word that is present everywhere/at all times. This presumed singular identity residing in Eternal Word/Jesus Christ correlates well with this holistic and systemic nature.

Beyond these general features of today's science, the next area of conversation would be ***nonlocality***. This is a feature of reality, you will recall, that emerged through investigations of quantum experiments, first notably in the EPR controversies[3] between Einstein and the Copenhagen theorists. As we have seen, however, the nonlocal features of physical science have proved to be much more widespread. Throughout these chapters, we have noted the presence of nonlocality in several other aspects of quantum theory, including the existence of dark energy and the possibility of multiple dimensions (hyperspace). Nonlocality speaks of an imperceptible facet of physical reality whose "breadth and depth" are unknown and immeasurable.

This imperceptibility within reality is also, of course, at the very heart of what Christian theology understands as the spiritual life. God permeates the universe unseen, that is, beyond our physical senses. The permeation of Christ, the Eternal Word, does as well, while still fully present in Christ's physical and historical reality. Along this line, we might reflect on the presence of Christ in word and sacrament.

---

[3] Recall from earlier discussions that EPR is named for Albert Einstein, Boris Podolsky, and Nathan Rosen.

Christology describes Christ present both in scripture and sacramentally as a true presence, not simply an emotional attachment or an intellectual reminiscence. This fully applies as well to the working of the Holy Spirit, present unseen but not beyond our experience at the edges of perception.

Entanglement is directly tied to nonlocality, which was the basic issue of the EPR experiments and was verified through them. Entanglement, you will recall, designates a nonlocal correlation that can exist between two quantum particles, sharing a single wave function that extends somehow beyond the four-dimensional limits of time and space.

The theological question lying underneath this is: What exactly can be entangled? If entangled particles separated theoretically by millions of miles can remain entangled and work as one system, can we in some analogical way (at least) be entangled with each other in some manner of consciousness? Can all of us be entangled with Christ? How is such entangling relevant to a theology of the Mystical Body of Christ? At the very least, entanglement has some significant metaphorical value in understanding how a true presence of the full person of Christ can be understood as existing in the fullness of the Church, its sacraments, and its scripture.

Moving from the expanses of the universe and to the basics of physical reality, the ***wave function*** lies at the heart of quantum theory. The wave function, prior to observation or measurement, exists in superposition, having the potential of being both wave and particle, but currently neither. As a wave it possesses in potential velocity and momentum, but if you were to look for it, it would have neither. Instead, if you see a particle, it would have location, something that it previously didn't possess. In its essential form, it has both.

How might this understanding of superposition be relevant in our attempts to wrap our minds around the two natures of Christ, divine and human? The wave function may offer a significant, though limited, analogy of how a single physical entity can have in potential two different manifestations. We must be careful here, however. While a wave function possesses the potential of being a wave or a particle, it cannot be both at the same time. Since Christian theology does not hold that Jesus would have lost his divine nature while being in his historical existence, nor his human nature in his risen state, superposition may remain a *faint* or distant metaphoric example of the Christ Union.

But this is not so clear in **quantum field theory**. To understand quantum field theory, we must again consider fields in general. Fields exist over a certain area around a source of potential energy, such as a magnet or an object having gravitational mass. The closer one moves toward the source of energy, the stronger the effect produced by the field. There are many types of fields, representing areas of different kinds of influence. Starting from biological theories developed by Rupert Sheldrake early in the twentieth century, Judy Cannato described something called a *morphogenic field*. She said, "It can be thought of as a field of information. A morphogenic field organizes the structure and activity of a form or system. It holds the energy, keeping it coherent."[4] She theorized a field of compassion, rooted in and characterized by love.

Quantum field theory, however, is different from other classic field theories. In quantum field theory *everything* consists of fields, and these fields are spread out across the universe. They are not limited by space, nor are they limited by time. Each wave function would exist in its own frequency and would take up no space until it was observed or measured. A physical space (including time) in theory can "hold" an infinite number of wave functions. Quantum field theory could offer a very strong metaphor for Christian theology in its argument for the pervasiveness of fields. This could be particularly important for questions of presence in Christology, for instance, the divine/human presence of Eternal Word/ Jesus Messiah, as well as the mystical presence of Christ in scripture, sacramental and Eucharistic theology, ecclesiology, and the theology of the Mystical Body of Christ within the Universal Church.

While all of these features of quantum theory, and probably others, could strike us as quite significant, there is one final cautionary note for us to hold on to. Much like philosophical theories, theories of physical science have historically come and gone. What past ages taught as factual conclusions to physical questions have, in many cases, either been disproved or superseded by more refined explanations. The best example of this, frequently noted, is how the entire discipline of physics was stunned in the early part of the twentieth century to see Einstein's theory

---

[4] Judy Cannato, *Field of Compassion: How the New Cosmology Is Transforming Spiritual Life* (Notre Dame, IN: Sorin Books, 2010), 30ff. See also Ilia Delio, *The Unbearable Wholeness of Being* (Maryknoll, NY: Orbis Books, 2013), 33–34.

of general relativity so rapidly replace Isaac Newton's explanation of gravity, which had been thought to be unassailable. We would not want to prematurely tie Christian theology in general or Christology in particular to any physical or philosophical theory so completely that it could not be salvaged without severe loss to the belief of the faithful.

Quantum Theory and the Church

The first question of this chapter was "Does quantum theory have anything of value to offer the Christian communities, and if so, where would that lie?" Even our brief focus on specific elements of quantum theory and Christian doctrinal beliefs can give a glimpse into the fruitful work that can be done in our story of the sciences and spirituality. In a general sense, of course, that is what the entirety of the book has been about. I hope, then, that the answer has largely emerged in the previous chapters and is no surprise for you at this point. A few aspects of quantum theory that can offer something specific to the nature of the Christian churches remain, and it would be helpful to point them out.

As we have seen, the early Christian communities of the first century waited for some time before the central theological issues around the person of Jesus the Christ were thoroughly explored. It would be centuries before the Church felt that it had arrived at a complete answer—if in fact they feel that way yet. Through the earliest centuries, the young faith community was also going through its own version of multiculturalism, discovering what its relationship with the Jewish community was to be going forward, finding its place within Greek culture and Roman government, and surviving an unpredictable series of harsh persecutions.

There were other tasks at hand as well, internal tasks that had to do with its own self-awareness and the formation of its own value system, tasks concerning what the Church felt itself to be and how it should function in order to remain resonant with its perceived mission. Dealing with these tasks occurred within a process that stretched over decades, and it took place on many fronts in the small communities that primarily extended around the Mediterranean basin. While Christianity has expanded, evolved, and developed over centuries, many of these same tasks have remained embedded in the daily life of each Christian community. Asking a question about the relevance of quantum theory to present Christian communities and into the Church's future rightfully brings us back to some of Christianity's earliest questions. I mention four areas below, although there were others, but these seem to me to be especially apt for how our contemporary churches may seek to deepen an awareness and appreciation of the physical world that surrounds and includes our communities of prayer and worship.

Quantum Theology and Koinonia (A Loving Community)

Koinonia is a Greek word that means both community and communion (oneness, fellowship). It embodies the commandment received from Jesus in his final discourse in John's Gospel. "This is my commandment, that you love one another as I have loved you" (John 15:12). Jesus showed love of others in all things, and his call to his disciples to do the same was unambiguous. The interaction of love moves reality toward an ever-deepening affinity, not just with family, friends, or people who intend good. It moves us toward all people, toward all creation.

It is hard to sustain such oneness of heart and mind. The early communities went through many personal and social difficulties. In the original Jerusalem community, the Greek-speaking Jews complained of unfair treatment by the Hebrew-speaking majority (Acts 6:1). The later admission of Gentiles into the early communities had to be settled by a council of elders in Jerusalem (Acts 15:1ff.). Paul was frequently in tense circumstances with some of the communities he was so instrumental in founding (1 Cor 11:17ff., Gal 3:1ff., for example)—all, common growing pains of close human interaction. Paul, however, continued to urge his communities to make consistently greater efforts to love. He writes to the community in Corinth, "Love is patient; love is kind; love is not envious, or boastful, or arrogant, or rude. It does not insist on its own way; it is not irritable or resentful; it does not rejoice in wrongdoing, but rejoices in the truth" (1 Cor 13:4–6). We do not give up on our attempts to love simply because we sometimes fail in our efforts.

As this is true between individuals, so is it true at a communal level. In Corinth (1 Cor. 12), Paul employed the metaphor of the human body to urge the community's members to set aside their petty jealousies and judgments. The hand cannot do without the foot, and the eye still needs the ear. The body's members have different gifts and responsibilities, all of which are necessary.

Through the ongoing Christian experience, oneness in *community* has often lived in tension with oneness of *belief*—as evidenced by the proliferation of Christian denominations. Jesus's metaphor of the vine and the branches in Chapter 15 of John's Gospel, mentioned above, speaks to this. Jesus doesn't say, "I am the trunk, and you are the branches." He doesn't say, "I am the root system ..." He says, "I am the [*whole*] vine; you are the branches" (15:5). Branches may go off in different directions, but that doesn't mean they are disconnected from the vine or from each other.

God's love for the Church reveals the good news/bad news of the Gospel. God resides within the Church and empowers it with love, but God also leaves us free to choose how much we want to cooperate with that empowerment. Often, as history has shown, we have made frequent choices not to cooperate. When we have chosen not to cooperate, unfortunately, our choices have mattered in real life historical outcomes.

But love's good news is overpowering. Growth in community, despite our human foolishness or worse, shows that the force of love still drives the agenda of faith around the world. Paul proclaimed to the community in Rome, "the free gift is not like the trespass. For if the many died through the one man's trespass, much more surely have the grace of God and the free gift in the grace of the one man, Jesus Christ, abounded for the many" (Rom 5:15). The universe is hardwired by the Great Plan of God to grow deeper in love. *Koinonia* as a fruit of God's sustaining gift reveals itself as a cooperative enterprise. The Spirit of God is at work within the Great Plan, and the Spirit continues to provide us with abundant opportunities for transformation.

Today the Church must realize that we are embedded in the world, and the world is embedded in us. Contemporary science shows this clearly. The universe and all its systems are interconnected. This fact must be lived out and proclaimed. If we dismiss or disregard it, we ignore it at our own peril. The Church of the twenty-first century, in a holistic and totally systemic reality, cannot remain the city on the mountain, believing itself to be untouched by the world's folly. The rest of the world will not wait around for us; it will continue to move forward, at increasing risk to itself. The churches need to take seriously the call to love creation. Love needs to be continuously incarnated, embodied in the goodness of the entirety of God's physical creation.

Quantum Theology and Katēchesis
(Religious Education)

When the first waves of converts came to the Christian community, first from Judaism, then from the Greek culture that surrounded those communities, they were, for the most part, fully grown adults, and they brought their entire families with them. The leaders of these communities understood that their converts' first experiences of faith and conversion were powerful but very fragile. Without support, the power that lies in such faith experiences is vulnerable. Further instruction, *katēchesis*, was an important way to provide this support.

This instruction is a direct part of what I have called formation. As you remember, it is distinguished from transformation, which is an action of God's Spirit. I have used *formation* in a very broad sense, as everything we have learned from all sources, good and bad, and incorporated into each life. Katēchesis is much narrower; it is instruction in the Christian life. Such instruction still encompasses quite a bit. It includes all that we would need to learn to live out fruitfully our religious faith. This kind of formation has always been important to the Church. Acquiring a full understanding of any religion requires a thorough foundation in such instruction.

We understand that we live in a world inundated by factual information and data. Most often, in these days, it comes more or less unfiltered. Anything and everything is available. Most of our news is provided to us with very little regard for peer review, which would at least help safeguard the value of its content. How do we distinguish all of the frivolous or even dangerous information from helpful knowledge? And how do we evaluate the vast amount of available knowledge, and integrate it in such a way that it leads us to wisdom? Speaking once more with Teilhard's writings in mind, Ilia Delio writes:

> Thinking is a spiritual act. It is that long, deep, hard look at reality where the knowing process becomes more than the vision itself. Thinking requires use of the intellect, as well as judgment, consciousness, and connectivity to the object of thought. It is not mere information but the synthesizing of information into ideas and insight. Thinking is the work of the spirit, not only the human spirit but God's Spirit. Each time the mind comprehends something it unites the world in a new way.[5]

---

[5] Delio, *The Unbearable Wholeness of Being*, 146–47.

We understand in theory that adult education is not the same as what would be presented to children. The education of children is an art and skill of utmost importance, but at some point our religious education opportunities must be transitioned into an adult curriculum. Regrettably, many Christian adults attempt to make it through the challenges of contemporary society with little more than a childlike understanding of their religion. In the world in which we live, which understands and functions at an adult level, we can no longer afford to keep Christians from an education suitable for adulthood. We must find better ways to educate our parishes and congregations in order to equip them adequately for the world they are already meeting and in which they must function, beyond the doors of our worship sites.

Part of what the early Christian communities came to understand of their faith had to do with its expansion. The early churches were missional. The good news of Jesus was to be spread. Evangelization was a large part of their journey onward. Evangelization in the global village we now inhabit must pass the scientific/technological test. Can we explain why the world needs instruction in faith and spirituality? If our answer is "to escape it," no one will listen any further. If, however, our answer is "to help transform our world into someplace worth the investment of our lives," we will find a cooperative audience that is anxious for our help.

This book has focused on contemporary science in dialogue with faith, but I am not speaking only of education in the sciences, including physics. That will certainly be helpful in a science-focused social milieu, but we are also called to understand history, civics, the social structure, psychological behavior, and a number of other subjects. Our world is totally holistic and interconnected. We meet and journey with all of these fields in our lives, and each will have an impact on our *spirituality*, on our lives lived in faith.

Quantum Theology and Paraenesis
(Moral and Ethical Instruction)

The early Christian communities, formed largely from foundations provided by the Jewish scripture and its strong ethical guidance, soon found themselves immersed in a Greek and Roman culture that was vastly more permissive and largely secular. For many Christians today, that may have a familiar ring. Most of the Gentile (non-Jewish) converts came from a variety of pagan religions that more or less flourished throughout the Roman Empire. They had many gods with many different names. The pagan gods were largely felt to have little interest in human life and behavior, which, after all, was scripted by the fates anyway. If the gods were placated, however, it might be possible to receive a hearing from them. Religion was, therefore, a tool close at hand that the Roman governmental structure could use to pacify the vast number of foreign peoples they governed. Rome was a warrior culture, and it had little real concern for the well-being of those under their rule. Beyond a strict obeisance to the emperor, pagan religious rituals were largely tolerated.

Gentile converts to Christianity came from this formational context. Culturally and ethically, conversion was a big leap for many. The dangers of backsliding were ever present. In this context, pagan religion, with its accompanying permissive sexual atmosphere, remained an ever-present source of temptation, potentially pulling converts to the Christian life back into what they had left behind. The sexual morality expected of the Christian communities, therefore, was strict by Gentile standards, and the Jewish model of family life was maintained. The early sexual morality was far stricter than the surrounding pagan culture, which often used sexuality in their religious rites. There was a great need for moral instruction. We meet this in many of the writings of Paul and the other early works of the New Testament (for instance, in 1 Cor 5:9ff., Gal 5:16ff., Rev 2:19ff.). Family life and the roles of men and women largely mirrored the Jewish and Greek cultures around them, in that they emphasized monogamy and the mutual love responsibilities of spouses.

In such an atmosphere, it is perhaps understandable that early Christianity was seen as an *escape* from what was surrounding it. It is understandable all the more because Christians were awaiting an early return of the Risen Christ. The gradual deterioration of the Empire in the first centuries of the Christian experience increasingly made it desirable to "check out" for the many people who were concerned about society's moral fabric. The Egyptian desert became a refuge for those who wished an exit from the secular society around them. The development of early hermit communities and solitary lifestyles expanded.

Is my description of moral life surrounding the early Christian communities hauntingly familiar? Are you maybe thinking that this escape to a hermitage could be the way to go? Quickly, I say, "Think again!" The first centuries of Christianity happened in a very different world from ours. One of the implications of my emphasis on living in a global village today is that *there is no place to go*. Yes, we have monasteries that follow sound and established rules of life. We have male and female communities of consecrated life, following charismatic figures like Benedict, Francis, Ignatius, and Teresa. We have beautiful retreat centers and shrines with exquisite panoramas. And, for the most part, they are all wired and connected. If you joined my community, in the first week, you would be asking for our Wi-Fi connection so you could check your social media. The global village is not just out there, it is also in our heads. It's in our social reactions and our conversations.

You may think all of that is bad news, and you long for the peace of solitude. I do, too, and the good news is that it is somewhere to be found. It can be found in the journey onward and the journey inward. It can be found in the deepening of consciousness. It can be found in transforming resonance. It is actually there now, waiting for you. But this realization doesn't necessarily shorten the journey. We still need to do the work, and the work takes discipline and the kind of ascetical practice I mentioned in the previous chapter.

The first ascetical practice is to be in touch with what lies in the present experience before us. That is a matter of awareness and of attending to what is now available, the first steps toward consciousness. Iain McGilchrist affirms attention to the present as a moral act in an interview quoted by Gay Watson:

> One can obviously see it as a moral act in certain circumstances such as caring for people, even being a therapist or being a doctor, just being a husband, wife, parent, the way you attend is important, has consequences for other people, how they perceive themselves, and how they see themselves in relation to you, and so as soon as one attends, and one can't not attend if one is conscious, one's engaged in a moral act.[6]

I have mentioned often that we live in a reality where everything is connected. But, from this perspective, that connection is a moral one. *If reality is totally interconnected, to that degree, you and I are responsible for everything.* The journey toward transforming resonance in time must embrace life in all its forms. That is shockingly radical.

---

6 Watson, *Attention*, 75–76.

This realization affects every important moral question before us today. It is both the recognition and the result of the interaction of love. It affects the questions involved in today's ecological debates. It affects the questions involving social justice and economics. And, motivated by the force of love, it leads us to consider the service we are invited to provide.

Quantum Theology and Diakonia
(Service)

The early Christian community that formed in Jerusalem shortly after the Resurrection of Jesus was highly communal. It was shaped on the belief that Jesus was returning soon, and it was important to prepare for that coming. The charismatic experiences that accompanied many converts were extraordinary, and trusting the descriptions of its development in the Acts of the Apostles, many people joined it almost immediately. The early Christian community was predominantly Jewish, and there was probably little expectation that it would soon change. But it was not monolithic.

Jerusalem was an urban center within the Roman Empire, and a wide variety of people had business concerns there or had come for Jewish religious ritual life, obviously along with their families. Greek was the language of the day among this group, and, for some time, Hebrew had become a liturgical language. Most native residents of Roman Palestine commonly spoke Aramaic. Language, as many of us know, is a common tension point in multicultural environments. It was, predictably, only a matter of time before those tensions surfaced.

All the close disciples of Jesus were from various parts of Roman Palestine, and they formed the leadership of the Christian community. They were not formally educated. The Hellenists, the Greek-speaking people, in contrast, were largely urban and "Roman-savvy." Whatever else was going on in the daily life of this community, it was quite probable that the fact that all the leadership was "part of *them*" was a cause of growing tension. Acts gives us an idealistic picture of this community. "There was not a needy person among them, for as many as owned lands or houses sold them and brought the proceeds of what was sold. They laid it at the apostles' feet, and it was distributed to each as any had need" (Acts 4:34–35).

It was not long, however, before this very system became a focal point of tension, and the Hellenist leaders, Greek-speaking Jews, began to raise objections as to how their elder members seemed to be overlooked. As a result, these Hellenist leaders were appointed for *diakonia*, the ministry of service (Acts 6). That these leaders, who felt comfortable debating theology in the synagogues, quickly expanded their ministry to incorporate many of the evangelical duties the apostles themselves were performing should not be particularly surprising. The designation "deacon" continued to develop in the early communities, taking on the qualities of both charismatic and formal offices. Paul refers to himself in some places as someone in *diakonia* (2 Cor 6:4 and 11:23), and the early communities had both men and women functioning as *diakonos*. For the early communities, rendering service was primary, particularly caring for the indigent members.

Furthermore, the Church as a whole is in service to the rest of humankind, just as Jesus saw himself as coming "not to be served, but to serve, and to give his life as a ransom for many" (Mark 10:45). If that is the Christian obligation and privilege, how are we to do that in a quantum world and universe? Clearly, it has immediate connection with what we are called to do as we seek to bring forth global and universal *koinonia*, the manifestation of the force of love. Today, we are called to be in *diakonia* to our communities, to all humanity, to other species great and small, and to our planet as a whole. As it is suggested by Jesus, this asks of us a role reversal: not to be served, but to serve. It is a call to humility. We have run out of time to continue our habit of waiting to be waited on. The enrollment of our service is long overdue.

Toward Embracing a Universal Spiritual Consciousness

Transforming resonance lays before us a threefold spiritual life plan. The first layer in this plan consists in work that is to be done in our own individual lives—the process of growing and deepening consciousness in the journey onward and the journey inward that each of us makes. The second layer unfolds in our relational and communal systems—in the faith commitments that we share and deepen with other significant people with whom we meet and bond throughout our lives. The final layer lies in the recognition that we have a moral imperative to work toward the good of the whole, toward the fuller development of the small portion of the entire universe that we can touch.

We also realize that these three layers are not successive. We don't work on one until it is complete and then turn to the next. Since none of these layers of our experience are ever complete within our life-span, and since real work on any one layer will necessarily affect both of the others, we must pursue them together, in a systemic and holistic way.

From a Christian point of view, this life plan is laid out in the gospel teaching of the two great commandments. Asked which commandment is the greatest of all, Jesus answered, "The first is, 'Hear, O Israel: the Lord our God, the Lord is one; you shall love the Lord your God with all your heart, and with all your soul, and with all your mind, and with all your strength.' The second is this, 'You shall love your neighbor as yourself.' There is no other commandment greater than these" (Mark 12:29–31).

These "commandments" to love are themselves holistic. The love of God is envisioned as a response of our whole person to the One who has given us everything. It is all a gift, and our responsive love is not required to keep the love coming. Responding to God's love is not a condition or requirement but must be a free choice. Each is invited to utilize cooperatively this free energy emerging from the interaction of love.

The same is true in regard to others. I am not forced to love others in order to continue God's free gift. Loving others resonates with the gift, and it is to our benefit that we do.

Jesus's commandment seems to presume that we already love ourselves, but many of us don't. If we don't, someone or something came into our lives at some point to shut off the positive regard we should freely have toward our own betterment. Loving work that we undertake toward restoring that natural resonance for our truest self is a work of discernment that enriches our entire spiritual program. But Jesus also reminds us that we are each given the gift of life, but it is a life to gain or a life to lose. He warns us concerning these two takes on life, "For what will it profit them if they gain the whole world, but forfeit their life?" (Matthew 16:26). Each of these commandments, therefore, has its own trajectory toward transforming resonance, even though they continuously relate and interact.

It would be wonderful if transforming resonance appeared with a symphony of violins, piano, woodwinds, brass, and percussion. We could call it symphonic consciousness, and we could spend the rest of our lives simply basking in the experience. We can still call it *symphonic consciousness*, but this silent music seldom takes on full orchestration. Instead, we meet it in small pieces and short times, in our moments of peace and of justice, in our times of social harmony, in our intimate encounters with each other, in our experiences of natural beauty, in rare occasions of global awareness—in all the occasions of our union with Mystery. Over time, our awareness can deepen, and the symphonic consciousness that is always there in the background of our existence makes its appearance with more frequency and greater promise—the growing fruits of our onward and inward journey.

In the fullness lying within the beyond of spacetime, we meet again and remain always present to the One who holds all things within the Divine Heart.

Bibliography

Armstrong, Regis J., J. A. Wayne Hellmann, and William J. Short, eds. *Francis of Assisi: Early Documents.* 3 vols. New York: New City Press, 1999–2001.

Bohm, David. *Wholeness and the Implicate Order.* New York: Routledge Classics, 2002.

Brewster, David. *Memoirs of the Life, Writings, and Discoveries of Sir Isaac Newton.* Vol. 2. Edinburgh: T. Constable, 1855.

Cannato, Judy. *Field of Compassion: How the New Cosmology Is Transforming Spiritual Life.* Notre Dame, IN: Sorin Books, 2010.

Carroll, Sean. *From Eternity to Here: The Quest for the Ultimate Theory of Time.* New York: Plume, 2010.

Catechism of the Catholic Church. 2nd ed. English trans. Washington, DC: United States Conference of Catholic Bishops, 1994.

Chalmers, David. *The Conscious Mind: In Search of a Fundamental Theory.* New York: Oxford University Press, 1996.

Delio, Ilia. *The Unbearable Wholeness of Being: God, Evolution, and the Power of Love.* Maryknoll, NY: Orbis Books, 2013.

Feser, Edward. *Philosophy of Mind: A Beginner's Guide.* London: Oneworld Publications, 2006.

Fowler, James W. *Stages of Faith: The Psychology of Human Development and the Quest for Meaning.* San Francisco: Harper Collins, 1981.

Greene, Brian. *The Elegant Universe: Superstrings, Hidden Dimensions, and the Quest for the Ultimate Theory.* New York: Vintage Books, 2000.

Greene, Brian. *The Hidden Reality: Parallel Universes and the Deep Laws of the Cosmos.* New York: Vintage Books, 2011.

Hillman, James. *A Blue Fire: Selected Writings by James Hillman.* Edited by Thomas Moore. New York: Harper Perennial, 1989.

Hillman, James. *The Soul's Code: In Search of Character and Calling.* New York: Random House, 1996.

Humphrey, Mark, Paul V. Pancella, and Nora Berrah, eds. *Quantum Physics* (Idiot's Guide series). New York: Penguin Random House, 2015.

Kaku, Michio. *The Future of the Mind: The Scientific Quest to Understand, Enhance, and Empower the Mind.* New York: Anchor Books, 2015.

Kaku, Michio. *Hyperspace: A Scientific Odyssey Through Parallel Universes, Time Warps, and the 10th Dimension.* New York: Anchor Books, 1995.

Kurtz, Ernest, and Katherine Ketcham. *The Spirituality of Imperfection: Storytelling and the Journey to Wholeness.* New York: Bantam Books, 1992.

Lommel, Pim van. *Consciousness beyond Life: The Science of the Near-Death Experience.* New York: Harper One, 2010.

Moore, Thomas. *Care of the Soul: A Guide for Cultivating Depth and Sacredness in Everyday Life.* New York: Harper Perennial, 2016.

Penrose, Roger. *Shadows of the Mind: A Search for the Missing Science of Consciousness.* Oxford: Oxford University Press, 1994.

Polkinghorne, John. *The Faith of a Physicist: Reflections of a Bottom-Up Thinker.* Minneapolis: Fortress Press, 1994).

Polkinghorne, John. *Faith, Science & Understanding.* New Haven, CT: Yale University Press, 2000.

Polkinghorne, John. *Quantum Theory: A Very Short Introduction.* Oxford: Oxford University Press, 2002.

Polkinghorne, John. *Science and the Trinity: The Christian Encounter with Reality.* New Haven, CT: Yale University Press, 2004.

Progoff, Ira. *At a Journal Workshop: The Basic Text and Guide for Using the Intensive Journal.* New York: Dialogue House Library, 1975.

Robinson, Marilynne. *Absence of Mind: The Dispelling of Inwardness from the Modern Myth of the Self.* New Haven, CT: Yale University Press, 2010.

Rohr, Richard. *The Divine Dance.* New Kensington, PA: Whitaker House, 2016.

Rovelli, Carlo. *The Order of Time.* New York: Riverhead Books, 2018.

Russell, Robert, et al., eds. *Quantum Mechanics: Scientific Perspectives on Divine Action*, vol. 5. Vatican City: Vatican Observatory Foundation, 2001.

Siegel, Daniel J. *Mindsight: The New Science of Personal Transformation.*
    New York: Bantam Books, 2011.
Tart, Charles. *Waking Up: Overcoming the Obstacles to Human Potential.*
    Boston: New Science Library, 1986.
Teilhard de Chardin, Pierre. *The Phenomenon of Man.* Translated by
    Bernard Wall. New York: Harper Perennial Modern Thought,
    2008.
Thompson, Curt. *Anatomy of the Soul.* Carrollton, TX: Tyndale House
    Publishers, 2010.
Thompson, Evan. *Waking, Dreaming, Being.* New York: Columbia
    University Press, 2015.
Tickerhoof, Bernard. *Paradox: The Spiritual Path to Transformation.*
    Mystic, CT: Twenty-Third Publications, 2002.
Watson, Gay. *Attention: Beyond Mindfulness.* London: Reaktion Books,
    2017.
Wilber, Ken. *A Brief History of Everything.* Boston: Shambhala, 2007.
Wilber, Ken. *Integral Spirituality: A Startling New Role for Religion in the
    Modern and Postmodern World.* Boston: Integral Books, 2007.

Index

on end time, 83
on metaphysics, 4, 49–50, 94
positivism, 43
postmodernism, 6
practiced mastery, 159
prayer
 and consciousness, 17, 102
 defining, 16, 34, 101–2, 156
 and determinism, 49
 and directionality, 56–57
 and faith, 17, 102
 forms of, 34
 and interconnection, 71–72
 vs. meditation, 17
 and movement, 102–3
 and objectivity, 35
 particularized, 34–35
 private *vs.* communal, 71–72
 and reality, 17, 49, 71
 and self-awareness, 137
 and spirituality, 16
 and stillness, 102
 and string theory, 102
 as superposition, 34–35
 as systemic, 71–72, 178
 and time, 49
 as wave function, 35, 72
prayer field, 72–73
precognition, 95
preconscious, 141–42, 150–51
predictability, 15, 28, 66
prefrontal cortex, 124, 126–27, 131, 138, 158–59
Primal Observer, 161
primordial soup, 37, 40
principle of equivalence. *See* equivalence
probability, 29, 32–33, 50
processions, 110
Progoff Intensive Journal, 164
protons, 32, 41
Providence, 116
Pseudo-Dionysius, 13, 137
psychoanalysis, 141
purpose, 51–52, 117
Pythagoras, 23

quanta, 26
quantum field theory, 43–47, 175
quantum mechanics, 24, 29
Quantum Physics (Idiot's Guide Series), 21n
quantum theory
 and Christ, 187–90
 and determinism, 100
 development of, 33
 and freedom, 100
 and gravity, 40, 42
 incomplete nature of, 88, 181
 laws of, 24
 measurement problem in, 28, 30, 133
 as metaphor, 188–90
 and objectivity, 11
 as paradox, 27
 and probability, 29
 and reality, 161
 and relativity, 40, 176
quarks, 32, 44, 88

radiation, 37
 Hawking radiation, 84–85
rationalism, 96
 See also Enlightenment
realism, 12–13
reality
 and holism, 64
 interrelational, 59–60
 nature of, 60, 62, 92
 and prayer, 49
reductionism
 on brain *vs.* mind, 128, 133
 on change, 51
 on consciousness, 139, 155
 definition, 14
 and evolution, 115, 154
 vs. holism, 61
 on love, 90
 and metaphysics, 43, 49, 52
 and multiverse, 79
 and values, 15
 See also determinism
Reformation, 6
reframing, 169